Wonderful
Little
Hotels
and
Inns

America's Wonderful Little Hotels and Inns

Edited
by
Barbara
Crossette

*drawings
by
Ron
Couture*

TC

Thomas Congdon Books
E. P. DUTTON
New York

For information contact:
E. P. Dutton, 2 Park Avenue, New York, N.Y. 10016

Library of Congress Cataloging in Publication Data
Main entry under title:

America's wonderful little hotels and inns.

"Thomas Congdon Books."
1.   Hotels, taverns, etc.—United States—Directories.
I.   Crossette, Barbara.
TX907.A618   647′.9473   79-14700

ISBN: 0-525-05370-0 (cloth)
ISBN: 0-525-03005-0 (paper)

Published simultaneously in Canada by Clarke, Irwin &
Company Limited, Toronto and Vancouver

10   9   8   7   6   5   4   3   2   1

First Edition

_____Contents

Part Three: South   155

Part Four: Midwest   179

Part Five: Plains, Northwest and Alaska   205

Preface and Acknowledgments

The guest registers of America's hotels and inns are documents of our social history, recording the movements of people who came to explore, settle, enlighten, entertain, enjoy or even fleece one part of the country or another. Taverns with food, drink and lodgings were the oases of the post roads that linked the Eastern seaboard colonies long before the American Revolution. The trails west were soon punctuated by saloon hotels and stagecoach stops around which centers of population and commerce formed. The railroads helped open the mountainous hinterlands to grand resorts. The car was followed by the motel.

What next? What of the 1980s? Happily a nation looking for its many and diverse roots seems to be rediscovering the inns and hotels of the past. From the California wine country to the smaller cities of the Midwest and the hills of New England, restorations and re-creations are multiplying, and people are being drawn back to some half-forgotten comforts: roaring fires, old furniture, bathtubs with feet, rooms with singular character not stamped from molds and innkeepers who make the traveler a personal guest.

And so this book.

America's Wonderful Little Hotels and Inns is a collection of travelers' own recommendations. It is a book about places to stay that people have found to be special, places that reflect the regions and people the hostelries sprang up to serve. This is a second-generation book. A few years ago Hilary Rubinstein, a

British author and literary agent who traveled widely in Europe and elsewhere, wrote in a London newspaper about a place of near perfection he had found on an island off Malta. His article brought him a flood of letters from Europeans wanting to share with kindred spirits the places they too had found. The result was *Europe's Wonderful Little Hotels and Inns.* Next came the question: Could this be done for North America? The evidence is here; the judgment is yours.

This book does not grade or classify hotels and inns. The recommendations you will read are very personal observations. You may disagree. You may find gaps—and there are gaps: Where, for example, are the places of character in Boston? Philadelphia? If you want to add your opinion, turn to the back of the volume and remove the pages inviting your comments. The comprehensiveness of future editions of this book will depend in no small part on the contributions of people like you, people who seek alternatives to the look-alike hotels and motels that seem to dominate the places we sleep both in this country and, increasingly, abroad.

The basic information on rooms, rates and such at the bottom of every entry in this book was supplied by the innkeepers, most of whom operate without the aid of a public relations staff. So not all the information you need may be there. Not all entries include directions for those in unfamiliar territory. Some innkeepers were more detailed than others in listing the special features offered by the places they run. If you need help with transportation, meals that follow a special diet, a place for small children or the family pet, all you need to do is ask. The best advice in any case is to write or call ahead before you set out for any of the places in this book. Some are very small—at least one has only one room—and many are very popular with a loyal set of "regulars" who reserve rooms as much as a year in advance. A few places demand a deposit on rooms; some have a two-night minimum requirement on weekends or in certain seasons. In vacation areas meals—either on the full American plan (three meals) or the modified American plan (usually breakfast and an evening meal)—are often the rule. Incidentally, languages spoken by the staff are listed for the aid and encouragement of foreign visitors who are often fearful of straying from well-worn paths in this notoriously monolingual country.

The hotels and inns in this book, by their very appearance here, fit no patterns. Many have fewer than a dozen rooms; a few have more than a hundred. Some are very cheap—it is still possible to sleep, surrounded by antiques, for less than $20 in the United States. Others are very expensive. Some are very old, some new. Some are tucked into country settings; others are in cities. Most of them, however, are presided over by people who care about them, people who may have rescued them and brought into them both their personalities and their family heirlooms. The keepers of small hotels and inns can make their own rules. You may have to dress the way someone else feels you should for dinner. On the other hand, there may be no tipping—and you may find a fresh rose and a bowl of fruit by your bed late in the evening. There are innkeepers who paint, and innkeepers who will sing to you, accompanied by dulcimer and guitar, as you dine or sit by a crackling fire. Chuck Swain, an innkeeper in Princeton, New Jersey, is a poet. No doubt his counterparts across the country would share the feelings he expressed when he wrote these lines about his Peacock Inn:

> The doors are slanted, the locks are stiff.
> The floors have settled, strong but bent
> Under the weight of fireplace stone
> And tall chimneys. Two hundred years
> Of North winds and locust leaves in the eaves;
> Summer sun and rain, the violent
> Autumn hurricane have conspired
> To weather, twist and toughen
> Each organic beam and rafter.
> Reverberations of running laughter,
> Of tears and subtle shades of sorrow—
> Elfin shudders of sublime delights;
> The ghostly tremors of old regrets, all
> Have shaped the fallen angle,
> Have crooked the floor and sunk the tile.
> But listen, there is love here. . . .

(Copyright © 1976 F. C. Swain)

A book like this has very many people to thank for its existence. There were the travel editors who brought this project to the attention of their readers in the United States and Canada. Several professional travel writers dug into their own experience to provide notes on some of their personal favorites, or revisited places that merited inclusion here. There were hotel managers and innkeepers from coast to coast who shared their thoughts and their guest registers. And then there were the travelers themselves. All kinds of people have written this book. The hotels and inns you read about here have been recommended by doctors, authors, lawyers, musicians, people who travel on business, a couple of Jungian analysts in their seventies, two United States senators, two Pulitzer Prize-winning journalists, the director of a film institute, distinguished professors, local historians—and many people who did not identify themselves at all beyond admitting that they were enthusiastic champions of one, several or many small hotels and inns. The hard work of searching and sifting, of researching and com-

municating with far-flung contributors was done by my associate in this project, David Wigg, without whose efforts the book
would not have taken the shape it did. Thanks are also due to
Hilary Rubinstein for his continuing encouragement. And to
Joanny McCabe, who made a manuscript of little more than a
pile of papers pasted, stapled and clipped together. Finally
there is my father, who introduced me to small hotels by telling
me tales of the inns of his rural Pennsylvania boyhood. He
taught me restlessness, and to him, for that, this book is
dedicated.

Part One

New England

Connecticut

Essex

Griswold Inn
Essex, Connecticut   06426
Telephone: (203) 767-0991

"It was a cold rain-swept evening in November when we first made our acquaintance with the Griswold. (The Griz, we now endearingly call it.) The warmth that greeted us is forever imprinted on our minds—roaring fireplaces, a charming reservationist and smiling, contented people ambling about. The Griswold is a special sort of place in the wonderfully quaint (but alive) village of Essex on the Connecticut River. You can lunch in the Library or the Gun Room (guns date back to the 15th century) or dine in the Steamboat Room where the mural floats gently up and down giving one the feeling of dining on the river. The bar is unbelievable—a one-room schoolhouse brought in to serve the purpose—with its crackling fireplace, pot-bellied stove, walls covered with old prints of steamships, humorous posters, mast lights, ships' bells and all sorts of impressive memorabilia. To top it off, there's an authentic antique popcorn machine on wheels that never gets a chance to rest. Then there's Nick, the bartender—a gem!

"The inn dates back to 1776. The rooms are exactly as they

should be—charmingly quaint and spotless. (We love climbing into the huge four-poster in Room 3.) For entertainment there's a piano player weekdays in the bar, and a very good small combo on weekends.

"There is a century-old railroad depot in Essex where one can take an antique steam train (the Valley Railroad) for an hour's nostalgic ride. Deep River, a village close by, has the Annual Fife and Drum Muster each July where dozens of units come to compete. At East Haddam (a stone's throw away) there is the Goodspeed Opera House, a restoration of a famed opera house originally built in 1876."

—Mr. and Mrs. Don Cooper; also recommended
by Charles L. Garrettson

Closed Christmas Eve and Christmas Day.
19 rooms, 8 with private bath.
Rates $20–$28, suite $34. Continental breakfast included.
Credit cards: American Express, Master Charge, Visa.
Bar, antique shopping, boating.

_____*Greenwich*

Homestead Inn
420 Field Point Road
Greenwich, Connecticut   06830
Telephone: (203) 869-7500

"The inn is housed in a farmhouse originally built in 1799. In 1859 it was moved to the top of the nearest hill, remodeled and named Homestead Inn. It has been in continuous operation as an inn and restaurant since that time. The original farmhouse still serves as the central portion of the inn. Although it was modernized in 1968, the inn still maintains its lovely colonial appearance, sitting high on its hill overlooking Long Island Sound in the elegant Belle Haven section of Greenwich. It has twenty-five rooms with air-conditioning, television and private baths. Although it is twenty-nine miles from New York City, a trip by car or train takes only forty-five minutes because it is located two blocks from Exit 3 of the Connecticut Turnpike. The inn thus serves as a convenient bridge between country and city tastes. It does not have the stark and sterile surroundings of a modern hotel or motel, yet the accommodations are pleasant and far more than adequate. The rooms have candlewick bedspreads, Boston rockers and other country-inn touches. Essentially a small estate, its buildings show the charming signs of age: creaky stairways, some doorframes that are a little bit crooked and a pipe that knocks a bit now and again. Yet, on walking in the morning, it is delightful to see birds circling above the tops of magnificent beech, red maple, birch and chestnut trees." — *Jim Smith*

Open all year.
25 rooms, all with private bath.
Rates $32 single, $40–$50 double.
Credit cards: American Express, Master Charge, Visa.
Bar, heated outdoor pool, parlor.
Italian spoken.

New Milford

Homestead Inn
5 Elm Street
New Milford, Connecticut   06776
Telephone: (203) 354-4080

"Situated just off the village green of this lovely New England town, about eighty miles north of New York City, the Homestead Inn offers two choices. You can stay in the main house, which was built about 1817, or in the adjoining motel rooms. The rooms are immaculate. A number of restaurants are within a mile or two of the inn—there is a good choice of fresh seafoods. Many executives, visiting local branch factories of their national organizations, find the inn a relaxing stop."
— *Paul B. Hatch*

Open all year.
15 rooms, all with private bath.
Rates $18 single, $22 double.
No meals.
Credit cards: American Express, Master Charge, Visa.

New Preston

Boulders Inn
Lake Waramaug
New Preston, Connecticut   06777
Telephone: (203) 868-7918

"I have spent parts of—and sometimes all—summer at the inn for the last fifteen years: Believe me, I love the place. An inn, I find, is only as good as its chef. Through the years there has never been a poor one here. Dick Love, of course, supervises the kitchen, and it is a credit to the three-generation family. The dining room is fine. All the rooms and cabins are kept sparkling clean. All the help—usually college girls and boys— are picked carefully. This is primarily a 'homey' place, a New England country place—not a modern hotel. There are others who come back year after year. The younger generation love the lake, the hiking, square dancing and the big barn for recreation. I love the fall best; the scenery is fantastic."

—Helen Shattuck

"I first went to Boulders Inn with my four young children (ages ranging from about seven to fifteen) at the enthusiastic recommendation of a close friend. There I found lovely surroundings conducive to both a quiet time and a social life with warm, friendly guests. The children were safe—able to enjoy swimming, grounds where they could hike and camp out and many other sports. In fact, we liked the summers there so much, we went back in the winters to enjoy the skating and sledding. Now my children are grown—some married—but we still return to Boulders to enjoy the delicious food, varied and attractively served."

—Jenny Lee Hanson

Open all year, except for early December.
24 rooms, all with private bath.
Rates $31–$46 per person including meals in summer. Lower winter rates, no meals included. Weekly rates and family rates.
Credit cards: Master Charge, Visa.
Bar, trails, tennis, boating.

The Inn on Lake Waramaug
New Preston, Connecticut   06777
Telephone: (203) 868-2168

"The inn has been in the same family since the 1890s when it was bought as a summer home. At that time, it was known as Lakeview. In 1951, Richard Combs bought out his grandfather's interest and renamed it The Inn. He has operated it ever since with the help of his family—the original building has only five guest rooms and an intimate family living room; there are no telephones or televisions in the rooms. The inn is immaculately clean and the food is traditional American and very good.

"The area around Lake Waramaug is picturesque and private (there are only three public inns on the twenty-mile lake coastline; the rest of the area is taken up by private homes). It is perfect for leisurely bicycling on the road around the lake or for canoeing or sailing. The inn provides both bicycles and boats for a small charge, as well as a free tennis court and 150 acres for strolling around or just sitting in one of many lounge chairs scattered around the lawns. Nearby are several state parks, horseback-riding stables, local museums, antique shops and charming New England countryside and small towns.

"The Combs have kept the inn decorated in a colonial style and filled the rooms with 18th-century pine and cherrywood antiques. They added an indoor pool and bar adjacent to the old building, built two separate guest lodges to accommodate a growing clientele and provided a boat dock and lakeside snack bar." —*Philip and Debbie Fretz*

Open all year.
24 rooms, all with private bath.
Rates $40–$55 single, $30–$40 per person double, breakfast and dinner included. 10 percent discount for 7 days or longer.
Credit cards: American Express, Diners Club, Master Charge, Visa.
Bar, indoor swimming pool, private beach, tennis court, free golf.
French spoken.
Located on north shore of Lake Waramaug off Route 45.

_____*Norfolk*

The Blackberry River Inn
Route 44
Norfolk, Connecticut   06058
Telephone: (203) 542-5100

"We discovered the inn in April. We both travel a lot and enjoy going out on Saturday night for dinner and trying out new places. We were first impressed with the friendly warmth and old-world atmosphere of the dining room and the lounges. The food and service were a second lovely experience. The specialty fish dish of the day was fresh and delicate and aromatic as any I've enjoyed in fourteen trips on the *S.S. France.* Later we spent some time in the lounge bar and were surprised to see that most of the 'help' had changed into street clothes and returned as customers. Several sang along with the pianist and became part of the entertainment. We think it highly complimentary that a staff can play together, work together and seem to enjoy them-selves together like one big happy family. The evening was a total pleasure.

"In a gigantic ice house, gradually being renovated, the après ski room is delightful, with its dropped hearth and plush car-peting surrounding a hooded fireplace where a group can sit around. It is so conducive to relaxing and companionable conversation. The lower level is now open as a boutique and there is space for hanging paintings by local artists. The barn is going to be used as an antique shop.

"The suite in which we stayed recently had most comfortable beds with a fireplace and extra couch for added comfort. The view was splendid and the bathroom was big enough to get lost in. Everywhere you will see beautiful paintings and hanging plants and a magnificent collection of Royal Doulton china. We can only say, if anything happens to change the situation, we will feel as if we've lost a very dear old friend."

—Anita and Dr. James Meagher

Open all year, but closed Mondays and Tuesdays.
14 rooms, 11 with private bath.
Rates $23 single, $30 double. Weekly rates available. 10 percent discount for senior citizens.
Credit cards: American Express, Master Charge, Visa.
Bar, heated pool, tennis, cross-country skiing.

Mountain View Inn
Litchfield Road
Norfolk, Connecticut   06058
Telephone: (203) 542-5595

"The Mountain View Inn is family owned and operated. Three generations work together to bring a warmth and hospitality rarely seen these days. The accommodations are clean and well maintained with many antique clocks and pieces of furniture that help keep the New England flavor of the inn. The food is prepared by Karl Jokinen, a superior chef trained in the Escoffier tradition, and is served by waitresses in period costume. A gourmet's delight. The inn is located in historic Litchfield County in the foothills of the Berkshire mountains. Norfolk is full of early American history and exemplifies a quiet New England town complete with village green and steepled church. Activities and facilities within short driving distance include antique shopping, swimming, boating, fishing, golf and downhill and cross-country skiing. Excellent music is available across the road at the Yale Summer School of Music and Art and at Tanglewood, one hour away."

—Dr. Richard A. Susskind

Closed every Monday, Tuesday and Wednesday from January 1 to May 1.
7 rooms, 5 with private bath.
Rates $30–$35.
Credit cards: Master Charge, Visa.
Bar, restaurant, hiking, cross-country skiing, lake swimming.

Norwalk

Silvermine Tavern
Perry Avenue
Norwalk, Connecticut   06850
Telephone: (203) 847-4558

A 200-year-old inn, the Silvermine is only an hour from New York City and a short distance from the Stratford Shakespeare theater and the Westport Summer Theater.

"There is a quaint dining room furnished with antiques. In summer, meals are served outside on a terrace amid trees and above a running brook. The food is tasty and well prepared."
    —_Ann Rosenberg; also recommended by Patricia Lievow_

Open all year, closed Tuesdays from October through May.
10 rooms, all with private bath.
Rates $17–$32 including continental breakfast.
Credit cards: American Express, Diners Club, Master Charge, Visa.

Old Lyme

Bee and Thistle Inn
100 Lyme Street
Old Lyme, Connecticut   06371
Telephone: (203) 434-1667

Old Lyme, founded by sea captains where the Connecticut River meets Long Island Sound, has remained conscious of both its natural setting—there are marshlands and beaches—and its colonial past. There are museums to visit, and there is the Old Lyme Historic District for walking and bicycling. On a five-and-a-half-acre plot in the district is the Bee and Thistle Inn, built as a judge's home in 1756 and renovated in 1920. It has been an inn since 1941.

"What could be more delicious than to be awakened by a rap on the door followed by two smiling, cheerful young girls each bearing a breakfast tray of fresh, carefully prepared dishes just the way you specified the night before? Home-baked bran muffins just out of the oven are individually wrapped to keep them hot. Orange juice is freshly squeezed moments before; coffee is in a sizable thermos pitcher with enough to last the morning. Tea is Lapsang Souchong served in old English teapots. The strawberries on your bran flakes are fresh and tender. The cheese omelet is loose and not browned because Gene Bellows, the genial host and chef, makes it a point the night before to find out exactly how you prefer it. (There is a masterpiece option known as 'mystery omelet' that gives one something to anticipate before drifting off in the huge, oversize four-posters.) And to cap it all is a long-stemmed vase with a cheery, freshly picked flower to help you awaken in the best of all possible moods. Such is life at the day's beginning for the lucky guests of the Bee and Thistle Inn.

"The inn itself sits back from the road amidst the towering trees that surround it. The yellow color with its white trim and the little circular porch off the front door somehow bid you welcome even from a distance. Inside the feeling is casual, relaxed, as though you already live there and a few old friends dropped by to spend the weekend. There are two parlors with a roaring fire in each and another fire blazes away in the main dining room down the hall. Classical music is going on the stereo in the office off the hall. Upstairs the tubs are so large you can actually submerge your whole body.

"The Bee and Thistle is not really an inn. It is the home of Gene and Barbara Bellows, their two daughters and the friends who come to visit. When you walk through the front door you become one of them. Barbara is a younger, infinitely more charming, Joan Baez. Talented, at ease, knowledgeable, she shares her music during dinner. The ballads she sings are refreshing, haunting and rhythmic. She accompanies them with her Contreras classical guitar and her dulcimer. The effect is a pleasant companion to the candlelit tables and quiet efficiency of the girls serving from the kitchen. When Barbara plays, everyone listens. The spell is contagious.

"There are a multitude of chores to do every day when you run a small inn. Gene somehow manages to see that all gets done. The remarkable thing about Gene, though, is that he is always ready to stop and chat. He is genuinely interested in the people who come to the inn. He enjoys finding out what it is that you especially crave and then helping you find it. Learning that I was an incurable jogger he suggested one of the most delightful scenic little lanes for my morning run that I have ever seen. Barbara loaned me her precious Contreras to play whenever I felt like it. Gene and Barbara are both that way, always ready to please. The feeling rubs off and the next thing you know you find yourself being more considerate to your mate and vice versa.

"Angie and I were married there in the woods not far from Old Lyme and the Bee and Thistle. It was a second marriage for both of us and we only had five old friends to help us celebrate it. The dinner afterward was right at the inn. We had champagne and all the trimmings but we were both deeply touched by two things. The first was a very special card of congratulations in Barbara's flowing hand. The other was a bottle of Cold Duck that Kathy and Pam, our breakfast-bearing buddies, had gone out and chipped in to buy us. Now I ask you, where else are you going to find the upstairs maid and the dining room waitress going out to buy you a bottle of Cold Duck just because you got married?" —*Jay B. Teasdel*

"We were pleased with our long weekend stay at the Bee and Thistle. A charming New England house converted to an inn, and improvements still ongoing. Our room was airy, comfortable and scrupulously clean, with more than adequate closet space and private bath. The management was warm and welcoming, and the staff enthusiastic and polite. Meals (breakfast and dinner) were delicious, with attractive breakfast trays served in one's room if desired.

"Old Lyme is a serene and interesting village, consisting of beautiful homes, an art gallery and historical house open to the public. Nearby is Long Island Sound and the Connecticut River."
—*Virginia U. Prout; also recommended by Marilyn Svihovec*

Open all year.
10 rooms, 8 with private bath.
Rates $24–$36. Weekly rates available.
Credit cards: Diners Club, Visa.
Bar, porch, dining rooms, fireplaces.

Old Lyme Inn
85 Lyme Street
Old Lyme, Connecticut   06371
Telephone: (203) 434-2600

"Mr. and Mrs. Milne make an art of innkeeping. They attend to every detail, from furnishings and tableware to the vegetables and meats purchased for the exquisite meals. Service is courteous and helpful. Many of the young people who work in the dining room are college and university students from neighboring communities. The atmosphere is pleasant, serene, efficient and slightly merry. The food itself is, in my opinion, the best that can be found between New York City and Boston. The wine list provides a range and quality not usually found in American restaurants. The Milnes are in the process of creating an American institution of great worth." —*Lee Hall*

Open all year, except for Christmas week.
5 rooms, all with private bath.
Rates $27 single, $30 double, including continental breakfast.
Credit cards: American Express, Carte Blanche, Master Charge, Visa.
Bar.
French spoken.

Ridgefield

The Elms Inn
500 Main Street
Ridgefield, Connecticut   06877
Telephone: (203) 438-2541

"To us this is like home, in the New England tradition. The Scala family, an extended family indeed, are friendly and eager to please; they like people. And so, when dining there you will be greeted by someone from the family or by the jovial and outgoing maître d', who welcomes you as an important guest. The several dining areas are cozy and interesting, and fit whichever mood prevails at the time. The food is fresh and tastefully prepared in the style of continental cuisine. In summer many of the vegetables come from the family garden, as do the flowers on the tables. The crisp hot buns, straight from the oven to your table, are superb. For those who are wine buffs, the wine cellar is among the best in the area. Simple, uncomplicated breakfasts are available.

"There are many unique and varied antiques to view—both in the dining and the sleeping areas. It is quiet and restful for overnight stays. The rooms have white ruffled tie-back curtains. And most important, it's a clean place. It is also within easy walking distance to the center of the village to some unusual shops with quality merchandise. Just up the street is the up-to-date library handy for browsing. It's pleasant to stroll up Main Street under the tall trees lining the street where one might be greeted in passing by friendly Ridgefield residents. Incidentally, this old town predates the American Revolution; the Elms dates back to 1799."   —*Charles L. Skelley*

Open all year.
10 rooms, all with private bath.
Rates $25 single, $35 double. Weekly rates.
Credit cards: American Express, Diners Club, Master Charge, Visa.
Bar.
Albanian, French, German, Italian, Portuguese, Serbo-Croat and
    Spanish spoken.

Turn to the back of this book for pages inviting *your* comments.

Riverton

Old Riverton Inn
Route 20
Riverton, Connecticut   06065
Telephone: (203) 379-8678

"The Old Riverton Inn is located in the northwestern part of Connecticut at the foot of the Berkshire Hills on the Farmington River. The inn was originally opened in 1796 by Jesse Ives, as Ives' Tavern, on the post route between Hartford and Albany. It was later owned by the Yale family and was known as the Yale Hotel. In 1937 the inn was restored to its earliest possible state. In 1954, because of increased business, the Grindstone Terrace was added. The floor of this room is made of grindstones that, according to records, were quarried in Nova Scotia and shipped to Long Island Sound and then up the Connecticut River to Collinsville to be used in the making of axes and machetes.

"There is an attractive Hobby Horse cocktail lounge and ten rooms for overnight guests. The upper lounge is filled with family pieces of furniture, many of them antique treasures. The dining room is furnished with Hitchcock chairs and tables, made in the factory across the river.

"The cooking of the inn is American style, with specialties of baked stuffed pork chops, Southern fried chicken and baked stuffed shrimp. The fish—sole and scrod—is all fresh. The atmosphere of the inn is relaxing, and its location excellent—ten miles from the Yale Summer School of Music and Art, less than an hour's drive from Tanglewood and of course across the river from the famous Hitchcock chair factory and museums."   *—Ruth Katzin*

"What you always thought an old-fashioned inn should be— simple, unpretentious, true to itself, picking up no false or faddish new styles. A reflection of the tiny community in which it has served since 1796, a town that time has passed by and is the better for it."   *—David Halberstam*

Open all year. (Dining room closed in January.)
10 rooms, all with private bath.
Rates $12.50 single, $10 double per person, $11 per person in twins. Breakfast included.
Credit cards: American Express, Master Charge, Visa.
Bar.
French, Italian and Spanish spoken.

Salisbury

Ragamont Inn
Main Street
Salisbury, Connecticut   06068
Telephone: (203) 435-2372

"The Ragamont Inn, on Route 44 in Salisbury, is owned by Barbara and Rolf Schenkel. It is a great place. The rooms are warm and intimate, with a colonial motif. Authentic antique furniture abounds—take a look at the old wooden chest dated in the 1700s near the front entrance. The main event for me, however, is the food. Rolf Schenkel is an artist in his kitchen. He puts a great deal of feeling into his cooking and because of the modest menu is able to devote unusual attention to each dish. Rolf starts by using the freshest of vegetables and meats. Many of the vegetables are grown in a garden behind the inn. He makes his own bread early each morning—always a treat—and he mixes his own salad dressing.

"Some of the places in the area are worth taking note of. The Sharon Playhouse offers professional productions of some of the popular plays and musicals. You can also walk to an art gallery and look at some strikingly creative paintings and sculptures. Most of the works are for sale.

"On Route 41 toward Sharon there is a beautiful view of a lake nestled between two mountains. And you can rent boats for fishing on Twin Lakes. For another kind of adventure, you can make a turn at the beautifully maintained old Salisbury courthouse, go past the huge stone caldron with its springwater and continue up Mt. Riga Road to the home of Mr. Brazee, the game warden—a warm person and a delight to talk with. He knows more about the area and its rich history than anybody, and with some coaxing (well, very little coaxing) Mr. Brazee will unfold some of it for you. (There is a humorous story about how Mt. Riga got its name.)

"Sometimes I get a little apprehensive about what would happen if everybody discovered this wonderful area in the northwest corner of Connecticut all at once. Would it be ruined? With relief I studied some photographs taken in the 1800s. The Ragamont Inn and Salisbury look almost the same now as then."

—_Danny Fiore; also recommended by George Gottlieb_

Open May 1 to January 1, but closed Mondays.
12 rooms, 8 with private bath.
Rates $10–$18 single, $22–$32 double. 10 percent discount on stays of a week or more.

No credit cards.
Bar, lake, boating, fishing.
German spoken.

White Hart Inn
Village Green
Salisbury, Connecticut 06068
Telephone: (203) 435-2511

"A relaxed, cheerful country mood is the essence of the White Hart. The proprietor, John Harney, is genuinely helpful in directing you to all the local pleasures. There are three dining rooms and a fine menu with home-baked breads and pastries (which can also be bought to take home). In the winter, I prefer the bar with its roaring fire. In the summer, the porch is delightful. This charming old inn has an interesting country store, and the bedrooms are typical 'country.' Salisbury is a delightful village and not at all 'touristy.' It is a big center for cross-country skiing, and since the Harney family are all ardent skiers, they will be helpful. Downhill skiing is also nearby. Summer is delightful with lovely country walks, (small) mountain climbing and several lakes within a few miles. You can usually judge an inn by the mood of the guests—at the White Hart they all seem relaxed, convivial and obviously enjoying themselves."
—*George Rooney*

Open all year.
20 rooms, all with private bath.
Rates $20–$32 single, $22–$38 double. Higher on holiday weekends.
Credit cards: Master Charge, Visa.
Bar, dining room, country store.

Woodbury

Curtis House
Main Street (U.S. 6)
Woodbury, Connecticut 06798
Telephone: (203) 263-2101

"For more than ten years Curtis House has been our halfway stopping point between Pennsylvania and our farm in New Hampshire. We get a good night's rest and good food. A longer visit for pleasure or business in the area is equally rewarding. The reasons are easy to understand:

"Woodbury is a beautiful, peaceful and unchanging New

England community. The inn itself, operating continuously since 1754, has the casual, homelike charm of those 18th- and 19th-century years. Look at the posters and pictures on the walls in the beautiful beam-ceilinged dining room with its stone fireplace. Curtis House prices are reasonable. The food is well above average. Try their lobster bisque, lamb chops or sweetbreads. You will be pleased with them, as well as with many other good American dishes. Inspect their rooms, some with four-poster canopy beds. Last but not least, get acquainted with the Hardisty family, who own and operate this treasure place, unique among inns. Mrs. Hardisty, well along in years, can be seen showing guests to a table or clearing one for the next party—truly a gracious lady. Meet the boys who spend long hours on the job and offer help well beyond that expected from an inn owner. An example of what we mean is this: During a gasoline crisis we arrived from New Hampshire late in the evening with the needle reading below zero. No gas stations were open. I explained our problem to Gary Hardisty. Without hesitating he said, 'I will drain the lawn mower. This should get you to Danbury where the stations are open twenty-four hours a day.' There is warmth and friendship in their relations to their guests. And humor. Witness the barrel of fall apples near the desk with a sign: 'First apple free. Additional apples $1.75 each.' "   —*James E. and Helen Louise Norcross*

Open all year. Closed Christmas Day.
18 rooms.
Rates $9–$25. Weekly and monthly rates.
Credit cards: Master Charge.
Bus transportation available to Southbury, four miles away. Taxi to inn, or call ahead to arrange to be met.

Captain Lord Mansion,
Kennebunkport

Maine

Camden

The Owl and Turtle Bookmotel
8 Bay View
Camden, Maine   04843
Telephone: (207) 236-4769

"The Owl and Turtle Bookmotel, located at the public landing where many of the windjammers embark, is surely one of the most beautiful bookstores anywhere. They have four motel rooms at the back, all of which look out on the bay. This is a most unusual combination—guests enjoy browsing amidst the thousands of books—and excellent for someone who is staying one night only. Breakfast comes with the room."

—Patricia Lievow

Open all year.
4 double rooms, all with private bath.
Rates $21–$28. Breakfast included.
Credit cards: Master Charge, Visa.
French spoken.

Whitehall Inn
52 High Street
Camden, Maine   04843
Telephone: (207) 236-3391

"This is the place where in 1912 Edna St. Vincent Millay re-
cited her reflective poem 'Renascence' and was spotted and sent
to Vassar by a rich woman. She wrote about Penobscot Bay:
'All I could see from where I stood/was three long mountains
and a wood;/I turned and looked another way/and saw three
islands in a bay.' There are pictures of the Millays in the lobby
of the inn, which was built as a sea captain's house in 1834. The
inn has fine antiques (a Queen Anne desk, grandfather clocks
by Seth Thomas and Hoadley) and one of those wonderful
porches, with rockers, that runs the entire length of the house. It
is old and therefore not for those who want everything modern.
Friends of ours find it musty, but we like its spacious rooms and
antique quality."   *—Patricia Lievow*

"Overlooking lawns and trees to the bay, the Whitehall is an
inn in the traditional meaning of the word, where friends meet
on wide verandas or, later in the season, around fireplaces or in
the Spirits Room. The Dewing family, Ed, Jean and their two
sons, Chip and Jonathan (a daughter Heidi lives in Boston), see
that everyone is comfortable. Within an easy walk is the town
and harbor of Camden, known for its windjammers. Nearer
still is a secluded cove with its own State of Maine charm—a
photographer's dream. Within an hour or so you can see Aca-
dia National Park, the 'Christina's World' of the Andrew
Wyeth painting and many old fishing villages."
                                             —Nancy Bradberry

Open June to mid-October.
41 rooms.
Rates July 1 to Labor Day $26–$34 single; $27.50 double per person,
     including breakfast and dinner. European plan also available. In
     June, September and October rates are slightly lower. Monthly
     discounts.
Credit cards: American Express, Master Charge, Visa.
Bar, tennis, shuffleboard, boats, bicycles.

Rates quoted were the latest available. But they may not reflect
unexpected increases or local and state taxes. Be sure to verify
when you book.

Clark Island

The Craignair Inn
Clark Island
Spruce Head, Maine   04859
Telephone: (207) 594-7644

"Here is a place that should be tried by those who appreciate plain living. I lived on this part of the Maine coast thirty years ago. Knowing the precise combination of rocks and water I wanted, I found it at the Craignair Inn—smack on a delectable cove with a stunning view of the open ocean and ledges warmed by the sun for swimming. The area is uninfected by the chain-hotel disease though only ten minutes from Route 1. Still, as I approached the inn, I wondered if there would be oil-cloth on the tables and dangling flypaper. Then I saw the fresh curtains blowing at the window of my simple room and sniffed the salt air, and I was reminded of the rooms one could get on the Mediterranean twenty-five years ago. New paint everywhere, and the sort of cleanliness that comes only from scrubbing. Most rooms share baths, and the big, old-fashioned ones are kept tidy by the other guests, who are better behaved than those in fancier spots. This do-it-yourself spirit may come from respect for the new family who operate the inn: father, mother, son and two daughters were all the staff I saw.

"Craignair is not for people who are dependent on motel and microwave. It looks like what it was: a boardinghouse for the workers in the granite quarries at Clark Island, which only recently ceased working. This is a chance to see a way of life of which many traces remain—and not in a museum. The inn's rates are commensurately modest. The food is adequate, a compliment if one recalls the tasteless condition achieved by other places. I saw no bar, meaning that the guest is spared the 'lounge' that has blighted Maine. No Muzak."   —_Peter Clarke_

Open all year.
16 rooms, 1 with private bath.
Rates $22 single, $19 double per person, including breakfast and dinner. July, August—$24 single, $21 double per person. Special discounts for groups of 10 or more, organizations and workshops. Discounts for children under 12 with parents.
No credit cards.
Directions: From U.S. Route 1 just east of Thomaston, take State Route 131 south 5½ miles to junction with State Route 73; go left on 73 one mile to Clark Island road; right 1½ miles to Craignair.

_____*Deer Isle*

Pilgrim's Inn
Deer Isle, Maine   04627
Telephone: (207) 348-6615

"Squatting on a gentle rise of land, the Pilgrim's Inn faces the unpredictable Northwest Harbor, which can fling its surf high over the rocks or feign contentment with the soft murmur of its relentless tides. A quiet millpond provides another kind of watery view from the back of the late Georgian house, and is a place where children might take turns in a rowboat. The deep-red clapboard inn, once the home of an ostentatious shipbuilder and politician, has accommodated summer lodgers since the early 20th century. Architecturally there is nothing similar to the imposing structure anywhere on Deer Isle, and the interior has undergone extensive renovations under the aegis of innkeepers George and Ellie Pavloff. Although guests are treated royally, life is essentially simple. Bedrooms are all equipped with wood-burning stoves and not everyone has a private bath. Interesting local art is displayed everywhere. Cocktails are served in the common room, which is the heart of the inn. Dominated by massive colonial fireplaces replete with Dutch ovens, it is furnished with sinfully comfortable furniture and lined with bookshelves. Enhanced by candlelight, small tables and waitresses in colonial costumes (music on weekends), dinner is elegant and artistic."   —*Marion Laffey Fox*

Open from May 1 to December 1.
10 rooms, all with semiprivate bath.
Rates $35 per person including breakfast and dinner. Special weekly rates.
Credit cards: Master Charge, Visa.
Bar, bicycles, badminton, horseshoes, rowboat.
French, German and Spanish spoken.

_____*Kennebunkport*

Captain Lord Mansion
P.O. Box 527
Kennebunkport, Maine   04046
Telephone: (207) 967-3141

"Kennebunkport is one of the most charming and quaint towns in Maine, situated near good sight-seeing, beaches and stores that sell antiques. Nestled about three blocks from the main square, overlooking a large expanse of lawn and marina, is the

Captain Lord Mansion. The mansion is a beautiful old house built during the War of 1812 that remained in the Lord family until 1974. The charm of the house has been maintained throughout by using many of the original pieces of furniture and other furnishings of the period. The owners, Beverly and Rick, are a delightful couple who are extremely helpful and offer a tour of the mansion to all arriving guests. The tour revealed large comfortable rooms, many of which have working, wood-burning fireplaces. Breakfast is included with lodgings. During the summer, the breakfast includes, among other things, fresh strawberries picked on the grounds as well as freshly baked zucchini bread and muffins that are out of this world. The inn attracts very interesting guests, and breakfast is a great way to meet them and to engage in interesting and lively conversation.

"During our five-day stay in Kennebunkport we overindulged in lobster and a great place for it is Nunan's Lobster Shack on the road to Cape Porpoise. Its decor is simple, and the atmosphere is very casual. The lobsters were the best that we had in Maine. You can phone a few days in advance for large lobsters."   *—Jon H. Manchester*

Open all year.
10 rooms, 8 with private bath.
Rates $44–$60 double, including breakfast.
From November through April a three-night stay gets a fourth night free.
No credit cards.
Directions: Take Exit 3 off Maine Turnpike. Turn left on State Route 35 to Kennebunkport. Turn left at Route 9 to Dock Square. Right on Ocean Avenue three-tenths of a mile and turn left.

Shawmut Inn
Ocean Avenue
Box 431
Kennebunkport, Maine 04046
Telephone: (207) 967-3931

"The Shawmut seems unable to decide whether it is an old seaside hotel or a motor lodge, so accommodations vary from the quaint to the motelish. But the location (well out of town) and the seclusion of this establishment perched on a rocky shoreline make it an attractive place to get away from summer crowds, while remaining within a short driving distance of Kennebunkport itself as well as other towns known for their craft shops and seafood. Shawmut's main lodge (with a seafront dining room), its motel-style annex and its cottages form a nice compound, with woods and beaches for walking, porches for sitting to watch the sea and recreational facilities for the restless. Morning here can be a breathtaking thing: a misty ocean dotted with lobster boats giving way to sunrise on the open Atlantic. The spectacle is soundless, except for the chugging of the lobster boats. For the rest of the day, nothing but the calls of birds—or the occasional voice of a child—disrupts the sound of the sea."

—*B. C.*

Open May 1 to October 31.
115 rooms, all with private bath, many with kitchen facilities.
Rates $40–$60. Off-season and weekly rates available.
Credit cards: American Express, Master Charge, Visa.
Saltwater pool, beach.
French spoken.

Poland Spring

Poland Spring Inn
Route 26
Poland Spring, Maine   04274
Telephone: (207) 998-4351

The waters of Maine's Poland Spring area have been praised—and bought—far and wide for more than a century, and the pleasant land from which they come has been a resting place for travelers for almost a century longer than that. First a stagecoach stop before Maine became a state (it was part of Massachusetts), Poland Spring grew by the turn of the 20th century into a community of hotels, a glittering resort—indeed something of a spa—frequented by the rich and famous. Its recent history has been less happy. By the time the present owner of the complex took over in 1972, many of the old buildings were in shambles and only a newer (albeit well-appointed) inn built in 1963 and a nearby motor hotel remained usable. So the owner, Mel Robbins, started with these, hoping, he says, to eventually restore the gracious older resort buildings as he goes along. They are still there to look at: monument to another age of leisure.

"We spent a lovely vacation at the inn at Poland Spring. It's a unique type of family hotel owned by a very friendly couple. The host, Mel Robbins, is a remarkable man, intelligent, witty and an extremely warm individual who made everyone feel very special! He is a very versatile man who kept us entertained with his many talents. The inn is situated on lovely grounds with beautiful scenery. There are a lot of activities if you want to get involved, or you can just relax and watch. The villages nearby are fascinating with their boutiques and flea markets."

—*Edith and Alec Scheffer*

Open from the end of May to the end of October.
105 rooms, all with private bath.
Rates $14–$24 per person, based on double occupancy, with MAP.
   Deposits required for certain holiday weekends.
No credit cards.
Bar, pool, tennis, summer theater and 18-hole golf course.

_____ *Southwest Harbor*

Claremont Hotel
Southwest Harbor, Maine   04679
Telephone: (207) 244-5036

"Located not far from the harbor and high above the southern end of Somes Sound—the only fjord on the East Coast—the Claremont commands magnificent views of the Sound and of the mountains of Mt. Desert Island. These are the mountains seamen watch for in navigating these waters. The hotel, now nearly a century old, has been entered on the National Register of Historic Places; but it is no relic, no outworn shell. The original building has been carefully and expertly restored, and a beautiful dining room with huge picture windows on three sides added at the back of the building. Also a new kitchen and laundry.

"The food is delectable; the beds the best we have ever encountered away from home. The public rooms are pleasant and comfortable. There is a well-stocked library, including a fine, big dictionary! The wide and spacious lawns surrounding the hotel are carefully tended. Tetherball, croquet and tennis are played. One notices a hammock suspended between two shade trees—apple trees, I think. It is obviously a good place for children and young people, and there are many of these. Down the hill, near the water and the hotel's dock, is the boathouse, where older guests may gather in the late afternoons for refreshment and talk of the day's activities—mountain climbing, golf, sailing, exploring—there is no end to what may be done on and from this island. Some of us consider it the most beautiful and interesting little island in the U.S.A. (See Samuel Eliot Morison's book—*The Story of Mt. Desert Island;* Boston: Little, Brown and Company.)

"The staff, carefully chosen, includes many college boys and girls. All do their best to make the guests happy. My special admiration goes to the proprietor, Gertrude McCue, who is vitally concerned to preserve and perpetuate a priceless heritage; and to the manager and his wife, Matthew and Joan Landreau, who so ably cooperate with her." —*Richard McClanahan*

Open Memorial weekend to October 15.
30 rooms, all with private bath.
Rates $38–$68. Breakfast and dinner included.
Special weekly rates.
Pets in cottages only.
Cocktails in boathouse, tennis, croquet, boats.
French spoken.
Directions: I-95 from Boston to Augusta, Maine. Route 3 east from Augusta to Belfast. Route 1 north (U.S. 1) to Ellsworth. Then Route 3 again to Mt. Desert Island and then Route 102 to Southwest Harbor where signs direct one to the inn.

_____*Sunset*

Goose Cove Lodge
Post Office
Sunset, Maine   04683
Telephone: (207) 348-2508

"When you follow the sign to Goose Cove, you drive on a winding road through woods and up hills until you think you have surely missed your turn. Finally the landscape opens. There is a lovely view of a Maine cove, Penobscot Bay and its wooded islands. Scattered through the woods are rustic but very comfortable cottages, all with fireplaces and a view to the water. Meals are served in the main lodge. The food is wholesome and simple. Seating is informal—around large tables—and this gives guests the opportunity to get to know one another. What has drawn us to Goose Cove Lodge on Deer Isle for many summer vacations is the lovely scenery, use of the sailboats and the walks along the trails through the mossy woods or along the rocky coast. Dr. Ralph Waldron, an author and naturalist now in his nineties, and his wife, Florence, owned the lodge and gave the place a very special flavor for many years. The new owners, Jo and Liz Kern, are following in the same tradition, and Dr. Waldron is going to assist them for as long as he is willing." —*Ann Rosenberg*

Open from early June to late September.
22 units, all with private bath.
Rates $34–$78, including three meals. Special off-season rates and weekly rates.
No credit cards.
Beach parties, library, nature trails, sailing, sea bathing.

Tenants Harbor

The East Wind Inn
P.O. Box 149
Tenants Harbor, Maine   04860
Telephone: (207) 372-8800 or 8908

The inn was built in 1890 in a small fishing village that was once an important shipbuilding center. Originally the building was part of a shipyard complex: Sails were made in it. After many years of standing vacant, it was restored in 1975 by Tim Watts.

"The small comfortable lobby invited you to stay awhile, share the excellent dining room fare and watch the fishing boats and yachts in the harbor across the broad expanse of lawn. The food is delicious and the fresh lobsters and other seafood make the short journey down the St. George peninsula well worth anyone's time. Conversely, if a tiny New England hamlet seems to be lacking in urban affairs at some times, then a few minutes' drive takes you to numerous art galleries and studios, craft shops or to the museum (with all the Wyeths represented) or to crowded Camden Harbor and its windjammer fleet. Port Clyde and Monhegan Island are only a short distance away."

—_Henry and Bettie Miller_

Open all year.
16 rooms, 2 with private bath.
Rates $12–$18 single, $18–$24 double.
No credit cards.
Beaches, skiing.

Wiscasset

Squire Tarbox
RFD 2, Box 318
Wiscasset, Maine   04578
Telephone: (207) 882-7693

"Westport Island is hardly an island at all. It's a turn off the road toward the Atlantic, between the Bath drawbridge that overlooks the old town's shipyards and the town of Wiscasset whose sea captains' and merchants' houses of the 18th century are worth a detour in themselves. The Squire Tarbox should be part of that detour. It's some three miles from U.S. Route 1, an elegant reminder of Maine's past, which grew rich on whaling and then felt the wealth slip away toward the more economically convenient centers of southern New England. The inn is a square, white, clapboard Federal house, furnished with antiques from the families of Anne McInvale and Elsie White, the owners. Its ample bedrooms each have a fireplace and the good beds are covered with handsome authentic quilts. As it should be, though, the two dining rooms and the kitchen are the center of the house. Anne is a superb cook with a special gift for the vegetable dishes that accompany and enhance the choice at dinner between a meat and fish course: tomato pudding, minted carrots, ratatouille or summer squash, depending on the season and harvest from their own and other gardens. Elsie makes an excellent dry martini and both the red and white house wines, *en carafe,* are good. The bread and breakfast muffins are fresh-baked at the inn. Elsie and Anne are both from Mississippi and, in choosing Maine for their venture into the inn business, are an exception to the trend of Americans migrating toward the Sunbelt. Their warm, unintrusive Southern welcome is a good part of this inn's charm. After Wiscasset, the campus of Bowdoin is nearby. The famous mail-order house, L. L. Bean, is in Freeport."   —*Patricia H. Painton; also recommended by Mr. and Mrs. Alan H. Bomser*

Open mid-May to mid-October.
8 rooms, 2 with private bath.
Rates $20 single, $30 double, including continental breakfast.
No credit cards.
Service bar.
From the south follow I-95 and U.S. 1 to Bath. North of Bath, Route 144 turns right off of Route 1. Follow 144 for eight miles.

_____*Yarmouth*

Homewood Inn
Drinkwater Point
P.O. Box 196
Yarmouth, Maine   04096
Telephone: (207) 846-3351

Homewood Inn is a cluster of buildings on the shorefront of Maine's Casco Bay. Centerpiece of the cottages and houses is the 1742 Maine House, one of the Yarmouth area's historic buildings.

"My husband and I have vacationed at the Homewood for three years now and find it perfect. The food is delicious, especially the Sunday night buffet and the Monday night clambake (lobster, bags of clams, corn on the cob and baked potatoes—all for a very reasonable price). The accommodations are very comfortable. We usually take a room in the guesthouse, over-looking the bay. The room is decorated with rustic furniture and charming prints and has a working fireplace (since we usually take our vacation in October, we use the fireplace at least once a day!).

"The lodge itself is very homey (complete with wood-burning stove), and we like to take a half hour every morning or evening to chat with whoever is running the desk—or just sit and read the books or magazines.

"The Homewood is located in a very untouristy area—and that's what we especially like about it. The pace is relaxed. The more active types can play tennis, shuffleboard or swim—but we prefer to walk on the beach with our dog (yes, they do allow animals), or jog through one of the Homewood's pastures or around the beautiful houses next to the inn."

—*Phyllis Schneider*

"My wife and I have traveled extensively throughout our country and Europe. We have yet to find (nor do we expect ever to do so) the ideal resort. However, the essence of a successful resort operation is the ability to please all age groups by offering a wide range of features and charm. The Homewood Inn at Yarmouth achieves this. Our family consists of three generations, my parents, my wife and my children. All of us look forward to Homewood each summer.

"For us, the isolated feeling of Homewood set on a point of land facing Casco Bay is one of its great advantages. Yet we are only ten minutes to historic Yarmouth, and only an additional twenty minutes to the Portland International Airport. Since my father and I cannot spend the entire summer with our family, the ability to 'commute' is essential for us.

"Although in recent years the Homewood restaurant operation has been somewhat curtailed, the food is still wholesome and well prepared, with gracious and eager-to-please waitresses. The small bar/lounge is a congenial meeting place for before or after dinner. Perhaps best of all, Homewood encourages the real essence of a family vacation, which means being together and enjoying each other's company in a setting of great natural beauty."

—*Jack Chris Kahn*

Open mid-June to mid-October. Some lodgings available in mid-May and late October, when dining room is closed.

44 rooms, including suites and cottages. Housekeeping facilities available.

Rates $25–$41 single, $27–$43 double, $52–$100 suites and cottages. 5 percent discount for visits of a week or longer.

Credit cards: American Express, Master Charge, Visa.

Bar, pool, tennis, croquet, shuffleboard, game room.

German spoken.

_____*York*

Dockside Guest Quarters
Harris Island Road
York, Maine   03909
Telephone: (207) 363-2868

"A few years ago my wife and I made the first of what has become an annual pilgrimage to New England in the fall. As we approached the beautiful little community of York, we consulted our automobile club directory to find a place to stay where we could get a shore dinner. We picked, based on its description and location, Dockside Guest Quarters. We drove along the harbor and over the bridge and causeway leading to the island on which Dockside is located, expecting to find an ordinary seaside motel. Imagine our surprise to arrive at a beautiful wooded setting and an old sea captain's home constructed in the 1700s. Dockside, a unique combination of the picturesque, historic, modern and comfortable, offers a constantly changing panorama of natural beauty and activity. There are views not only of the harbor, but also of the Atlantic Ocean. The traffic of fishermen and yachtsmen in their vessels is always interesting. Some of the sunrises we have watched from our favorite room—14—were so spectacular that we will never forget them. There are interesting walks through the woods and along the rocky cliffs. Our contact with the local people, mostly seafarers, has always been cordial. The traditional 'Down East' reserve shown to visitors has not been our lot. Nearby there is the spectacular Marginal Way walk from the picturesque art colony at Perkins Cove to the resort town of Ogunquit, numerous harbors and inlets and the famous Nubble lighthouse, said to be the most photographed one in the United States."   *—Kenneth F. Kniskern*

"The atmosphere of Dockside resembles that of Cowes, on the Isle of Wight. You enter by a leafy lane, passing the inner harbor of yachts and fishing boats and the marina on the way to the Main House. You are now on board, welcomed by the hosts, David and Harriette Lusty and family. Mr. Lusty owns a sloop, and both he and his sons have won many trophies for yacht racing. Therefore it will not surprise you to learn that all terms used here are of a nautical nature—even the golden retriever's name is Brig. The quarters have individuality—whether you choose the 'Crowsnest,' the 'Quarterdeck,' the 'Lookout' or a room in the Main House. All face seaward.

"York and the surrounding area are most interesting. Indians, who called the area Agamenticas, were hard hit by a plague and deserted the neighborhood by 1623. In 1630 settlers from Bristol, England, moved in and, in 1638, when permission was granted for them to trade with their home city, they named the area Bristol. In 1640 Sir Fernando Georges made Bristol a chartered city and gave it the name Georgeana, though he never did come to the New World. In 1652 the colony of Massachusetts took control of the province of Maine, and Georgeana was reduced to town status and renamed York.

"Seafood dishes are the main items on the menu at Dockside, though roast duckling is the specialty of the house. A continental breakfast is served at moderate cost. Each morning at breakfast the weather is chalked up on a blackboard, and conversations about that break the ice between the shy traveler and the more experienced guest. Soon maps are hauled out and ideas are exchanged." —*Joyce and Ken Tuddenham*

Open May 26 to October 15.
20 rooms, 19 with private bath. Efficiency suites available.
Rates $15–$44. Special weekly rates and rates for families.
Credit cards: Master Charge, Visa.
Cocktail deck, marina, rental sailboats and runabouts.

___Massachusetts

Brewster

The Bramble Inn
Route 6A
Brewster, Massachusetts   02631
Telephone: (617) 896-7644

"On historic Route 6A in Brewster, the Bramble Inn offers good food and comfortable lodging as well as a gallery of local art work. Restoration of this Civil War period home revealed the wide and mellow pine floorboards and the narrow staircases. Many antique furniture pieces grace the foyer and dining areas. Candles burning on small tables in the gallery lend warmth to the intimate dining atmosphere and invite patrons to linger over both paintings and such tempting dishes as Cape Cod chowders, quiches, crepes and fruit-and-cheese trays.

"The rooms on the upper floor are spacious and sunny, and accented with antiques. It is delightful to discover a pot of coffee and a tray of doughnuts in the hallway each morning. The inn's location allows easy access to any spot of interest on the Cape. Brewster itself has a fascinating old general store, a fine needlework shop and uncrowded beaches, all within walking distance of the inn. Nearby are the Cape Cod Museum of Natural History, the New England Fire and History Museum and the Stony Brook grist mill." —*Jean Driver*

Open May to October.
3 rooms, sharing 2 baths.
Rates $19.50–$25.50, including coffee and doughnuts at breakfast.
No credit cards.
Art gallery, tennis courts adjacent.
French and Russian spoken.

Concord

The Colonial Inn
48 Monument Square
Concord, Massachusetts   01742
Telephone: (617) 369-9200

For students of American literature and history Concord has always held a special rank among towns. Here, today's pilgrim finds the Old North Bridge, Walden Pond and the cemetery where Emerson, Thoreau, Hawthorne and the Alcotts are buried. Together the towns of Lexington and Concord—where that "shot heard round the world" was fired—like to think of themselves as the starting point of the Revolutionary War.

"Concord is one of the prime visitor destinations in the United States, and the Colonial Inn is in a prime location to see everything, facing the famous green and easy to find when entering town. The inn has a variety of accommodations. The food is good. There is plenty of parking space. Attractive shops and many historical sights are within walking distance."
—*Dorothy and Link Moore*

"For over thirty years my wife and I and our three children have visited the Colonial Inn, which has been owned and operated by the Grimes family for many years. We like the young manager who, through marriage, is now a member of the owner's family. The inn is at the end of Concord Green, presenting an authentic colonial front to the beautiful expanse of grass and trees. Apart from being ideally situated for visits to Concord and its environs, it is a base for the short trip by car or frequent rail service into Boston. The north and south shores are also readily accessible. Several interesting dining rooms and bars at the inn have always added to our pleasures. Victorian furniture and old prints and paintings give a pleasant atmosphere to the whole. The large bedrooms on the front, facing the green, are our special favorites." —*Stuart C. Henry*

Open all year.
60 rooms, all with private bath.
Rates $25–$30 single, $30–$35 double.
Credit cards: American Express, Carte Blanche, Diners Club, Master Charge, Visa.
Bar.
French, German, Italian, Polish and Spanish spoken.

Hawthorne Inn
462 Lexington Road
Concord, Massachusetts   01742
Telephone: (617) 369-5610

"The inn, in Concord's historic district, is across the street from The Wayside, Nathaniel Hawthorne's home on the battle road between Lexington and Concord. The room was furnished with antiques, and each bed had a homemade quilt on it. Our room had a bay window that looked out on well-kept grounds with many trees. The innkeeper and owner, a delightful young artist named Gregory Burch, was a marvelous host. He joined us at breakfast, which consisted of fruit and juice, homemade baked goods, coffee and tea. All this was included in the price of a room, which was very reasonable."   —*Mrs. Meredith Szostek*

Open all year.
5 rooms, no private baths.
Rates $18 single, $25 double, including continental breakfast.
No credit cards.

East Orleans

Nauset House Inn
Beach Road
P.O. Box 446
East Orleans, Massachusetts   02643
Telephone: (617) 255-2195

"I am essentially a homebody. I don't transplant easily, and when I go away for a vacation I like to find a place where I can keep my roots wrapped in warm, receptive soil, continue to enjoy the creature comforts (and the comforts of the creature, as the Irish say) and breathe an atmosphere where I won't wither. Such a place is Nauset House Inn, a rambling, attractive group of buildings with invitingly decorated rooms. The approach of the host and hostess, Jack and Lucille, is a happy blend of savoir- and laissez-faire. One does exactly as one pleases. I like to walk along the beach or, in bad weather, to read beside the huge hearth with its log fire, or converse with guests and friends there. The magic of this inn is not performed with mirrors. Breakfast helps. The French toast is itself deserving of a toast, and the quiche is beyond the reach of stock superlatives. Although breakfast is the only meal served at the inn, Jack will help you make reservations for dinner at any one of a number of excellent restaurants in the area."

—*T. R. Milligan; also recommended by Folke B. Lidbeck*

Open April 1 to November 15.
14 rooms, 9 with private bath.
Rates $18 single, $23–$35 double.
Credit cards: Master Charge, Visa.
Beach, bicycling, hiking, national seashore park, set-up bar.

Ship's Knees Inn
Beach Road
East Orleans, Massachusetts   02643
Telephone: (617) 255-1312

"For the uninitiated to Cape Cod's historic landmarks, its winding two-lane roads like Route 6A (bypass the Mid-Cape Highway 6, as you'll never see the real Cape this way), the beautiful hydrangeas everywhere and the roses of Falmouth, a quiet, small, distinctive place to spend the night—and preferably several days—is East Orleans' Ship's Knees Inn, an old sea captain's house on Beach Road about a mile from Route 28. It is only a matter of several minutes' walk to Nauset Beach, one of the loveliest on the East Coast. We became acquainted with this inn through friends who had also spent several days here in October, as we did. Our room had a private bath, and was furnished with many antiques. It was relatively quiet at this time of year: One deterrent at the height of the summer season is the continual stream of cars on Beach Road bound for Nauset Beach. There are no meals served, so it is required to drive to town for all food in the fall.

"Distances are so short on the Cape. Fifteen minutes away is the Salt Pond Visitor Center of Cape Cod National Seashore, with Nauset Marsh trail. A bit beyond that is the site of the French cable station built in 1890 to house the trans-Atlantic cable from Brest. Provincetown is a mere half-hour drive beyond that. To the west of East Orleans are the captivating towns of Chatham, Harwich Port, Falmouth and Woods Hole, the home of the Oceanographic Institute and Marine Biological Laboratories.

"Cape Cod is filled with fascinating antique and craft shops.

The North Shore, on Cape Cod Bay, has the interesting town of Sandwich, where the famous glass was once made, and little towns such as Yarmouth, Brewster and Barnstable. But be prepared for a slower pace and perhaps closed restaurants after mid-September."   —*Marion Jacques*

"The tree-filled town of Orleans is a mixture of all that is New England, from the rambling dwellings to the picket fences, white clapboard New England churches and Cape Cod and Victorian homes. Orleans has maintained its idyllic country look. Ship's Knees is a charming and neat clapboard country inn, within view and a pleasant brief walk of Nauset Beach. Nauset Beach's awesome beauty, its miles of sand dunes and clear blue ocean, is breathtaking and unforgettable.

"As for the inn itself, I am completely taken by the colorful individuality of each room. The bright flowered sheets and towels and colorful bathrooms give one the feeling of being a special guest in someone's home. The inn abounds with early Americana, from braided rugs to the antique furniture and wall arrangements. The atmosphere and feeling of Ship's is unquestionably the best of Cape Cod and New England. The innkeeper, Dee, is young and enthusiastic and makes her guests feel welcome and very much at home. She has been most helpful in guiding and suggesting places that are suitable to each guest's interests. Although the inn does not serve meals, a continental breakfast of coffee, muffins, doughnuts and assorted breads was available in the summer. A wide variety of restaurants to suit all tastes and discriminating palates are close by. The area abounds with local artisans and shops that would tempt even the strongest. Their pottery, paintings, glass (Sydenstricker in particular), weaving and jewelry are unique. Of course the antique shops are nonpareil."   —*Roseanne Donovan*

Open all year.
19 rooms, 5 with private bath. 3 rooms and 1 efficiency apartment in Cove House, all with private bath. 2 housekeeping cottages.
Rates $14–$40. Cottages $300–$325, weekly in summer, $30–$36 a day off-season. Breakfast included from mid-June through Labor Day. Special rates off-season.
No credit cards.
Tennis court, picnic facilities with barbeque grills, working fireplaces in rooms.

Where are the good little hotels in Boston? Philadelphia? Omaha? Dallas? If you have found one, don't keep it a secret. Write *now*.

Edgartown

The Edgartown Inn
Box 1211
N. Water Street
Edgartown, Massachusetts   02539
Telephone: (617) 627-4794

"The inn is situated one block up from Edgartown harbor on Martha's Vineyard. Its location puts it within easy walking distance of the shops and restaurants as well as the ferry that takes five minutes to reach the island of Chappaquidick. Because of its popularity during the summer, we return year after year right after Labor Day to find the pace much less hectic. There are geranium-filled flower boxes and comfortable lounging furniture on the open porch and inside. The shelves are filled with books and magazines and there is a lot of original art. All the breads and cakes served for breakfast are made daily, filling the inn with tantalizing aromas. You can eat in the dining room with its whaling artifacts and antiques, as well as on the enclosed patio."   —_Fran Bergere_

Open April 1 to November 1.
19 rooms, 13 with private bath.
Rates $12–$20 single, $28–$40 double.
Only breakfast served.
No credit cards.
French spoken.

Falmouth

Elm Arch Inn
Elm Arch Way
Falmouth, Massachusetts   02540
Telephone: (617) 548-0133

"The Elm Arch Inn is in the center of historic Falmouth, in a quiet area convenient to everything, including several beautiful beaches and the excellent Cape Cod restaurants in the vicinity. Woods Hole is only a few miles away, with daily steamers to Martha's Vineyard and Nantucket Island. The Elm Arch Inn, built in 1812 for Silas Jones, was bombarded by the British frigate _Nimrod_ in 1814. The wall in the former dining room still carries the scar of the cannonball. The inn and the Richardson House have a variety of fine accommodations, all in charming early American decor. A swimming pool surrounded by beautiful old trees and spacious lawns is right next to the inn. There is a homelike atmosphere in this truly old Cape Cod inn, a fine place to stay and enjoy the tranquility of the early American tradition."

—*Eric H. Boyer*

"Harry Richardson and his wife, Flossie, carry on a family tradition that happily began over fifty years ago. Their hospitality, warmth and friendliness create an atmosphere that is congenial, relaxing and most conducive to an enjoyable change of pace, any season of the year. No two rooms in the inn are exactly alike; each one has been thoughtfully and creatively decorated in colonial fashion. The Richardsons have a boundless knowledge of Cape Cod and an unending list of fascinating and interesting things to do and see. Although meals are not served, several fine restaurants are located within a very short walking distance."

—*Mr. and Mrs. James F. Donovan*

Open all year.
25 rooms, 12 with private bath.
Rates $12–$15 single, $16–$30 double.
No credit cards.
Swimming pool.

Harwich Port

The Melrose Inn
601 Main Street
Harwich Port, Massachusetts   02646
Telephone: (617) 432-0171

"The Melrose Inn welcomes visitors to Cape Cod from lilac time to the cranberry season. Redwood chairs and benches on flagstones beneath lovely shade trees front the white, yellow and green wooden building. Flowering shrubs encircle the inn. A wide, green lawn is on one side. In a garden setting, at the end of a flagstone path, is a heated swimming pool. A short walk along a pine-edged road leads to the inn's lovely beach house, on a sea rose-bordered sandy Nantucket Sound beach. In both the inn and the beach house, crackling log fires glow in fieldstone fireplaces on spring and autumn evenings. The Cape cranberry from the nearby bogs is featured in many forms on the menu. Charming floral arrangements in unusual vases grace each table. Ruffled, white Cape Cod curtains dress the dining room windows. Magnificent tall ships, cruising on a smooth sea at sunset or plunging into white-capped waves, adorn the walls of the dining room and the guest rooms. These paintings are T. Bailey's oil translations of Masefield's 'Sea Fever.' Owned and managed since 1921 by the Gerald A. Smith family, Cape Codders, the Melrose Inn radiates warmth, charm and hospitality.

Choice objects from the family's European, Asian and African travels are of special interest. Mrs. Gerald Smith's letters acknowledging reservations end with 'until we greet you.' Personal attention and interest are traditional."

—*Katherine Tucker*

Open mid-May to mid-October.
100 rooms, 80 with private bath.
Rates $15 single, $45 double. Special rates on request. MAP and AP available.
Credit cards: Master Charge, Visa.
Bar, cocktail lounge, heated pool, private beach.

Holyoke

Yankee Pedlar Inn
1866 Northampton Street
Holyoke, Massachusetts   01040
Telephone: (413) 532-9494

"Just fifteen miles north of the tinsel and cookie-cutter world of motels in the Springfield area is a true oasis—the Yankee Pedlar Inn. The rooms are distinctively and tastefully furnished in traditional colonial style; some rooms have canopy beds, and everything is polished and sparkling clean. After settling into one of these rooms, visit the warm pine-paneled dining room. There, through the doorway, you can view the spotless kitchen with its gleaming copper pots."   —*Stephen E. Van Zandt, Jr.*

Open all year except Christmas Day.
47 rooms.
Rates $20–$26 single, $26–$32 double.
Credit cards: American Express, Diners Club, Master Charge, Visa.
Bar, nightly entertainment.
French, Italian and Polish spoken.

Lenox

Wheatleigh Inn
Lenox, Massachusetts   01240
Telephone: (413) 637-0610

"The Wheatleigh Inn in Lenox, Massachusetts, is a most unusual hostelry, having originally been an Italian palazzo given as a wedding gift from an early tycoon to his daughter. This mansion has magnificent rooms with decorations of the period, including a stained-glass window over the staircase in the style of Louis Tiffany. The proprietor of this inn is David Weisgal, who is very much concerned with good food, and many visitors in the area come to Wheatleigh for the meals. One of the features of the cuisine is the Sunday night buffet. Dinners are planned on the early side so that guests can get to the famous Tanglewood concerts, less than a mile away. Lenox and the surrounding Berkshire countryside is one of the most beautiful sections of New England, with rolling hills and trees throughout the area. Stockbridge, Williamstown and other historical and cultural centers can be reached by car in about an hour."

—Earl Morse; also recommended by Wallace W. Meyer

Open all year.
18 rooms in summer, 11 in winter, all with private bath.
Rates $30–$80. Special weekend rates.
Breakfast included.
Credit cards: American Express, Master Charge, Visa.
Bar, tennis, pool.
French spoken.

Whistlers Inn
5 Greenwood Street
Lenox, Massachusetts   01240
Telephone: (413) 637-0975

"When I think of Whistlers Inn I remember with affection the warmth and hospitality of the family that runs it—and the irresistible library it houses. I plan to return a few times next summer so that once again I can open those great Dutch doors that admit one to this rambling Victorian mansion and see the welcoming faces of Mr. and Mrs. Richard C. Mears, their family and staff. And I am sure that their little daughter, Laura, will be holding her Maltese dog, Butchie, in her arms—a most enchanting bundle of white fur. Whistlers Inn was the home of the nephew of the painter James Whistler. It is perched on a hill across from an old cemetery and an old church—should you wish to reflect on the past and the future. There are fourteen rooms in the mansion—a few small, but mostly large and roomy, furnished in the old style, but with all the modern amenities (except TV). A curved staircase leads to the rooms one flight up. There are no meals served, except breakfast, although the Mears family has ambitious plans to correct this as time goes by. But the inn is only a short walk to several Lenox restaurants. Ah, yes, the library—it is a veritable plum pudding of books, old and new, hundreds of them, on almost every conceivable subject from mysteries to medieval philosophy, and especially rich in literature, history and political science. Lots of soft chairs and soft lighting, and classical music playing from the music room next door. If you're not careful, the library could seduce you away from the many other cultural attractions of Lenox and the surrounding area." —*Terry Dewhurst*

Open all year.
14 rooms, 12 with private bath.
Rates $30–$50, including continental breakfast.
No credit cards.
Art gallery, dining room with Louis XIV furniture, library, music room, sunken garden.
French, German, Polish, Spanish and Swedish spoken.

_____*Nantucket*

Jared Coffin House
29 Broad Street
Nantucket, Massachusetts   02554
Telephone: (617) 228-2400

"Nantucket Island is blessed with some of the finest warm-water beaches in the northeastern United States, blissful bicycling and an overabundance of good restaurants (dieters, stay away!). Nantucket is also blessed with a number of hostelries that merit inclusion in an anti-motel guide, but paramount among them is the Jared Coffin House.

"The origins of the Jared Coffin House date back to whaling days, when the original building, built in 1845, was an opulent private home. That building, embellished by a number of small additions, was restored about ten years ago at tremendous expense by the Nantucket Historical Trust, with the goal of re-creating the aura of a bygone age. The restoration achieved its goal.

"A number of the hotel's rooms (but by no means all) are furnished with priceless antiques. Most noteworthy (and delightful) are the rooms with elegant, finely carved four-poster canopy beds, adorned with crewel embroidery hand-done by island ladies. The public areas of the hotel are graced with Oriental rugs and works of fine art. Accompanying these surroundings (lest you fear you have intruded into a plutocrat's private museum) is an atmosphere of extraordinary warmth and friendliness, not to mention courtesy, extending from chambermaids to waitresses to the front desk and to the owners themselves. Phil and Peg Read (Peg is a native Nantucketer) are committed to maintaining 'the Jared' as a very special place.

"Let there be no mistake: The Coffin House has been 'discovered' by those who value fine personal hotels. Reservations are a must, and for the summer season and other peak holiday periods, they must be made well in advance. We have found the hotel especially delightful during the off-season. In an age of crass commercialism, however, it is a truly civilized place at any time of year."   —*Richard Hugh Linden*

Open all year.
46 rooms, all with private bath.
Rates $20–$25 single, $40–$55 double. Special rates in January, February and March.
Credit cards: American Express, Diners Club, Visa.
Bar with live entertainment year round.
French spoken.

The Ships Inn
13 Fair Street
Nantucket, Massachusetts   02554
Telephone: (617) 228-0040

"The most important thing about Nantucket is just being there, though getting there and finding moderately priced accommodations can be trying. This island offers more to the senses than any other sea-trapped sand hillock you could imagine. Fifty square miles of beaches, dunes, moors, ponds and even forests (you may spend years on the island and never suspect their existence, much less visit one) surround one of the largest collections of lovely old dwellings in the United States. Ships Inn was built in 1912 by Captain Obed Starbuck—as in *Moby Dick*. It stands on the site of the house where Lucretia Mott, the abolitionist, was born. Across the street is the Episcopal Church and beyond it, on Orange Street, is the Unitarian Church where Ishmael heard Father Mapple preach the night before he signed on for the last voyage of the *Pequod*.

"But the inn's charm is contemporary as well as antiquarian. It is a typical whaler's mansion—center entrance, two windows on either side, two full stories. Its twelve rooms (ten doubles and two singles) are neatly and adequately if plainly furnished. Some of the rooms do contain furniture of the period. The singles share a bath; the doubles all have private baths. In the basement, which you may enter from the outside through a tiny but lovely planted patio garden, is the Captain's Table, where Nantucket standbys are prepared with more than usual care and imagination. (On our last visit, the chef was a Thai, and he introduced a mildly exotic flavor to bluefish, scallops, quahog chowder and other island fare.) Steaks, lobster and lobster tail, duck, swordfish and lamb are other frequent menu items. Dinners range from $8 to $12.

"Ships Inn is open most of the year, though Bar and John

Krebs, the charming couple who run it, try to spend some time in America, as the islanders call the mainland, in winter."

—*John Ravage*

Open Easter through Thanksgiving.
12 rooms, 10 with private bath.
Rates $16 single, $38 double from June 15 to October 31, including breakfast. Lower rates at other times.
Credit cards: American Express, Master Charge, Visa.

The Woodbox
29 Fair Street
Nantucket, Massachusetts   02554
Telephone: (617) 228-0587

"If you can imagine an inn run by Margaret Rutherford, you know the Woodbox. The proprietor, Marie W. F. Tutein, is a very generous and good-hearted person who has made a life's work out of cultivating her eccentricities. Thanks to her, the Woodbox is what it is—a special place on a special island. There is nothing quite like this inn, and when you are there you feel different. Maybe that has something to do with the reassurance that comes from being in a place that has survived time itself. The Woodbox takes you back 270 years, to when Nantucket was a sparsely populated sandspit thirty miles out in the lonely Atlantic, still the home of half a dozen Indian tribes, and long before the prosperity of whaling allowed the famous mansions of Nantucket to be built. The inn has low, beamed ceilings; dark, glowing paneling; antiques, old paintings and samplers, and candlelight. Upstairs are rooms and suites, many with fireplaces. Across the street in an annex are more rooms, less quaint but quite serviceable. The food is simple but well prepared. Mrs. Tutein is turning over the management of the Woodbox to her son, Dexter, a cordial and capable host."

—*John Wulp*

"The Woodbox sits at the point where Fair Street (which, with its pretty houses, is indeed fair) makes a picturesque bend. A pleasant thing to do after a good dinner is to stroll along Fair and then amble off to one side or the other into the maze of moon-dappled lanes, smelling the roses on the evening air, listening to the church-tower bells and looking discreetly into the beautiful interiors of homes whose owners have been hospitable enough to leave the curtains open."   —*Tom Congdon*

Open May through October.
9 rooms.
Rates $21–$25 per person per day.
No credit cards.

Newburyport

Benjamin Choate House
25 Tyng Street
Newburyport, Massachusetts   01950
Telephone: (617) 462-2808

"If you had been a traveler in the American colonies in the 1700s, chances are you might have spent some time in Newburyport. At that time it was not only the second largest seaport in America, but also host to such celebrities as John Adams, Lafayette, Benedict Arnold, Aaron Burr and George Washington. Although the colonial townsfolk have long since been laid to rest, their mansions, cobblestone streets and cemetery, with many fascinating epitaphs, remain. The place to spend an overnight visit is definitely the Benjamin Choate House, a three-story Federal home built about 1801. The home, meticulously researched by Rose Ann and Paul Hunter, the innkeepers, is furnished with four-poster beds, antique pieces and huge fireplaces."   *—Mary Clifford and Richard Bosch*

Open all year.
5 rooms, 2 with private bath.
Rates $18–$30 in summer, including breakfast. Lower rates from September to spring.
Only breakfast served.
No credit cards.

New Marlboro

Flying Cloud Inn
New Marlboro, Massachusetts   01230
Telephone: (413) 229-2113

In the Berkshires, where cultural activities and natural beauty vie for the traveler's attentions today, 18th-century shipwrights built a sturdy farm home near the town of New Marlboro. The home, on 200 acres of meadows and woodlands with a trout-stocked pond, is now the Flying Cloud Inn, named, appropriately, for a clipper ship.

"Summer and winter the Flying Cloud enfolds its guests in its warm 18th-century farmhouse atmosphere. Located far from the nearest town, Great Barrington, its isolation and the innkeepers' awareness of surrounding nature and the changing seasons give this place the special attraction it has for us. No conventional resort entertainments (except tennis courts) detract from the sense of closeness to the elements. The innkeepers for the last few years have achieved the right balance of service and 'leave-the-guests-alone' to bring about a completely relaxing retreat. The good food and varied wine cellar assure complete satisfaction. The limit of about twenty guests brings them together easily and informally. After a few visits the Flying Cloud becomes a home away from home. The surrounding country offers hiking, skiing, music festivals and lovely scenery to be enjoyed while tramping through snow and the glorious autumn foliage."   —*Joseph E. Poser*

"One can write glowingly of the antique-furnished four-poster bedroom for lovers at the Flying Cloud. And one can write, too, of the lovely *à la Provence* cooking with just the right gourmet touch. But the personal feelings of a frequent visitor to the Cloud can only relate to the tranquility, congeniality, comfort and hospitality that prevail. Surrounded by the beauties of nature and the sound of good music from an excellent, but subdued hi-fi system, one can literally fall into the lap of relaxation and 'come down' rapidly from the travails of a week in the city. We've always considered the Cloud our summer place. Its qualities make it our home in the country. Close to the interesting areas surrounding it, filled with art, antique shops and music, the Flying Cloud with its tennis, hiking paths and lovely pond gives you your choice of doing everything or doing nothing, which is indeed sometimes preferable."

—*Harold W. Melson*

Open May through October and December through March.
9 rooms, 7 with private bath.
Rates $40–$50 double, including breakfast and dinner. Weekday reduced rates available.
No credit cards.
Bar, tennis, ponds, cross-country skiing and ice skating.
Spanish spoken.

_____*Princeton*

The Inn at Princeton
Box 342
Mountain Road
Princeton, Massachusetts   01541
Telephone: (617) 464-2030

"Sometime in the 18th century, when the fear of the Indian frontier had reasonably subsided, a Bostonian known as the Rev. Dr. Prince resigned from his Congregational congregation and pushed west and north some sixty bird-flight miles to the slopes below Mt. Watuschett. There he bought up several hundred acres and founded a village named for himself: Prince-ton, no kin to the one in New Jersey. Princeton, Massachusetts, has been attracting a few runaway Bostonians and other New Englanders ever since. Today it contains a score or more of late-18th-century and early Federal houses of simple charm, well kept without a Williamsburg-type benefactor, as well as Victorian and 20th-century things. The Princetonians are a quiet folk, almost as though they wanted to live without crowds, with their rustling leaves and cool, clean air. Population less than 1,000 probably.

"Princeton is a lovely weekend or stopover village for motorists on their way to or from Maine, let's say, who wish to avoid the vast traffic problems of Boston. From the south or west one ignores the Massachusetts Turnpike after Sturbridge. Route 31 winds interestingly about thirty-two miles to Princeton—and the getaway route to Maine leads east, later. In Princeton the place to sleep, dine and breakfast is the Inn, half a mile or less up the slope from the post office. Once the summer estate of a Boston millionaire, the old place was rescued from a pleasant but indigent commune of hippies in the mid-1970s by a pair of Massachusetts schoolmarms and restored in the spirit of the days of President William Howard Taft. Half a dozen huge double bedrooms with lofty ceilings and splendid beds."

—*John Tibby*

"Suzanne Reed and Elizabeth Sjogren have, in a few years, clearly made the re-creation and new creation of this inn a joyous and cherishing life work. Everywhere you look there is something lovely to see; a glance into a charming dining room, spread over several parts of the downstairs and on outside into a patio by the garden in summer, a living room with fireplace that is for 'living' as well as for admiring, a gift shop that evokes nothing of the standardized hotel. On the stairs you pass a Victorian doll's house, a show-treasure to come back and back to.

"In a time of bustling, plastic 'eating places,' the inn's dining room is a revelation. You are welcomed by one of the owners, who brings the young chef over to the table as part of the welcome, and they discuss with you a menu of specialties with the enthusiasm of artists and the grace of hospitable hosts. The owners have sought out a head chef and a bakery chef from one of the very best training programs in the United States."

—*David Mallery*

"It is the smaller, more personal touches that legitimize use of the word 'special' in describing this inn. Such touches as breakfast trays decorated with guestroom-matched wallpaper, help-yourself bowls of fresh fruit thoughtfully placed in the second-floor foyer and carefully tended fires in the entry hall fireplaces reflect the true character of this inn experience."

—*Dianne M. Foster*

"I don't know how the innkeepers were able to instill the sense of 'time' that encompasses one so warmly—but they have done that in exceptional measure. Each room (we went on 'tour' when there were no other guests!) is done authentically and differently—some brass beds, some gorgeous old dressers, an antique shawl draped over a velvet love seat, a handmade cradle with a teddy bear inside, patchwork and lace—we wanted to spend a night in each. There are fireplaces, a sun-room, lovely and comfortable common rooms to sit and read, talk or just dream in. And what a dining room! Absolutely exquisite food! We had a lovely, crusty onion soup, a steak with Béarnaise sauce, fresh vegetables and a mousse in an edible bittersweet chocolate cup. What a delightful surprise it was—and from our table by the garden window, a view of the twinkling lights of Boston, fifty miles in the distance."   —*Susan Nance*

Open March 15 to December 31.
5 rooms, all with private bath.
Rates $35 single, $45 double, continental breakfast included.
Credit cards: American Express, Master Charge, Visa.
Dinner served Wednesday through Sunday.
Hiking trails, cross-country skiing.

Provincetown

Bradford Gardens Inn
178 Bradford Street
Provincetown, Massachusetts   02657
Telephone: (617) 487-1616

"The visitor traveling to the tip of Cape Cod and the Bradford Gardens Inn goes along the Cape's rocky spine at the end of a sandy spit and reaches Provincetown where trees live buried up to their 'chins' in the dunes. The town, with its harbor and surrounding dunes, cliffs of multicolored sands and grassy moors, imparts a feeling of tranquility. I visit Bradford Gardens Inn frequently and during all seasons. In summer, after an early run or swim, there is a grand breakfast served in the rose garden, where I usually can pick up a backgammon game. In the winter the cape is quiet and isolated—travelers are few—a different feeling from the summer season. I arrive with my books and find the fire lighted in my room."   —*Joan Lang*

"My first reaction to Bradford Gardens was warmth. You feel at home when you meet the innkeeper—Jimmy Logan. He is young, charming and eager to answer all your questions. When you live at the inn—it was built in 1820—you find it has a quiet atmosphere surrounded by a New England grandeur. There are interesting paintings by artists indigenous to Provincetown. You see antiques from all over the globe because Jimmy is an avid traveler. You can lounge by the fireplace in his living room, where a gourmet breakfast is served. Each of his rooms has a character of its own, such as the Jenny Lind bedroom, which has a spool bed. What moved me most was the presence of fresh flowers each day from his garden, and sometimes a goody on your pillow at night. You can relax in his rose garden or swing in his blue swing—in fact, we practiced for *A Streetcar Named Desire* in it.

"You can park your car and walk up and down Commercial Street visiting the monument, the harbor, the stores and restaurants. (All the menus are in his living room and he gives you hints on what to order—he even makes your reservation.) We used the outdoor grill for a lobster dinner one night and other evenings enjoyed our cocktails in the rose garden."

—*Mary Meehan*

Open all year.
20 rooms, all with private bath.
Rates $32–$65 double, including breakfast.
No other meals served.
Credit cards: American Express, Master Charge, Visa.

_____*Salem*

The Coach House Inn
284 Lafayette Street
Salem, Massachusetts   01970
Telephone: (617) 744-4092

"The Coach House looks more like a house than today's more conventional inns and motels. The antique-furnished hallways and winding stairway give an atmosphere of warmth. The room in which I stayed was clean and spacious, with plenty of closet space, and gave out the same homely warmth I experienced at the entrance to the inn. It was simply, but adequately furnished. The private bath I had was also very clean and large, with a small refrigerator. The room had a color TV, but no phone. Each guest is given two keys—one for the room, and the other to the building, to use after all the entrances are locked for the night. I appreciated the literature I found in my room about the town and its many historical sites, in addition to the pamphlets listing all the restaurants in Salem."   —*Leila Dabbagh*

Open March 1 to December 15.
20 rooms, 14 with private bath.

Rates $22–$26 single, $30–$36 double. Special weekly rates and
group rates for students.
No meals served.
Credit cards: American Express, Master Charge, Visa.
French spoken.

Sandwich

Daniel Webster Inn
149 Main Street
Sandwich, Massachusetts   02563
Telephone: (617) 888-3622

"After a three-week stay in Plymouth, we started to venture
down Cape Cod along the seaboard and soon came across the
quaint town of Sandwich, of glass fame. The inn is new—it was
rebuilt after a fire—but the theme is very much New England.
We were treated to meals served on pewter dishes by waitresses
clad in period garb. Our room had deep shag rugs and furnishings that lent an almost family atmosphere. All in all, our weekend stay has since become the highlight of our month in the
area. The village of Sandwich has a beautiful park area with all
trees and shrubs labeled with their Latin and common names.
There are excellent restaurants nearby, where fresh seafood was
superbly cooked."   —Andree Zeritsch

Open all year.
25 rooms, all with private bath.
Rates $42–$52. Lower rates from mid-September through May:
$26–$36 from November through mid-April.
Credit cards: American Express, Master Charge, Visa.
Tavern, entertainment.

Scituate

Inn for All Seasons
32 Barker Road
Scituate Harbor, Massachusetts   02066
Telephone: (617) 545-6699

"The town of Scituate is about thirty miles south of Boston on
the South Shore, about halfway to Cape Cod. Since Plymouth
is only a few miles farther south, the whole area is steeped in
Pilgrim history. Driving north on the main street of Scituate
Harbor, one passes many specialty shops as well as those one

would expect to find in a center of commercial activity. Continuing north, the harbor itself becomes visible with its large dock and many commercial boats. Somewhat farther north the commercial activity begins to fade and the view is now of many pleasure craft at anchor or berthed in either public docks or at the Scituate Yacht Club. In the summer season the pleasure boats dominate the view.

"Turning north on Barker Road there is a large barnlike building identified by a marker as the Barker House. Immediately on the right is the Inn for All Seasons, almost completely hidden by many years' growth of shrubbery. The first thing that strikes the newcomer is the inn's unique door. Ornately carved with a large sculpture, the inn announces itself. From then on—whether spending the night or enjoying a meal—one continuously experiences a feeling of personal service."

—*Boyd Harris*

Open all year.
7 rooms.
Rates $22–$26 single, $27–$34 double, continental breakfast included.
Credit cards: Master Charge, Visa.
Bar in Victorian parlor.

South Sudbury

The Wayside Inn
South Sudbury, Massachusetts   01776
Telephone: (617) 443-8846

"If you have a good imagination you can almost feel the 18th-century stagecoaches on the Boston Post Road that passes the Wayside Inn. This fine 17th-century hostel, once called The Red Horse Inn, played a part in the making of colonial history during the Revolutionary days. It was immortalized in Longfellow's poem 'Tales of a Wayside Inn' and still contains a special exhibit to his memory. The inn has changed little since its early days except that it has blended an antique flavor and decor with necessary modern room comforts to provide an unusual hotel. The dining is equally great, with a wide variety of items and special 'Revolutionary War' drinks for stouthearted individuals. Dinner is served in one of many period rooms often lit only by candles and presided over by the innkeeper, Frank Koppeis. A stroll around the grounds or the town of Sudbury will reward you with sights and pleasures seldom available outside museums: an operating grist mill, the schoolhouse from 'Mary Had a Little Lamb,' a typical New England church and many other sights blended into the colorful landscape all year round."

—*Calvin P. Otto*

Open all year except Christmas Day.
10 rooms, all with private bath.
Rates $20–$25.
Credit cards: American Express, Carte Blanche, Diners Club, Master Charge, Visa.
Bar, cross-country skiing, bicycling.

_____*Stockbridge*

The Red Lion Inn
Main Street
Stockbridge, Massachusetts   01262
Telephone: (413) 298-5545

The inn was built in 1773 as a stagecoach stop on the route linking Albany, Hartford and Boston, and the year after was the site of a convention of protesters from the Berkshire country towns, angered by the use of articles imported from England. After a disastrous fire in 1896, the inn was rebuilt, and since then there has been extensive restoration.

"Stepping into the Red Lion Inn is like stepping into a Currier and Ives print—a nostalgic return to the past with all of its charm, warmth and history. The inn was completely restored a few years ago but much of its antique furniture and fixtures were retained to keep its authenticity, even to the old rope-operated elevator. Old hat collections, comb collections, pictures, pewter, china, mirrors and clocks fill the nooks and crannies, halls and walls. History buffs will be delighted to realize that they may be sitting at a table where William Thackeray, Charles Dickens or Abraham Lincoln dined and that they are staying at the same inn where Nathaniel Hawthorne, Henry Wadsworth Longfellow, William Cullen Bryant and five presidents laid their weary heads.

"Tanglewood, Norman Rockwell's museum, the Ice Glen and many other interests keep the traveler busy in Stockbridge, but the Red Lion has plenty for its guests to do right under its own roof. Good food, a swimming pool, the Widow Bingham Tavern and the Lion's Den, the gift shop or lunch in the flower-laden courtyard, then some quiet conversation on the huge front veranda relaxing in an old rocking chair before retiring to your room containing a large four-poster, an old-fashioned chest of drawers and country curtains at the window."
—*Betty G. Mower*

Open all year.
103 rooms from May 1 to November 1, 28 rooms from November 1 to May 1.

Rates $18–$52.
Credit cards: American Express, Diners Club, Master Charge, Visa.
Pets $7.50 a day.
Heated outdoor pool.

_____*Whitinsville*

The Victorian
583 Linwood Avenue
Whitinsville, Massachusetts   01588
Telephone: (617) 234-2500

"Whitinsville is gracefully off all main roads, some twenty-five miles southeast of Worcester and some fifty road miles from Boston (my guess)—a wonderful weekend or trip-breaking place for those driving northeast or southwest and praying to avoid the Lost World of Boston traffic. In Whitinsville the place to stay is the Victorian, a stunningly successful restoration of a mid-Victorian mansion overlooking a clean-looking little river and one of the town's original mills: Astonishingly it is still a busy mill. Astonishingly, too, for those who have read about the decline of New England mill towns, Whitinsville nowadays carries the air of a rather sparkling and prosperous place: some Greek Revival houses among the Victorian and a proudly spreading building belonging to its historical society.

"In the inn's vast bedrooms the furnishings are delicately, not heavily Victorian in style; and the sheets, pillowcases and towels have been rested in lavender sachet. The baths and showers, meanwhile, are some of the finest mid-1970s equipment anybody could care to luxuriate in. There are a few other non-Victorian touches: In one upstairs hall stands a gleaming upright Victrola, circa 1922, in perfect working condition, with a rack of records from the twenties. On the turntable was 'The Sheik of Araby' without a speck of dust.

"Breakfasts run to English country style, with choices required on an order sheet the night before. Dinners are no less than ★★★ and the chef offers surprises of the day. Excellent tournedos of beef were exactly as rare as ordered."

—John Tibby

"Being from San Francisco, we both were dubious that any place outside of that area could truly lay claim to an authentic Victorian atmosphere. How mistaken (and vain) we were—and how royally pleased! The Victorian, built originally in the 1880s as a private home by the founder of Whitinsville, is richly decorated with antiques and furnishings that made us feel as if we had left the 20th century at the front door and briefly stepped into the adornments of the Victorian 19th century. Our favorites were the commanding center staircase of luxuriously oiled wood, the library dining room (where we were at liberty to browse and borrow at will among valuable old volumes), the original brass chandeliers throughout the inn and the Armour Room (the room we had)—complete with functioning fireplace, high arched windows and window seats, tooled leather wall coverings, king-size bed with brass head stand and fresh apples on a crystal platter to greet us each evening.

"The surrounding countryside well illustrates the reputation New England has for autumn foliage. We thoroughly entertained ourselves touring the back roads. Old Sturbridge Village is an easy drive from the Victorian, and should not be excluded from a day's outing."   —*Scott and Luree Miller*

Open all year.
7 rooms, 4 with private bath.
Rates $20–$45, including continental breakfast.
Credit cards: American Express, Master Charge, Visa.
French spoken.

New
Hampshire

Chocorua

Stafford's-in-the-Field
Chocorua, New Hampshire   03817
Telephone: (603) 323-7766

"The sun was setting and the light of day was beginning to fade. My two companions and I looked at our watches and saw it was ten minutes to six. We were lost in the woods and our greatest concern was that we would miss dinner at 6:30 at Stafford's-in-the-Field. We did not miss dinner and thank goodness, because it was a marvelous breast of chicken with cheese sauce that was absolutely delicious. My wife, Nancy, and I have been to Stafford's-in-the-Field—just below the White Mountains, a short drive from Mt. Washington, the highest peak of the state—twice recently: once with our sixteen-year-old son in July and again with friends from Chicago in October.

"You drive up the road on a long driveway and approach a large comfortable house with a front porch that has rocking chairs on it. The tone is set by the host, Fred Stafford, originally a farmer from California. He and his wife, Ramona, who supervises the fantastic foods served at the Stafford's, with help from their two sons and a daughter when they're not away at school, have been running Stafford's-in-the-Field for about fourteen years. There is a large main house which has a dining room, Fred's office, sitting room, library and one bedroom. More bedrooms (some with baths, some without) are on the second and third floors. Next to the house there is a large barn, beautifully preserved. Behind the house are three or four cottages, one of which we occupied on our October visit. That cottage has two bedrooms; it was very clean, with a rustic decor, a nice size living room with a fireplace, which we enjoyed, and one full bathroom. The house in which we stayed during our July visit had a tremendous amount of charm: The decor took us back about 150 years. On the July visit, we saw Fred and his sons stenciling a room, and we were delighted to see the beautiful finished product on our return in October.

"Dinner is soup, a main course, sometimes salad and your choice of incredible desserts. The guests mix before dinner. Fred might have several tables together or a long table of twelve to fourteen people. If you like photography, bring lots of film. I rose at sunrise one morning to take pictures in the woods behind Stafford's, which has well-marked cross-country ski trails. (I got lost anyway.)"   —*Fred and Nancy Weil*

Closed from November 1 to December 26 and in April and May.
8 rooms, 2 with private bath, and 4 cottages.
Rates $32–$35 double per person, including breakfast and dinner.
No credit cards.

East Hebron

Hillside Inn and Cottages
East Hebron, New Hampshire   03232
Telephone: (603) 744-2413

"This charming inn, originally a farmhouse, lies between Bristol and Plymouth. Across the street from the inn are several cottages that complete the complex: They are not particularly attractive on the exterior but are very convenient for people who travel with children and animals. A large addition was put on the main building about five years ago. It in no way detracts from the appearance of the original building. The rooms in the main area as well as those in the addition are beautifully appointed. A bar off the main lobby is a recent addition. Until two years ago no liquor was served at Hillside. The dining room is a delight. Many antique treasures are displayed there and in the lounge areas. Hillside could have boasted of serving some of the best food in New England until a couple of years ago. The change in management at that time was unfortunate. The menu is too extensive for a small inn, and the food is not well prepared. Welcome touches, such as finger bowls after each meal, were eliminated. Everything, however, is neat, clean and attractive. The view of the gardens, the barn and of the lake from the dining room are pleasing.

"Located on the shore of Newfound Lake, the inn offers swimming and boating. Two tennis courts are available. Paths through the property are lighted at night. There is little activity in the area. If peace and quiet are what the traveler wants most, Hillside has both to offer."   *—Kay Wilder*

Open all year.
19 rooms, all with private bath.
Rates $15–$20 single, $25–$38 double, cottages (sleeping 4–6) $38–$50.
Credit cards: Diners Club, Master Charge, Visa.
Lounge, tennis courts, recreation room.

Eaton Center

Rockhouse Mountain Farm
Eaton Center, New Hampshire   03832
Telephone: (603) 447-2880

"This is a working farm in the White Mountains, purchased by the Edge family in 1936 to be run as an inn. The setting is spectacular and the view breathtaking in every direction—mountains, lakes, rivers, ponds and fields. Most people take day trips, but my husband refuses to leave the farm, commenting that there is no more beautiful vista anywhere. Children find it a paradise too—there are horses and ponies to ride, geese, turkeys, ducks and pigs to feed, milking to watch, hayrides, swimming and boating. The farmhouse is filled with family antiques, not things acquired to impress. The evening meal is always an occasion, with fresh flowers and candlelight and the most superb food served beautifully. Then there are the Edges themselves—Libby, John, Johnny, Betsi Edge Ela and her husband, Bill—an intellectual family, well read, widely traveled, interested in everything and delighting in physical work."
                                       —Mrs. F. G. Evangelist

"In summer there are all kinds of exciting things to do. Children have their own dining area where the smaller are cared for by the bigger ones. But the beauty of Rockhouse reaches its peak in the fall, with maples, aspens and oak of every color. Johnny always has a bright and friendly fire glowing in the big stone fireplace where we all gather. Every family falls in love with this inn—we are now in our third generation."
                                       —John and Dorothy Francis

Open mid-June to November 1.
18 rooms, 6 with private bath.
Rates $30 single, $25–$28 per person double, including breakfast
  and dinner.
No credit cards.
Set-up bar.
French, German and Spanish spoken.

Fitzwilliam

Fitzwilliam Inn
Fitzwilliam, New Hampshire   03447
Telephone: (603) 585-9000

"The Fitzwilliam is the closest I've ever come to the postcard
image of a New England inn. The living room walls are charmingly stenciled, the stair has a comforting creak, the bathtubs
have feet and I don't ever recall having a key to my room.
(Keys may exist, but it has never occurred to me to ask.) I arrived a bit early for Christmas last year. The tree was trimmed
with homemade and other ornaments, bowls of greens were arranged on tables in the halls, and in one of the guest rooms a
small cat had settled himself to sleep at the foot of the bed. The
rooms are small but cozy, with painted furniture and hooked
rugs. Numbers 3 and 4 are the nicest—corner rooms with fireplaces and a rocking chair or two. The dining room turns out
hearty servings of good New England fare—brook trout with
almonds and roast beef head my list of favorites.

"On Christmas Eve, the Wallace family (all very musical)
were home for the holidays and gathered around the living
room piano. One elderly guest was dozing in the wing chair by
the fireplace; another guest stitched away on his needlepoint.
The rest of us joined in the carol singing, and I wondered if our
music was providing the background for the dreams of the
children who had been tucked in bed upstairs."
                                    —*Ellen Peterson Morris*

"How fortunate for us to arrive in New Hampshire in early October at the height of the fall foliage display, and to stay at the
Fitzwilliam Inn, an inn that has been in continuous operation
since 1796. My husband had just accepted employment in the
nearby town of Keene, so we spent a month at the inn in transition. And what a marvelous temporary home it was. The staff
at the inn, owned and managed by Barbara and Charlie Wallace, with apprentices Martha and Steve Jones assisting, is one
congenial family. Many of the Wallaces' personal belongings
are used throughout the old-fashioned, comfortable rooms. In
the dining room, the large fireplace and wide oak floorboards

add to the pleasant atmosphere. The rather limited menu is excellent, daily featuring homemade soups and Barbara's culinary talents of fresh bread and luscious desserts. George, the cook, excels in preparing fresh swordfish that literally melts in your mouth."   —*Frances M. Mitten*

Open all year.
22 rooms, 7 with private bath.
Rates $10–$16 single, $14–$20 double. Special weekly rates—seventh day free.
Credit cards: American Express, Master Charge, Visa.
Bar, pool.

Francestown

The Inn at Crotched Mountain
Mountain Road
Francestown, New Hampshire   03043
Telephone: (603) 588-6840

"This charming brick colonial house, with a wing built in 1822, faces intimate mountains, excellent for hiking or skiing. On the other side there is an unimpeded forty-mile view of rolling hills and meadows. Later we were told that our elevation was a pleasant 1,300 feet. On arriving at the inn, we were greeted by a delightful young man, who introduced us to our lovely New England room. He proved to be the host and owner. The next day, after a pleasant night's rest, we found the swimming pool, a wading pool and two tennis courts. We had been told they were championship courts, and indeed they were. On a late September visit we found the inn ideal for rest, healthy recreation and excellent food. I am sure that other times of year are equally delightful."   —*Kenneth J. Cooper*

Closed from the last weekend in October to Thanksgiving Day, and from the end of the ski season to Memorial Day.
8 rooms, 4 with private bath.
Rates $19 single, $31 double.
Breakfast served; dinners from Monday to Saturday.
No credit cards.
Dining room liquor license, tennis, pool.
Chinese and Spanish spoken.

If you would like to amend, update or disagree with any entry, write *now*.

Franconia

Franconia Inn
Route 116
Easton Road
Franconia, New Hampshire   03580
Telephone: (603) 823-5542

"The rooms are immaculate, and each time we returned from outings we found that little elves had straightened up our vacationers' mess. Fresh fruit in the room, fresh flowers daily, beds turned down at night and thick, thirsty fresh towels are the most visible signs of the attitude that prevails. The dining room is filled to overflowing with Magie Blakeslee's luscious green plants. The food is excellent and attractively served. The members of our group are addicted to tennis and we found the four clay courts in excellent condition. The location of the inn makes it ideal for day trips into the beautiful White Mountains. We did some walking, some climbing and some driving through spectacular countryside. We are not skiers, so I do not know what the inn is like during its peak season. I can only say that as an off-season, autumn respite we thoroughly enjoyed our stay."   —*Phoebe Liss*

Open December 15 to April 1; June 20 to October 15.
29 rooms, 10 with private bath.
Rates from $28–$47 single, $25–$38 double per person, including breakfast and dinner. Special 3-day and 5-day rates.
Credit cards: American Express, Diners Club, Master Charge, Visa.
Bar, cross-country skiing, pool, tennis.

Lovett's Inn
By Lafayette Brook
Profile Road
Franconia, New Hampshire   03580
Telephone: (603) 823-7761

"Lovett's has made few concessions, thank goodness, to the onward march of mediocrity and sameness that today characterizes so many of the travelers' lodging places in this country. True, Charlie Lovett—who with his wife, Red, has directed the destinies of this charming North Country inn for some thirty years—yielded mildly to the changing times in 1956 by adding the word 'motel' to the sign out front alongside Highway 18, making it read, 'Lovett's Inn and Motel.' A storm of protest arose from Lovett's repeating guests—whose large numbers attest to the excellence of the place—against this capitulation to postwar change, and the word 'motel' disappeared from the sign the following year, never to be seen there again.

"Other changes at Lovett's through the years have been relatively few and, for the most part, well advised. For several years now guests have been offered the alternative of bathing in a small swimming pool filled with solar-heated water instead of being compelled to indulge their aquatic whims in the pond across the road, which is fed with icy spring water from Lafayette Brook. A few years ago Charlie Lovett attended an auction of the furnishings of one of the great Newport cottages, and returned to Franconia with a magnificent curved, marble bar. By his own admission, this acquisition was an extravagance—it earned him the disapproval of his wife for a time—but the marble bar became the focal point of the charming and intimate barroom at Lovett's. It now contributes strongly to the feeling of well-being and sociability which one experiences on entering this small haven.

"Lovett's food demands special mention in any description of the inn. In the opinion of this writer, there is no more savory cuisine to be encountered *anywhere*. At dinner the guest is confronted with a choice of seven or eight tempting entrees, ranging on a typical evening from broiled fresh swordfish to 'heavy western sirloin.' The only problem is in making a choice from so many delectable possibilities. The salads are simple, but without peer, being made with lettuces and herbs gathered that very day from the salad garden just outside the kitchen. What can one say about Lovett's desserts? Simply that they will break down the resistance of the most iron-willed dieters. I think that a reasonable rule of thumb for the guest at Lovett's would be to figure on two to three added pounds of weight for each week spent in residence!"
—*A. Wells Pettibone*

"Tucked in a small valley in the splendor of the White Mountains is this unpretentious country inn. The surrounding towns of Franconia and Sugar Hill are unspoiled villages with examples of well-maintained and charming 18th- and 19th-century homes and farms. The fall foliage season offers magnificent color, harvest fairs and fetes. Downhill ski areas abound and newly created cross-country trails lead the adventurous into lovely winter woodlands. In the summer the state and national parks provide hiking, camping, climbing and swimming. Scenic wonders for the photographer or painter—gorges, flumes, mineral caves and a cog railway to the top of Mt. Washington—are nearby. Arts and crafts shops welcome visitors. Historic spots include one of the first successful iron forges in New England. Accommodations at the inn vary from private rooms in the restored farmhouse to separate motel units to simple 'barn' accommodations for singles and teen-agers who share baths and showers and enjoy a special camaraderie. Charlie Lovett presides in the attractive cocktail lounge, introducing guests and mixing a superb martini."   *—Mrs. James H. Cannon*

"Anyone who has ever stopped at Lovett's will tell you what a rare combination of rest and activity you find there, all adding up to exceptional enjoyment. When the World Cup Ski Competition was held in this country a few years ago, it was Lovett's that was chosen to accommodate the French team."
     —John T. Harman; also recommended by Dorothy Ebi

Open December 26 to April 1, June 28 to Columbus Day.
25 rooms, 18 with private bath.
Rates $24–$34 per person, including breakfast and dinner. European plan also available. Winter packages.
Credit cards: American Express, Visa.
Bar, swimming pool, cross-country skiing, hiking, tennis, golf.

Hancock

The John Hancock Inn
Hancock, New Hampshire   03449
Telephone: (603) 525-3318

"Surrounded by mountains, Hancock is a thriving community of friendly people, and the John Hancock Inn is truly the heart of this community. In the many visits we have made to the inn in the past five years, we have made many friends among the people of the town and surrounding areas. We feel very much at home, and of course much of this feeling is due to the warm, welcoming atmosphere created by Pat and Glynn Wells and their children. And one can't overlook the great meals prepared for us by chef Dick Doucette and the staff. For anyone interested in early New England towns this is the area to visit— time and progress have not brought ugly structures of metal, glass and neon. Hancock is much as it was before the turn of the century. The beautiful old buildings are treasured and maintained. The inn itself has been in operation since 1789. Norway Pond and the old cemetery, both within two minutes' walk of the inn, will appeal to camera buffs and historians."
     —Marjorie S. Burns

Open all year except one week in spring, one in fall.
10 rooms, all with private bath.
Rates $22 single, $30 double.
Credit cards: Master Charge, Visa.
Lake swimming, skiing.

_____*Hanover*

Hanover Inn
Hanover, New Hampshire   03755
Telephone: (603) 643-4300

"Throughout my drive from New Haven, Connecticut, to Hanover, New Hampshire, in September, I was enthralled with the beauty of the rolling hills and the beautiful farm scenery. I-91—a concrete maze that would normally turn me off—was a beautiful drive, especially north of Springfield. I thought: 'Well, this will soon end: Dartmouth, another college campus lecture and another couple of nights in some dingy hotel called the Hanover Inn.' As I entered the front door, I was absolutely amazed by the charm of old New England. The lady behind the desk was perhaps the most courteous and pleasant registration clerk I had ever encountered. Grabbing my few bags and getting onto the elevator, I couldn't help but compare this charm with the finest of small northern Italian pensions or Bavarian zimmerhauses which I had stayed in during the 1960s. I opened the door to my room and WOW! There was the most elegant colonial room in which I had stayed in my entire life. The quilted bedspreads, the antique chests and dressers, the beautiful colonial wallpaper, the dormer windows, not a speck of dust anywhere. After unpacking, I found the sitting room adjacent to the main lobby an absolutely fantastic place to sit with the evening paper, unwind and relax. And, dinner was superb. What a joy it was to return to my room, look out the window and see the moonlit Dartmouth campus across the street and hear the chimes of the clock echoing in the background."
—*Dr. Gilbert L. Whiteman*

"The twin-bedded room is small but adequate. Furnished with reproduction Hitchcock furniture, it has a warm feeling. The desk is well supplied with stationery, postcards and information on the area. And we cannot help but notice that the pale gold comforters folded at the foot of each bed are exactly the same color as the pattern in the wallpaper. The hallway leading to the elevator is a disappointment. On the strategically placed tables are identical arrangements of poorly made artificial flowers. They seem incongruous and tend to detract from the overall picture. All is forgiven as we enter the elegantly appointed dining room. The unusual salad bar holds two round tiers of beautifully prepared foods, artistically displayed. One can have that plus a bowl of soup for only five dollars. We decided to have the regular dinner, too, and were delighted with the excellent service plus the quality of the food. Every table was being used, but the tables were placed far enough apart so that conversation from other tables did not bother us at all. Ages of the diners ranged from one to about eighty, with no single age group predominating. We slept soundly and woke up refreshed. Breakfast in the coffee shop was pleasant enough. We were relaxed, knowing our car had been parked in the hotel's garage overnight." —*Kay Wilder*

Open all year.
100 rooms, all with private bath.
Rates $36–$46 single, $42–$54 double.
Credit cards: American Express, Diners Club, Master Charge, Visa.
Cocktail lounge, outdoor terrace.
French spoken.

_____*Jackson*

Christmas Farm Inn
Jackson, New Hampshire   03846
Telephone: (603) 383-4313

"As one proceeds north through Mt. Washington Valley on Route 16, a side road leads through a quaint covered bridge into Jackson. Through the village and up a steep hill, you notice a large, well-kept white farmhouse. Here, high on the slope of one of the area's lesser mountains, with outstanding views of Mt. Washington and the Moat Range, are the main farmhouse (really several buildings in one), an expanded Cape Cod cottage (Red House), a large barn, a sugar house and a log cabin—the Christmas Farm Inn. Enter the main house and find a typical old New England-style decor, functional and attractive. Off the hall and 'lobby' are two small living rooms, a spacious dining room and a small lounge. Upstairs, bedrooms are obviously meant primarily for sleeping. It is very much like a visit to Grandma's, provided yours lived in the country. The other buildings offer newer and more spacious rooms (Red House), privacy (Sugar House) and family or group accommodations (Log Cabin).

"The real charm of an inn is the friendly warmth and hospitality it can offer. The new owners of Christmas Farm Inn, Bill and Sydna Zeliff, and their three sons, Jim, Mike and Willie, seem more like old friends than innkeepers and they have selected their staff carefully to ensure that this feeling prevails. Add to this a significant number of repeat guests and the casual evenings in the living room before the fireplace or in the cozy lounge are indeed enjoyable.

"Children are welcome, of course, but they are expected to take noisier activities to the game room in the barn. Food has always been of prime importance at Christmas Farm and 'just plain good.' Bill and Sydna have improved on this through an expanded menu. Although lunch is not served, a sandwich 'trail lunch' is available. Enjoy the homemade soup, salad bar and the entree, but save room for desserts. These are varied but always include the popular 'Christmas Farm Sundae' (New Hampshire maple syrup over vanilla ice cream decorated with nonpareils). If your vacation activities are not strenuous, order the child's portions or be prepared to go on a diet when you get home."   —*Mr. and Mrs. Donald Chesebrough and family*

Open May 1 to October 31; December 15 to March 31.
22 rooms, 20 with private bath.
Rates $31–$40 single, $52–$70 double, breakfast and dinner included. Special family rates and 5-day midweek packages.
Credit cards: American Express, Master Charge, Visa.
Cocktail lounge, game room, pool, putting.

The Dana Place Inn
10 Pinkham Notch Road
Jackson, New Hampshire   03846
Telephone: (603) 383-6822

"Just above the village of Jackson on Route 16 leading toward Mt. Washington, lies Pinkham Notch and the Dana Place Inn. With the majesty of Mt. Washington as a backdrop, the Dana Place seen from its apple orchards on the Ellis River Trail presents one of the prettiest views anywhere in the Northeast. We have been frequent visitors to the inn over the past several years. In winter our lives revolve around cross-country skiing, and there is no finer anywhere for our money than in the Mt. Washington Valley's Jackson Ski Touring Foundation and Appalachian Mountain Club networks. Our visits have not, however, been limited to snow season. The Dana Place is an ideal headquarters for hiking in the White Mountain National Forest; in the summer the inn offers tennis in the shadow of Mt. Washington, a swim in the pool or, even better, in the natural pools of the Ellis River and Winneweta Falls, which flow nearby. The inn itself has comfortable, cozy rooms, an elegant dining room, personalized service from all the staff and a special warmth created by Betty and Mal Jennings, the innkeepers. The Valley keeps you coming back to the Valley. The Jennings keep you coming back to the Dana Place Inn."
          —*Lee and Margaret Phillips*

"Breakfast is a hearty meal and dinners are truly outstanding. There are three dining areas, each with a charm of its own. An open fire lends warmth to the central area while hanging baskets and glass walls provide interest in the others. The hiking possibilities around the inn are limited only by the energy of the visitor. There are gentle walks beside a lovely trout stream on the grounds and for the more ambitious, a mountain to climb across the road and hiking trails as far as anyone cares to go. Within a few miles there are several streams for the trout fisherman, early summer being the most productive time for this activity."   *—Yetta G. Samford, Jr.*

"The Dana Place Inn is really a small resort, offering two tennis courts, a private beach on the Ellis River that runs through the property, access to the network of hiking trails that crisscross the region, splendid views of the surrounding White Mountains and the best food in a hundred-mile radius. Several acres away, but on the estate property and within a few steps of the tennis courts, are privately owned condominiums whose owners sometimes rent them for brief periods through the Jenningses. But it is the food that primarily attracts both overnight guests and local diners. A resident chef keeps getting better and better, and probably will wind up as a partner. The fare is standard cosmopolitan, featuring the usual range of fish, fowl and meat, but it is done with unusual touches: The biscuits are baked on the premises and served hot, the butter is laced with orange rind, the salad dressing contains almond slivers, the dessert sundae is served melted and potable, the soups and sauces are proprietary and the salads are made of spinach rather than lettuce. Trail lunches often contain pâtés and puddings, olives and cheese, sandwiches and pies. The new chef has enabled the inn to surpass the Bernerhof Restaurant on Route 302 in nearby Bartlett as the gastronomic capital of the area."   *—Michael Glueck*

Closed late October to mid-December, early April to late May.
14 rooms, 6 with private bath.
Rates $18–$29 single, $26–$44 double, including breakfast.
Special ski packages.
Credit cards: American Express, Master Charge, Visa.
Cocktail lounge, piano bar, swimming pool, river pool, fishing, tennis, cross-country ski trails, hiking.
French spoken.

Jaffrey

Woodbound Inn
Post Office
Jaffrey, New Hampshire   03452
Telephone: (603) 532-8341

"On the shores of Lake Contoocook at the base of Mt. Monadnock, nestles a lovely old country inn—the Woodbound Inn in Jaffrey. Woodbound has something for all seasons, all travelers, all ages: hot buttered rum served in front of a huge fireplace, sleigh rides, skating parties, skiing and oyster stew and sugar on snow at a winter cookout; hayrides, lemonade parties on the lawn, water skiing, swimming, boating and beach luncheons in summer; square dancing, cornhusking bees, a golf course and a trout stream. Delicious, fresh food keeps folks fortified for all of the events and a groaning weekly buffet table provided by Woodbound's fantastic cook, Dot Flagg, satisfies every appetite. A children's program in both summer and winter makes it possible for parents to enjoy a leisurely vacation, too. All activities are served up with warmth and tender loving care by innkeepers Ed and Peggy Brummer, son Jed and daughter-in-law Mary Ellen."   —*Betty G. Mower*

"Woodbound Inn is a family-owned and operated country inn catering to family-oriented people. The rooms are comfortable, clean, attractively furnished and well maintained. Pine-paneled lakeside cottages with fireplaces offer excellent accommodations (with a view) for family groups. Congeniality is the keynote of the Woodbound Inn, and second and third generations return to enjoy the Brummers' hospitality. We are going back for our seventeenth family vacation and a June wedding for one of our daughters—all at Woodbound."   —*Constance H. Eng*

Open June 8 to October 9, December 26 to January 2, weekends in February and March, last two weekends in May.
25 rooms, 11 cottages, 17 with private bath.
Rates $35–$40 single, $28–$36 per person double, $27–$37 per person in cottages. Includes all meals. Weekly rates in summer, special rates for senior citizens in June and for ski packages in winter.
No credit cards.
Lake beach, boats, tennis court, par-3 golf course, ice skating, ski tours. Set-up bar.

_____*Littleton*

Beal House Inn
247 Main Street
Littleton, New Hampshire   03561
Telephone: (603) 444-2661

"While its white clapboard exterior is not prepossessing, its interior is delightful. The place is furnished with antiques, most of which are for sale. I suspect the building dates from the era of toilets out back, but now modern facilities are tucked into each room most ingeniously—no two alike. And no two rooms are the same in size, shape or furnishings. If you wish to sleep in a glamorous canopy bed or opt for a nostalgic brass one, you can be accommodated. Or, if one of you snores and the other takes umbrage, you can choose a pair of connecting rooms. Breakfast in front of the roaring fire is a must. Oh those tender, crisp waffles with all the genuine Vermont maple syrup you want or scrambled eggs served under an antique glass hen. And don't miss the coin silver flatware, pewter serving dishes and old red-and-white table linen. The town has the usual shops and country-type houses and is not inspiring, but its location in the center of the most beautiful and spectacular part of the White Mountains, as well as some excellent eateries and antique shops, makes it a great place to stay or to jump off from."

—John M. Belding

"The inn is situated on the main street of Littleton, a town in the northern part of the state close to the Vermont border and very near to the scenic Connecticut River Valley. The mountain slopes of both Vermont and New Hampshire are nearby and the air is said to be the purest in the country."

—Dr. John A. Roque

Open all year.
15 rooms, 9 with private bath.
Rates $14 single, $16 double.
Breakfast only served.
Credit cards: American Express, Carte Blanche, Diners Club, Master Charge, Visa.

Plymouth

Deep River Inn
Highland Street
Plymouth, New Hampshire   03264
Telephone: (603) 536-2155

"A serendipity for us was the discovery of the Deep River Inn in Plymouth, the gateway to New Hampshire's scenic ski areas. Not on the highway, or even on the main street of the town, the inn is set in thirty-six acres of wooded park, gradually being made into an all-season resort. Facilities are comfortable motel-style. The menu and food are good. But the special charm is the atmosphere created by the owner-hosts, Betty and Bill Gosselin—and their young-adult children. A stay here is refreshing."

—Dorothy and Link Moore

Open all year.
20 rooms, all with private bath.
Rates $22.95 single, $29.95 double. Special off-season and group rates.
Credit cards: American Express, Master Charge, Visa.
Cross-country skiing.
French spoken.

_Shelburne

Philbrook Farm Inn
North Road
Shelburne, New Hampshire   03581
Telephone: (603) 466-3831

"Sometime when your New England explorations lead you to U.S. Highway 2—which stretches all the way across northern Vermont, New Hampshire and Maine—you will find as you pass along the White Mountains that you are surrounded by forests of white birch trees. A few miles east of Gorham these trees line the road and arch overhead, making a virtual birch bower. These are known widely as the Shelburne birches, and you are now within a few miles of Philbrook Farm Inn. Watch carefully for North Road, turn left and follow the inn signs over the Androscoggin River bridge. No adequate description of this century-old inn can be written within the limits of this space. The inn, always owned and operated by the Philbrook family, has a large, beautifully furnished parlor at its east end and an attractive, spacious dining room at the west end. After meals many guests seem to gravitate to a smaller sitting room in between, where the fireplace is rarely without a flame. Other guests will congregate on the front porch where the view sweeps across fields, with cattle grazing, to the New Hampshire-sized mountains of the Moriah Range.

"Between meals the inn serves as home base for a dozen or more half-day auto trips—north through Berlin to explore genuine backwoods country, east into nearby Maine, west into nearby Vermont, south through one of the White Mountain notches to shop in Jackson and the Conways. The Appalachian Trail runs within a few miles of the inn, and many guests spend between-meal hours hiking over well-marked paths."

—*Robert Dixon*

"Connie Philbrook Leger and Nancy Philbrook are the fourth generation of the Philbrook family to be the keepers of this rambling white, hospitable, warm and friendly inn. Hikers have a field day at Philbrook Farm Inn. The sophisticated mountaineer can test his strength on many peaks of the Presidential Range a few miles off, or ramble more casually on the less formidable climbs of lower mountains. Winters are cold and snowy but skiers have their choice of downhill tough or easy trails within a few miles. Cross-country experts on their slender 'boards' have many miles of woodland paths. And snowshoers, in a modern revival of that lost art, have the best of everything. There are pleasurable snowshoe walks through few or endless miles of protected woodland paths, sheltered from bitter winter winds. Fishermen can ply their art on nearby streams or ponds. The Androscoggin River above Milan has fast-moving white water, and above it the deep slow-moving water winds peacefully through the thirteen-mile woods.

"So much for the outdoors! It is the pleasant, peaceful living, delicious food, comfortable beds and fine company indoors that make Philbrook Farm what it is. The traveled and the knowledgeable gather at this unusual inn, where good companionship is the order of the day. The walls of the living rooms are packed with a library of New Hampshire history and a variety of literature. There is a good reference library about birds, New Hampshire's flora and fauna, science, literature, medicine and the arts.

"The furnishings of the inn have been collected over the past hundred years or more by the Philbrook family. There are Shaker pieces, comfortable rockers and elegant maple spool bedsteads. Fine home cooking emerges from Nancy's kitchen, so tasty that weight watchers' diets are soon forgotten. Whole families converge upon Philbrook Farm Inn year after year, sometimes three generations of them at a time, where they unite for a gathering of their clan."

—*Dr. Theodore and Alice W. Badger*

Closed October 31 to December 26.
19 rooms, 6 with private bath.
Rates $18–$30 per person, MAP.
No credit cards.
Transportation from Gorham bus stop on request.

_____*Sugar Hill*

The Homestead
Sugar Hill, New Hampshire   03585
Telephone: (603) 823-5564

"The Homestead made such an impression on me when I first saw it that ten years later it is the 'magic place' I think of every morning. A remote village where I spent summers as a boy is now caught in the tentacles of a superhighway. But Sugar Hill satisfied me because I needed a place that hadn't changed. I now go back once or twice a year.

"Luckily, my cousin was a friend of the Serafinis (the owners), and for our first visit we were able to take the Chalet, one of the Homestead's outbuildings. We had the whole thing to ourselves, upstairs and down, which meant two fireplaces and two tremendous living rooms as well as a kitchen where we cooked our own food. The last was a necessity. If we had eaten at the inn, we couldn't have staggered up the high mountains.

The Chalet is a curiosity. The lower part is stone from nearby fields, and the upper consists of virgin timber, logs hauled from miles away and held together with a variety of iron fittings. Under the row of mullioned windows opposite the fireplace, upstairs, is a long bookcase for nights or rainy days. Outside is a balcony facing the White Mountains.

"When I stepped out on that balcony and saw the wild flowers and birches and the spire of a tiny church in the foreground, soft-colored meadows here and there, I was at peace. Lafayette was right in front of me, with Kinsman off to the west and Mt. Washington remotely in the east. An ancient telescope was fixed on a brass plate inscribed with distance and direction of the nearest mountains.

"I felt *among* the mountains, not perched over them. The setting, in fact, is indispensable. Buildings are not placed willy-nilly, but have evolved to make snowy winters endurable. Since the inn is well above the mists of Franconia Notch, it is a joy at all seasons.

"The Chalet is only one aspect of the inn. Where else could you dine on handmade plates with a different scene on them at each meal? Meet foreigners who come back year after year? Be smiled on by non-Hilton waitresses who—by some magic of the Rip Van Winkle gorges and notches hereabouts—have remained real, live human beings? Choose your dessert from a handwritten list mounted in a gold frame placed on the table? Eat Best Ever pie? This is not contrived nostalgia. The things that count—service and personal attention—have simply not been mechanized. (If tintinnabulation is your desire, the departing guest is rung off the premises, the staff dropping whatever they are doing and seizing the nearest bell.) Somebody is doing the work and a thousand details—willingly. Such duties, to be bearable, require love. And that is what the Homestead has to offer."

—Peter Clarke

Open Christmas to April 15; late May to November.
17 rooms, 7 with private bath.
Rates $28–$40 single, $26–$30 per person double, breakfast and dinner included.
Special rates for children under 12 and for extended visits.
No credit cards.

Turn to the back of this book for pages inviting *your* comments.

Sunapee

Dexter's Inn
Stagecoach Road, Box W
Sunapee, New Hampshire   03782
Telephone: (603) 763-5571

The main house was built in 1801 by Adam Reddington, a craftsman who earned his living making the bowls in which the sailing ships carried their compasses. It was remodeled in the 1930s by Samuel Crowther, a financial adviser to President Hoover. The house became an inn in 1948.

"The inn is a beautiful old house, with seventeen rooms, all of them spotlessly clean. Fires crackle in open fireplaces on chilly nights and there is a large library. For the summer there are several tennis courts, a swimming pool in a woodland setting, spacious lawns, pine groves, secluded walks and old-fashioned gardens."

—*Carroll S. Byrd*

"I have been a guest at Dexter's every summer and several autumns since 1972. The inn is small and intimate, the guests pleasant and considerate. The staff remains much the same year after year and warmly greet each guest by name. The innkeeper, Frank Simpson, a gentleman in every sense of the word, quietly goes about the business of making your stay at Dexter's a memorable one. Whatever your interests, Frank is always available to give suggestions for enjoyable side trips or day-long excursions. Shirley Simpson, Frank's wife, is the creative force behind the scenes—supervising the immaculate kitchen and bringing her special decorative touches to individualize each room. Returnees often ask to be in the 'tulip room' or the 'antique room,' the 'four-poster room,' and so on. Win King, the housekeeper, is cheerful and friendly. She is also talented at needlework and many of her creations are sold in Dexter's little gift shop. Her husband, Bill, keeps the grounds and buildings in good shape. One small example of Frank Simpson's devotion to his guests: My husband was eager to gather dried grasses and cattails, to make a table arrangement for our home. On the last day we needed only thistle to make our collection complete. Frank thought there might be some near the barn. In the confusion of leaving, we neglected to look for it. A week after we arrived home, a shoebox filled with thistle came from Frank.

"The surrounding area has much to offer—excellent gift and antique shops, an extremely well-stocked ski shop and a woolen mill store are ten minutes away. An outstanding championship golf course, Eastman, at Grantham, is a mere fifteen minutes away. A fascinating side trip is to Ruggles Mine, an open pit mica and feldspar mine on top of a mountain. Mineral picks may be rented there; all you need is a sturdy bag to carry away your finds. Hanover, home of Dartmouth College and Hopkins Center is but thirty minutes away from Dexter's. Manchester, an interesting old manufacturing city, is a pleasant hour's drive and it offers New Hampshire's newest shopping mall in addition to many factory outlet stores. In the Mall, there is an intriguing shop called Brookstone, home of the hard-to-find tool—said to be one of the few stores in which *men* actually browse!"   —*Julia Steere Koeck*

Open mid-June to mid-October and December 26 to mid-March.
17 rooms, all with private bath.
Rates $37–$45 single, $54–$67 double, including breakfast and dinner.
5 percent discount for 5-night visit, 7 percent for 3 weeks.
No credit cards.
Bar, bird sanctuary, pool, tennis, ski trails.

Waterville Valley

Snowy Owl Inn
Waterville Valley, New Hampshire   03223
Telephone: (603) 236-8383

"Does the mythical inn of the Bing Crosby-Irving Berlin movie *White Christmas* really exist? For our family, the answer is a resounding YES! For the past several ski seasons, we have spent our Christmas and February vacations at the Snowy Owl Inn in the center of Waterville Valley, two and a half hours from Boston and six hours from New York City. Although the Snowy Owl was only recently built, its inspired combination of wood and stone projects the warmth of an early New England inn, but with all of the modern conveniences. Of particular interest to the weary skier or traveler is the effective soundproofing of the rooms, the extremely comfortable beds and the saunas. Furthermore, all rooms have individual temperature control, telephone and private bath and there is a much-welcomed washer and dryer on the premises. But beyond creature comforts, it is the wonderfully relaxing atmosphere of the place that is for us its main attraction. The ambiance of the Snowy Owl is a direct reflection of the relaxed but dedicated natures of the owners of the inn, Tish and Roger Hamblin, and their staff.

"Waterville Valley offers a complex of recreational facilities unequaled in the East. At nearby Mt. Tecumseh, which may be reached by a free shuttle bus, there are thirty-two downhill slopes, day and night ice skating and a cross-country skiing center. And for the nonathlete there is a very comfortable base lodge where one can relax and read all day without feeling guilty, while still keeping an eye on the skiing members of the family. The summer offers the additional delights of swimming, fishing, hiking and a sporty local nine-hole golf course.

"A few caveats: The Snowy Owl serves a delicious continental breakfast, but one must go to nearby restaurants or to the base lodge cafeteria for other meals. Therefore, if possible, make dinner reservations and plan to dine early during peak seasons. Also, because of the paucity of New Hampshire's quaint state-owned liquor stores, it is strongly suggested that you bring your own libations and snacks."

—*Tony, Vicki and Dick Bram*

"I think the main reason why my family and I and all the tourists love the Snowy Owl is because of the friendliness of all the other people staying there. Also there is a place for everyone. My father can sit outside our room and read that book he never had time to get into, my mother can get busy with a jigsaw puzzle, and of course my brother and I can entertain ourselves with pinball, Ping-Pong, candy machines and more. It's also a really cozy place to come back to after skiing and warm ourselves up with a little hot chocolate." —*Julie Bram (age 11)*

"Ski areas are notoriously hard on buildings, but the Snowy Owl, the newest and handsomest of the inns in the valley, manages to balance function and durability with freshness and warmth. Some details to be noted: thick bath towels, live, healthy and abundant plants in all public areas, stoked fires in fieldstone fireplaces, alert desk girls and a slightly frivolous 'owl's nest' at the top of a long winding staircase from which one can view the entire valley. While some of these items do not seem extraordinary, let me assure you in the realms of ski resorts they count as luxuries. Instead of conceding to pragmatism and expediency one feels as if the Hamblins treat the inn as if it were an extension of their home."

—*Frank C. Henry, Jr.*

Open June 15 to October 20, Thanksgiving to April 15.
37 rooms, all with private bath.
Rates $26–$36 single, $37–$46 double, including breakfast. MAP available in winter. Weekly rates and special rates for senior citizens.
Credit cards: American Express, Master Charge, Visa.
Heated pool in summer, golf, saunas.

Do you know a hotel in your state that we have overlooked? Write *now*.

_____*Whitefield*

Spalding Inn Club
Mountain View Road
Whitefield, New Hampshire   03598
Telephone: (603) 837-2572

The growth of the railroads spurred the development of the resort hotels—vast places with large staffs, where families could spend an entire summer. By the 1940s the railroad era was over—the car was replacing the train and changing the nature of vacations. Families went away for one or two weeks or spent the time traveling over long distances. One by one the elegant, leisurely resort hotels began closing, until today there are very few of them left. The Spalding Inn Club carries on the tradition—it provides every possible activity in a grand atmosphere. The tables are still set with fingerbowls, white linen and silver napkin rings. Men are expected to wear jackets and ties in the main dining room for dinner, and the women are expected to wear dresses or suits. There is a busy social program, including putting, tennis, card parties, concerts, entertainment, poolside lobster bakes and steak roasts. The inn has become well known for its fostering of lawn bowling and has provided its manicured lawns for the United States championships.

"Each year since 1963 my wife and I at springtime look forward with happy anticipation to be with the Spalding family and their guests. The inn is immaculate, the food carefully served."   —*George E. Gregory*

Open from June 1 to late October.
70 rooms, all with private bath.
Rates $56–$64 single, $40–$48 double per person, $56–$60 suites, including three meals. Special family rates and extended stays.
Credit cards: American Express, Master Charge, Visa.
Bar, lawn bowling, tennis, swimming pool.
French and German spoken.

The 1661 Inn,
Block Island

Rhode Island

Block Island

The 1661 Inn
Spring Street
Block Island, Rhode Island   02807
Telephone: (401) 466-2421

"I fell in love with Block Island in 1957 and every year I go back to it, finding the familiar places and discovering some wonderful new things about the island: its history, geology, the mysteriously quiet places. All the lighthouses, the bird sanctuary—breeding place and dying place for gulls—the placid ponds and pounding surf, the tones and colors of the water according to the weather, the wail of the foghorns, the heavy morning mists, exciting storms and lazy warm sunshine. Flying over, it looks like such a little island, yet when you are bicycling up some of the hills toward the bluffs, it seems endless.

"The summer people fill the place to overflowing and life comes to the island. Rich and poor, young and old, families, lovers and lonely ones take on a new breath. Each can find his own way, with nature, biking, hiking and swimming. There are places to eat, drink and be merry. If you have your own boat or cottage, you can catch your dinner and cook it the way you want. The island is what you make it. The Abrams and the inn

73

are now a regular part of my life. I've been there in the fall at the closing of the season and it is so beautiful. Calmer and clearer. Some day I may visit during the winter and maybe never leave."   *—Ding Gerry*

"Block Island is reached by ferry boat. If you like single-engine planes, you can fly. We took the boat. From Pt. Judith, Rhode Island, it is a ride of about an hour and a half and most enjoyable. The 1661 Inn is about half a mile from the dock. It looks exactly as it does on the postcard, freshly painted. It is on a rise well above the sea with a great view to the east. There are two small ponds between the inn and the sand cliffs bordering the blue, blue ocean. There are swans in these ponds. It is as picturesque as it sounds. Chefs can come and go in any place, but the meals we have been served during our two stays at the 1661 could not have been beaten. Good variety of meats and seafood with homemade muffins and pastries. There is a charming small bar in the inn, but the best way to have your predinner drink is to sit on the porch and enjoy that fabulous view. The Abrams family may not want this advertised, but they do allow dogs, and we took Daisy, our well-behaved golden retriever. Our Daisy has had two vacations of her dreams on Block Island. Wonderful walks, glorious swims almost to Spain and holes dug on the beach almost to China."

—Mrs. J. Leslie Rodgers

"The 1661 reminds us of the Italian expression, *e dolce far niente,* meaning 'how sweet it is to do nothing.' In this case, just strolling along the countryside or biking, enjoying the unexpectedly beautiful beaches or reading a good book on the inn's old-fashioned porch. The inn has the atmosphere of the small, family-owned inns on Britain's Scilly Isles. During the complimentary wine and cheese hour, guests have the opportunity to chat with the hosts and get acquainted with each other. We also like the intimacy of the Settlers Pub, just off the antique-filled living room. We look forward to seeing the paintings, especially the Winslow Homers from the Abrams' collection on the walls. The Abrams family tend a two-acre vegetable garden, across the road, where everything is organically grown."

—Mr. and Mrs. J. T. Lemkowitz

"Dear Judy,

"Though more than a month has elapsed since our great weekend at Block Island, I'm writing to tell you what a satisfying time we had there, and to make you regret that you did not accompany us. Judy, the 1661 Inn is a conversation piece; it's old. Each room's door bears a neat sign, proclaiming it the Samuel Staples Room, the William Barker, the David Kimball, the William Edwards—and naturally, one has to know the story behind the names of these revered Block Island VIPs who were aldermen, whaling captains or early settlers. Just across the street from 1661 is the ancient Manisses—a hotel with a long and colorful history. The building has been sadly neglected, and after more than two years of research and planning, it is being renovated. The Abrams family did a lot of the work themselves, and only this past year the Manisses cafe/bar/restaurant was opened. The innovative installation of a pair of antique fireplaces, fine Victorian woodwork salvaged from old mansions and an enormous mahogany bar found in an Albany antique barn, along with walls of unusual paneling, have created a warm, rich, elegant atmosphere that manages to harmonize perfectly with a new terrace sidewalk cafe.

"The 1661 Inn isn't an attraction for people out for a high-power planned resort vacation, Judy; there aren't any structured activities, pool parties or organized calisthenics programs! But for the honeymooners who sit for hours on the Mohegan Bluffs, for the camera 'nut' who sloshes through the marshes seeking an elusive egret, for the contented middle-aged couple (us!) who spend a fascinated afternoon in the inn's fertile acre of lush herb garden and vegetable farm, for the dedicated fishing enthusiast who lugs his gear to the rocky jetty at 6 A.M., the 1661 Inn and Block Island provide a backdrop of true charm and simplicity. In sun or rain, it is a healthy place to be. We're going back next year. And we are looking forward to having you with us. Love, Mom and Dad."

—Bernice and Sam Gourse

Open Memorial Day to Columbus Day weekend.
21 rooms, 5 with private bath.
Rates $19 single, $15.50 per person for double occupancy, including breakfast.
Credit cards: American Express, Master Charge, Visa.
Bar, badminton, bicycling, croquet.
French, Portuguese and Spanish spoken.

Spring House Hotel
P.O. Box 206
Block Island, Rhode Island   02807
Telephone: (401) 466-2633

"Many of the buildings on Block Island are of the late 1800s to early 1900s outside, but more modern inside. The beaches are among the best in the world and are known for their fine and, in many places, black sand. (The black sand is supposed to be good for arthritis.) The water is as clear as can be and the waves are generally not rough. There is also a beach for surfing. The Spring House sits on top of a hill only a short walk to the center of town. The hotel supplies bus service to the state beach where you can rent a bathhouse (or you can change at the hotel). The hotel grounds are spacious and beautifully kept and the views from the wide veranda (with its old-fashioned wooden rocking chairs) are magnificent. From one end of it you can see the Montauk, Long Island, light to your right and the Pt. Judith, R.I., light to your left and in front the coastal and European-bound ships. The inn is now run by Douglas and Kandi Mott, a delightful young couple. The rooms are plain and in some cases quite small—but then one does not go there to spend much time in a room. Some have private bathrooms. The public rooms are comfortably furnished, and there is a small bar. The dining room is very large and the food is excellent and plenti-ful. The staff, mostly college boys and girls, are courteous and friendly. Many of them first came to the island as children with their parents.

"Block island is a fifteen-minute flight by small plane from Westerly, about an hour by ferry from Pt. Judith and two and a half hours, also by ferry, from New London, Connecticut. If you are planning to bring your car to the island, an advance reservation must be made. It is also advisable to make your re-turn reservation at the same time."   *—Margaret Givens*

Open from June 20 to September 6.
75 rooms, 25 with private bath.
Rates $25–$32 single, $44–$58 double, including breakfast and din-ner. Special weekly rates.
Credit cards: American Express.
Bar.

Surf Hotel
Block Island, Rhode Island   02807
Telephone: (401) 466-2241

"If you're looking for an impeccable, totally informal, rambling Victorian beach hotel where there is overstuffed comfort with good breakfasts and dinners, where checkers, chess and good books make up the evening's entertainment in a communal liv-ing room, and you don't mind a pair of lhasa apsos living in a corner of the front desk, and a shining crescent beach out the back door, and you like old-fashioned wooden porches for watching the sunset, and a communal refrigerator for storing beer, wine and luncheon meats for picnics—if you can accept all this, combined with friendly owners who let you enjoy your vacation or weekend quietly and in peace, try the Surf Hotel (and don't miss the moosehead in the dining room). Next door is a bike rental shop, and pedaling the length and breadth of the seven-by-three-mile island is the best way to discover the many coves and beaches that, at the south end of the island, rest at the base of the majestic Mohegan Bluffs. The Surf is a few steps from Block Island's tiny commercial street, and across the street from the excellent Block Island Library, which gives lending privileges to tourists." —*Mark Bloom*

Open from Memorial Day to Columbus Day.
40 rooms, none with private bath.
Rates $10–$18 single, $20 double. Special weekend and weekly rates. Breakfast and dinner $10.
No credit cards.
Bicycling.
French spoken.

Newport

The Inn at Castle Hill
Ocean Drive
Newport, Rhode Island   02840
Telephone: (401) 849-3800

"Our exposure to the inn dates back to World War II when, going into Newport to offload torpedoes, I admired its beauty from Narragansett Bay. It is named after the Castle Hill light, which guards the eastern entrance of the bay. We were recalled to the Navy for the Korean War and liked the area so much that we spent every summer and fall vacation there. We saw the transition from a quiet hotel with no bar, operated at a low key as sort of a private club for its distinguished owner, Mr. J. T. O'Connell, to its present active state with guests from all over the world. They come to enjoy the natural beauty, private swimming coves and the vantage points where you can observe all the sea traffic entering and leaving the Narragansett Bay (from tankers to international sailing craft)."
—*Marshall and Miriam Monsell*

"Our favorite time to visit the inn is after the season in September, before the rush in May, and anytime in between. 'Our' room, overlooking the Atlantic Ocean and the bay, is furnished in mahogany and chintz and has a private bathroom large enough to accommodate four additional guests. Friendly fog-horns lull us to sleep after a busy day of swimming, tennis and buying antiques. Sunday brunch is a tradition. Bloody Marys, Eggs Benedict and Sawmill Sundaes—served on the patio and accompanied by music and song. Brunch tends to extend into early evening when everyone gathers in the lounge for a sing-along around the piano. Our recently married daughter and

son-in-law claim that, excluding their honeymoon, their weekend at the inn was the best vacation ever."
                                    —*Mr. and Mrs. Martin M. Temkin*

Open all year.
10 rooms (increased to 34 in the summer, 31 with private bath).
Rates $26.50–$75, including continental breakfast. Special weekly
    rates for beach cottages.
Credit cards: Master Charge, Visa.
Bicycle rentals, private beaches, 32 acres of grounds.

_____*Tiverton*

Stone Bridge Inn
1 Lawton Avenue
Tiverton, Rhode Island   02878
Telephone: (401) 624-6601

"One of the oldest inns in the United States (built in 1794),
Stone Bridge has a lobby architecturally distinguished by unfinished, original cedar posts that support the ceiling. Upstairs,
the bedrooms are large, modern and blessed with a spectacular
view. The inn overlooks the water, and the sight of countless
boats maneuvering the scenic Sakonnet River is a welcome
change from the tailgates on the parkways from New York. A
small saltwater beach lies across from the inn; larger beaches a
few miles away afford almost total privacy. Commercial fishing
boats come in at Sakonnet Point, fifteen miles south, to unload
their daily catch for market. Fort Barton, for history buffs and
those who appreciate a breathtaking view, is within walking
distance. Newport, with its famed fine mansions and interesting
boutiques, can be reached in fifteen minutes. The inn specializes in fresh native seafood, although a wide selection of
chicken, steaks and salads is also available. While the portions
are large, the price of dinner is not. In addition to the standard
dining rooms, a dinner theater has been added for the entertainment of summer guests.

"The inn caters to a discriminating clientele, including boating people who come ashore for dinner. How this was made
possible is an interesting tale, albeit apochryphal. It seems the
owner, Helen O'Connell, had always wished there was some
way to entice people in boats. But there was no place for skip-
pers to dock. Legend has it that the resourceful inn owner dwelt
on this problem to such an extent that she inspired the hurri-
cane of 1938. When the devastating storm was over, Stone
Bridge, directly opposite the inn, had been washed away. All
that was left—sticking out into the water as if it were a pier—
was the long approach to the main bridge arch. Overnight,

Helen O'Connell had her long-sought marina. To this day she claims it was an answer to her daily prayer."

—Charles E. Rodgers, Jr.

Open all year.
20 rooms and 2 apartments, all with private bath.
Rates $22 single, $25 double; $5 each additional person. Special rates out of season.
Credit cards: American Express, Carte Blanche, Diners Club, Visa.

Wakefield

Larchwood Inn
176 Main Street
Wakefield, Rhode Island   02879
Telephone: (401) 783-5454

An inn with a Scottish accent that holds a "Bobbie Burns" night every year. It is close to the Pine Top and Yawgoo ski areas.

"One of the few remaining unspoiled old New England inns, the food, service and comfortable rooms are a real and memorable pleasure. The grounds with their flowers, unusual shrubs and trees supply charm and quiet."   *—George Gidge*

Open all year.
11 rooms, 7 with private bath.
Rates $12–$18 single, $18–$30 double.
Credit cards: American Express, Carte Blanche, Diners Club, Master Charge, Visa.
Bar, dancing.
German and Spanish spoken.

Watch Hill

Ocean House
Bluff Avenue
Watch Hill, Rhode Island   02891
Telephone: (401) 348-8161

"The Ocean House, gracious and spacious, is an imposing white-columned building in Watch Hill, an exclusive southern Rhode Island resort. This regal hotel has played a role in the social history of the area. In its early days, elegantly attired guests arrived in horse-drawn carriages and, later, in chauffeured limousines. Built by George Nash in 1868, it has wide verandas, a glass-enclosed porch, a ballroom, colorful flower arrangements and wicker furniture. The hotel's location on an excellent beach, with a view of the Watch Hill Lighthouse, is a special attraction. The dining room faces the sea, and luncheons are served under colorful umbrellas on the marine deck."   —*Katherine Tucker*

Open only in July and August.
59 rooms, all with private bath.
Rates $32–$42 single, $60–$70 double, including breakfast and
    dinner.
No credit cards.
Bar, marine deck, entertainment.

Weekapaug

Weekapaug Inn
Weekapaug, Rhode Island   02891
Telephone: (401) 322-0301

"We have not missed a summer since 1943 when a group of sixteen friends from New Jersey arrived for a two-week stay. Mrs. Nicolson and I feel that Weekapaug must be unique among inns. We are waited on by the handpicked group of college boys and girls who consider themselves lucky to be chosen—everyone smiles at Weekapaug. Of course, the heart of the entire operation is Sydney and Bob Buffum whom we have watched grow up from children. They can handle any emergency without excitement and with the maximum of efficiency, and come up smiling. The greeting from them when you arrive sets the spirit of the inn. Carrying out the rule of three generations of innkeepers, Bob buys nothing but the best, whether food, linen or equipment; then Wes, the master chef, turns the raw food into superb meals. What do we do besides eat? At 9:30 every morning the men and women play bocci, tennis, golf or shuffleboard, then down to the fine two-and-a-half-mile crescent beach."   —*H. Whitcomb Nicolson; also recommended by*
                                                     Virginia G. McCulloh

Open from mid-June to after Labor Day.
50 rooms, all with private bath.
Rates $75–$80 single, $65–$70 double per person, including three
    meals. Special family rates.
No credit cards.
Bottle club, sailing, tennis.

Saxtons River Inn,
Saxtons River

Vermont

Arlington

The Arlington Inn
Arlington, Vermont   05250
Telephone: (802) 375-6532

"As a commercial photographer, I have used many inns all over the country and the Arlington is the nicest one I know. The bedrooms are packed with original antiques; there is a four-poster and a high-back stencil bed, and a bedroom downstairs with a door that opens out onto a lawn. The chef shops in the local market to get what's good at the time, and the menu changes with the season—a nice touch. There's a little English bar with a grandmother's dropleaf table and a backgammon board, where in winter you can sit and watch the snow come down on the maple trees outside. My girlfriend, Anne, tells me that if she ever gets married, she wants to do so walking down the main staircase of this inn."   —*Peter Vaeth*

Open all year.
12 rooms, all with private bath.
Rates $23 single, $35 double, $39 suites, $50 cottage house. Special
  midweek rates.
Credit cards: Master Charge, Visa.
Bar, cross-country trails, fishing, tennis.

_____*Bethel*

Greenhurst Inn
Bethel, Vermont   05032
Telephone: (802) 234-9474

"The inn is a beautiful old Victorian home, completed about 1891. The innkeepers, Pat and Guy Smith, are so cordial, always welcoming us personally and inviting us to sit by the fire when we come back after a day of leaf-watching and back-roading. Pat serves wonderful breakfasts in the dining room with its round oak table with a built-in lazy Susan. Her biscuits, thin pancakes with Vermont maple syrup and her homemade jellies or warm applesauce (from their own apples) are some of the little extras that make the inn such fun. We like Greenhurst because it is quiet, full of antiques and books. Pat is a collector of old books and we always enjoy browsing through them and often find some we want. My husband this year found a biography of Albert Schweitzer and I an out-of-print edition of Robert Frost's poetry.

"The inn is on the outskirts of Bethel (formerly a mill town) which has been undergoing a facelift and looking better each year we have gone back. There are many lovely old homes being restored, some new shops and some of the old ones. If you're looking for crowds, head for Woodstock (beautiful but full of leaf-watchers in the fall, skiers in winter and summer people in the summer). We drove through Woodstock (at snail's pace due to the traffic) en route to lunch at the Bridgewater Mill—an old woolen mill now converted to shops and a lovely place for lunch (or dinner) called the Weaving Room. We had excellent homemade soup served in attractive Bennington pottery bowls, delicious homemade bread and well-prepared sandwiches. The dessert menu sounded great but we were too full to sample it.

"My husband wanted to add that his reason for enjoying Greenhurst is that he really relaxes there away from a busy practice of psychiatry. Ashley the coon dog greets every guest. And then there are Pat's cats—Denver, a large yellow male; Mercedes, a dark-brown female; a calico cat whose name escapes me, and Sue Ann, about whom Pat tells such funny stories. I would like to write a book called *Pat's Cats*."

—*Mrs. John Hanni*

Open all year.
8 rooms, 2 with private bath.
Rates $14–$18 single, $18–$26 double. Special weekly rate.
Breakfast only served.
No credit cards.
Old and rare book shop on the premises, tennis.

Brandon

The Brandon Inn
On the Village Green
20 Park Street
Brandon, Vermont   05733
Telephone: (802) 247-5766

"Since 1786, Brandon has had an inn for all seasons. In winter, when the snow is postcard pretty on the eaves of old houses and steepled churches chime the hours, ski-tired guests, back from mountain slopes and Robert Frost's woods, gather before the ever-burning wood fire to read or talk or sing to the accompaniment of innkeeper Al Mitroff's guitar. In spring, new syrup on the chef's secret-recipe French toast lures late risers to early breakfast. The chef himself, after carving the evening roast, the centerpiece of his sumptuous Saturday night buffet, emerges with violin to serenade all. In summer, there is Sunday music in the bandstand on the green and concerts on the lawn behind the inn, where guests can listen in the shade of patriarchal trees. In fall, the fire is relit, and Al and Trudy Mitroff welcome weary leaf-peepers, returned from mountain gap and gorge, to their dining room, where Trudy's prize-winning arrangements of candles, leaves and flowers, reflected in sparkling glass and silver, echo the brilliant, changing foliage outdoors. Al offers the best of wines to suit his imaginative menus.

"Whatever the season, the inn is a timeless place: It is old Vermont, defying fad and fashion. There, townspeople and travelers enjoy together local events (such as concerts, an occasional lecture or art exhibit and the annual flower show), returning again and again for anniversaries, family celebrations and friendly reunions. Nearby, in addition to central Vermont's extraordinary natural beauty, there is always something interesting to see: a reenactment of the Battle of Hubbardton, a horse show, ski races, a collection of strangely carved stones that may tell a story of ancient inhabitants from across the sea, antique shops, a marble quarry, the view from the gondola to the top of Killington, the Shelburne Museum. We make the trip from Wisconsin to Brandon as often as we can; whenever we arrive, we are sure to meet others whose company we have enjoyed before."   —*Janet and Gareth Dunleavy*

Open all year.
55 rooms, 50 with private bath.
Rates $34–$44 single, $30–$40 double per person, including breakfast and lunch. Special weekly rate—5 percent discount. Special 10 percent discount from April 1 to July 15 and November 1 to December 22.

Credit cards: American Express, Carte Blanche, Diners Club, Master Charge, Visa.

Bar, chip and putt green, fishing stream, summer theater, swimming pool.

Czech, French, German, Hungarian, Polish, Russian, Slovak and Spanish spoken.

Churchill House Inn
RD 3
Brandon, Vermont   05733
Telephone: (802) 247-3300

"This inn is our winter retreat. We escape from New York City, usually in late January because that's when ski touring is best, and drive north to where the snow is still clean and the air is cold, dry and smelling of pine. The inn borders on state forest land, and this is part of what makes it special; Churchill's guests can fall out the back door, hitch up their skis and be off into the woods. Ski touring or cross-country skiing, for the uninitiated, involves trudging through the forest on skinny skis for miles and miles, returning to the inn exhausted and hungry. Now the good part. First, before leaving in the morning . . . breakfast. Mike and Marion Shonstrom, innkeepers, share the cooking chores along with some very good local talent. The calorie count is high but the pancakes, French toast and anything else attempted (Mike tosses some very fine sour cream pancakes) are superb. If you haven't made an all-day trek, and return to Churchill for lunch, you will be greeted by the overwhelmingly rich smell of Marion's soup. Since you have most likely burned off your breakfast calories, it's okay to indulge; there will usually be some homemade French bread to enjoy as well. Dinner will inevitably surpass the culinary delights of the earlier meals. But enough of food.

"The Churchill House Inn is an old farmhouse that has been renovated; but not too much. Necessities, such as hot water (for aching muscles) and steam heat (for sleeping comfortably through the night), are abundant, but the atmosphere remains. In the den, logs are ablaze much of the afternoon and evening, until the last skier is tucked away. A final morsel of Vermont cheddar or a last glass of cognac can always be found by Mike or Marion for anyone who hasn't had enough dinner. Finally, a word about the congenial atmosphere. Conversation flows easily and naturally; guests of all ages, all professions and from all parts of this country and Canada seem always to be at ease. Mike and Marion are artistic in their ability to begin conversation, or to keep it moving. We believe they genuinely enjoy what they are doing. Guests can usually goad Mike to the piano (it doesn't take much). Once seated, melodic tunes from fifties' rock-and-roll fill the inn, ending with a smashing version of 'Blueberry Hill.' "

> —*Suzanne and Marc Lamberg; also recommended by Mr. and Mrs. W. Reid Thompson*

Open from December 15 to April 1 and from May 15 to October 25.
11 rooms, 3 with private bath.
Rates $38 per person, including two meals. Special family rates.
Credit cards: Master Charge, Visa.
Cross-country skiing, ski touring trails, trout stream.

Chester

Chester Inn
Chester, Vermont 05143
Telephone: (802) 875-2444

"The New England breakfast is included with your room. A very special lady comes in early every morning to bake the many kinds of good muffins. Tom Guido is the chef and he is a fine one. Betsy Guido is the hostess in the dining room. John and Eleanor, who have been with the inn over the years, even with former innkeepers, are a real plus. She is sometimes lady-chef, waitress or cashier, and John is bartender, wine steward, assistant manager and 'night watch' for the late bell. Their daughter also helps out. For the early risers, the cleaning ladies will get a cup of coffee for the guy who can't wait till the dining room opens. Then there is that nice waitress, Nancy, whose husband owns a cross-country ski shop; they teach cross-country skiing. The Guidos have two darling young children and young guests are welcome—baby-sitters are available.

"Last January we drove up for Super Bowl weekend. (Most of our friends were going to New Orleans for the Super Bowl weekend.) The weather was so stormy and snowy out of New York we thought we would never get there. Next morning, when we found our car in front of the inn in a snowdrift, Tom helped us dig it out.

"Chester is an interesting, quiet village. There is the Flamstead Store, where silk-screened fabric, hats, skirts, totes and bags are a specialty. The old stone houses on the edge of the village are of historic interest. You can get to lots of other interesting places from Chester. We enjoy golf at the Windham Country Club. There are interesting shops, several churches and the market store. Ski areas, flea markets, shopping centers, mills and a cheese factory are all nearby. Each day at 5 P.M. the Baptist Church chimes play a hymn. At twilight, a short walk away, you can spot a deer."   —*Margaret and Ervin K. Wax*

Open all year, except for April and first two weeks in November.
31 rooms, all with private bath.
Rates $16–$18 single, $25–$30 double, including breakfast.
Credit cards: Master Charge, Visa.
Bar, cross-country skiing, tennis.

_Chittenden

Tulip Tree Inn
Chittenden, Vermont   05737
Telephone: (802) 483-6213

"The food isn't the only reason for our love affair with this inn,
but it is scrumptious—wonderful homemade breads, soups,
elegant desserts—and it is served with the grace of a fine
French restaurant and the warmth of your grandmother's Sunday night dinner. Gerry and Barbara Liebert, the innkeepers,
are delightful people—the Thanksgiving before the inn opened,
they invited their extended family up for a turkey dinner and a
testing of beds. The family gave the Tulip Tree high marks, and
we concur. We have sampled many comfortable rooms. Situated in central Vermont, the inn is a glorious spot for cross-
country and downhill skiing in winter, foliage trips, biking,
fishing and canoeing during the spring, summer and fall."
—*Pamela J. Seigle*

Open all year, except for part of November or December and part of
   May.
10 rooms, 4 with private bath.
Rates $23–$30 per person, including breakfast and dinner. Special
   weekly rates.
No credit cards.
Beer and wine license, swimming pool.

_Craftsbury Common

The Inn on the Common
Craftsbury Common, Vermont   05827
Telephone: (802) 586-9619

"In a small town atop one of Vermont's green hills, the inn
overlooks a patchwork of well-kept farmlands, cow barns,
country roads and woodlands, all interspersed with clearwater
streams and ponds, and with Mt. Mansfield in the background.
The building is set back of lovely old maples and looks very
much like the substantial white clapboard homestead it was
before Michael and Penny Schmitt converted it to an inn a few

years ago. In doing so they succeeded to a remarkable degree in preserving an informal country home atmosphere—with family portraits on the walls and overflowing bookcases—while at the same time weaving in an unusual assortment of amenities. Dinner in the evening—at which superior dishes are served with delicately flavored wines, family style, at a pair of tables set with silver and candles—not only is delicious, but also socially refreshing and stimulating. The same mixture of simple country atmosphere with the best attributes of modern American life is reflected in the individualized bedrooms. There is a flower garden, tennis court and swimming pool in summer. In winter a large supply of cross-country ski equipment is available for the guests' use."   —*Nathan B. Talbot*

Open from about May 15 to October 20, and from December 21 to March 10.
12 rooms, 1 with private bath.
Rates $35 single, $22–$30 double per person, including breakfast. MAP rates $47 single, $34–$43 double per person. 25 percent discount for children under 9.
Credit cards: Master Charge, Visa.
Clay tennis court, cross-country skiing, English croquet, swimming pool. As there is only one bath, guests are given a terrycloth robe to use during their stay.

Dorset

Barrows House
Dorset, Vermont   05251
Telephone: (802) 867-4455

"Barrows House, a typical Vermont inn, is in the center of a typical Vermont village that is worth the visit in itself. The rooms are most comfortable and very clean, situated in the inn itself and in several other buildings on the grounds. However, if there is a party going on, you should avoid the room directly over the bar. Charlie Schubert, who looks after the place, and his wife, Marilyn, who tends to see to your comfort, are most hospitable and make every effort to see to your comfort. There is a large swimming pool and two excellent tennis courts. The food is prepared by Sissy, a young woman of unmatched abilities. You will never find crisper vegetables or such exquisite fish."
—*Charles L. Newberry*

Open all year, except from November 1 to November 15.
27 rooms.
Rates $30–$42 single, $60–$72 double, including breakfast and dinner.

No credit cards.
Cross-country ski shop, heated swimming pool, sauna, tavern.
French and German spoken.

Grafton

Old Tavern at Grafton
Grafton, Vermont   05146
Telephone: (802) 843-2375

"We first visited the Old Tavern in the summer of 1961 on the very enthusiastic recommendation of friends at Martha's Vineyard. We have returned two or three times a year since. Each season has an appeal all its own, but perhaps the most beautiful of all is the fall foliage season. We have watched the restoration of the original tavern of 1801 to its present structure and it has lost none of its original charm. Excellent meals are served in a setting of early America. The town carries one back to the 1800s and establishes that slow and peaceful pace of life. A walk of a quarter mile in any direction will lead to a quiet country road or into the woods where you are certain there is not a town in miles."   —_Jean E. Cutting_

Open all year, except for April and Christmas.
34 rooms, all with private bath.
Rates $30–$50.
No credit cards.
Bar, cross-country skiing, natural pool.
German spoken.

Lower Waterford

Rabbit Hill Inn
Lower Waterford, Vermont   05848
Telephone: (802) 748-9766

"The Connecticut River flows placidly here between Vermont and New Hampshire. Right on the edge of the river valley, looking over the river toward the New Hampshire mountains known as the Presidential Range, is the village of Lower Waterford, called the 'white village' locally. Back in the 1800s someone purchased the village and painted all the houses white with green shutters. Though properties have changed hands over the many years, the color scheme has become unwritten law. The focal point of the village is Rabbit Hill Inn (there is a Rabbit Hill behind the inn), a rambling 1830 Greek Revival structure whose front is dominated by four Doric columns that originally, as four huge New Hampshire pine trees, were hauled by a team of oxen across the frozen Connecticut River. Don't let the impressive front with its pillars and three levels of verandas intimidate you. Inside are large, sun-filled rooms, fireplaces (in the bedrooms, too!), overstuffed chairs, soft beds, wide pine-board floors, two antique grandfather clocks and, of course, the owners and staff. Both Ed and Nancy Ludwig and their staff (all locals) will in no time have you feeling less a guest and more like some related cousin who has dropped by. The food is a surprise—an excellent cuisine from steak to lobster. Ask for one of Gladys's homemade pies, delivered fresh to the inn each afternoon in a wicker basket by her husband. The house salad dressing is a secret that Ed won't part with.

"On our first visit, we felt guilty at not doing anything. But in a village of less than a dozen buildings, including the church, inn and library (operated on the honor system: no librarian), what is wrong with just going for walks or sitting on the veranda watching the mountains change colors and listening to the birds? The Rabbit Hill Inn offers cross-country skiing facilities, but we're sure the Ludwigs secretly prefer guests who sit sensibly by a crackling fire, enjoying a warm drink and sharing good, relaxing conversation." —*Dennis and Barbara Cavendish*

Open all year.
20 rooms, all with private bath.
Rates $19–$29 single, $24–$34 double.
Credit cards: Master Charge, Visa.
Bar, cross-country skiing, sleigh rides.
French spoken.

Manchester

The Reluctant Panther
Manchester Village, Vermont   05254
Telephone: (802) 362-2568

" 'One of the most civilized establishments in the Western Hemisphere' is the way a friend once described the Reluctant Panther. And it is. Both for the ingenuity of its marvelously eclectic decor (each room is like a page from *Architectural Digest*) and for its remarkably innovative menu (whole trout served ice cold with mayonnaise and capers; delectable smoked pork glazed with cherry sauce). And for the myriad personal touches: telephones in each room, delightful old claw-foot bathtubs, enormous thirsty towels and the world's greatest houseperson, who goes about in the early hours making things immaculate with all the stealth of the animal for which the inn was named. The sum of all these parts gives the Reluctant Panther an ambiance entirely its own. Basically it is an extension of the personalities of the owners—Joan (she cooks) and Wood (he hosts) Cornell. Over the years they have fashioned an image that is innovative and highly contemporary but at the same time warm, comfortable and real. The Cornells are not pretend people and, despite the urbanity of its striking mauve exterior, the Panther is more homelike than many traditional New England inns that cloak themselves in calico and old copper."

—Neil Quinn

Closed April and May, and from November 1 to December 20.
7 rooms, all with private bath.
Rates $25–$40.
No credit cards.
Cocktail lounge.
French and German spoken.

Newfane

The Four Columns Inn
Newfane, Vermont   05345
Telephone: (802) 365-7713

"After driving through the beautiful green and white village of Newfane, you reach the lovely Four Columns Inn and park in the spacious driveway. Madame Anna Chardain greets all of her visitors and if you have visited before, the same room will be waiting for you. If you wish to be left alone, the peace and quiet are amazing. We have entered the inn at mealtimes, with the dining room filled, and not heard a sound. Indeed 'our' room is directly over the dining room and we have never been able to tell if it was crowded or empty below. From the windows of our room, we look out on the magnificent Windham County Courthouse, the Grange building and a lovely, spired church, surrounding a tree-lined village green. The inn's rooms are large and airy and the decorations are mostly early American with some lovely prints. Mme Chardain's raids on the local flea markets have shown results at the inn. The rooms are spotless, the bathrooms sparkle.

"Food is too commonplace a term to describe Chef René Chardain's offerings. Rainbow trout, pheasant and guinea hens are raised on the grounds. The veal and shrimp dishes are superb, and the steaks are fabulous. We think that we have had each of the dishes on the menu, and know that there was not one that we would hesitate to recommend to our family or friends or order again for ourselves. The wine list, I am told by those who know better than I, is small but excellent. The main feature of the dining room, besides the copperware and the 12-inch service plates, is the fireplace and the log fire in winter. The chef sallies forth from his kitchen to talk to old friends, to inquire of the food and to see for himself 'if all goes well.' The maître d', Wesley Chardain, is pleasantly helpful and will discuss the menu, take the orders and prepare some of the flambés at your table, as well as supervise the entire room with an eye for perfection."   —*Marion and John Herman*

Open from the end of May through October, and from the end of
   December through April.
12 rooms, all with private bath.
Rates $30–$45.
Credit cards: American Express, Master Charge, Visa.
French and German spoken.

Old Newfane Inn
On the Common
Newfane, Vermont   05345
Telephone: (802) 365-4427

"The food is superlative, the service impeccable, yet the inn remains entirely 'country' in feeling despite a largely French (or at least continental) menu. The proprietors, Mr. and Mrs. Eric Weindl, are European and the maître d' (at the time of our visit) was Colombian. The service in the dining room was in the hands of American women who knew precisely what they were doing and did it very well. Our room (number 23) was comfortable, immaculate and quiet. I must say, however, that a few guests whose rooms were not at the back of the house found that some kitchen and dining room noise filtered upward. Our only ungratified wish was for an open fire in the spacious, attractive guest-sitting room during the beautiful but chilly October weather of our visit.

"Newfane itself is a tiny, attractive village where there is, thank God, nothing whatever to do. We brought a bag of books, hearty appetites and warm sweaters, and spent a blissful week. If fanfare and hoopla are your goals, stay out of Newfane and its charming inn. If peace, quiet, exquisite landscape and the best food imaginable give you pleasure, go there."
                    —*Dr. and Mrs. Francis Silver*

Open from the end of May to the end of October, and from the mid-
   dle of December to the end of March.
10 rooms, 8 with private bath.
Rates $36–$44.
Credit cards: Master Charge.
Bar.
German and Spanish spoken.

Poultney

Eagle Tavern
RD 2
Poultney, Vermont   05764
Telephone: (802) 287-9498

"I would think there are few, if any, inns of comparable age—
1785—that retain all the character, charm and flavor of that
era, even though the modern conveniences are at hand. The
original ballroom of the inn is now converted into the owner's
master bedroom which you can see if you ask. In the cellar,
with an outside door, there is an authentic Revolutionary War
taproom. This has brick walls and floor and a marvelous fireplace. Ida Mae Johnson runs the Eagle Tavern with great love
and care. All the rooms are comfortable, immaculate and of
course full of 18th-century charm."   —_Howard R. Berger_

"We have been visiting Eagle Tavern since 1954, and the third
generation has now slept in Horace Greeley's bed! Greeley
spent his early years in Poultney, and lived at the Eagle Tavern
when he was a printer's devil at the _Northern Spectator_. He, of
course, went on to found the _New York Tribune_. The first two
generations in our family were printers and we now wonder if
Horace's influence will rub off on our thirteen-year-old son who
slept there for the first time this year."
                              —_Frances and John Ratcliffe_

Open all year.
4 rooms, 2 with private bath.
Rates $15 single, $30 double.
No credit cards.
No meals.
Old brick taproom.
French spoken.

Proctorsville

Golden Stage Inn
P.O. Box 218
Depot Street
Proctorsville, Vermont   05153
Telephone: (802) 226-7744

"In the depths of a Vermont winter, the Golden Stage Inn is a
throwback to the early 19th century. It is situated close to the
main road leading to Ludlow and the nearby ski areas, but just

far enough away to provide tranquility and relief from the noise of traffic. The driveway, walled with four-foot snowbanks, leads to a typical white clapboard New England house with a porch on two sides. The interior is pleasant and old-fashioned without the discomfort sometimes found in old hostelries. In fact the inn has been modernized without losing its charm. There is a good fire and comfortable furniture in the large living room, where guests can sit to thaw out after long days on the ski slopes. Inner warmth is also available in the bar, where Tom Schaaff, the innkeeper, functions as barman for an hour or so before dinner each evening. Wende Schaaff provides her guests with plenty of imaginative and tasty meals. In fact the cuisine is one of the memorable parts of the Golden Stage, and there is always enough for even the hungriest teen-ager.

"The bedrooms and bathrooms, as might be expected, are comfortable and modernized. No motel color TVs in the rooms—but who needs a TV when there is good company downstairs? If the kids want to watch TV, there's a set in the bar. There are fireplaces in the bedrooms—including one with a superb double mantelpiece. The Golden Stage is a matter of minutes from the Mt. Okemo ski area, close to several others and perhaps forty-five minutes from Killington."

—*R. G. Bardsley*

"Passing through what seemed like endless valleys, hamlets and villages covered in deep snow reflecting occasional streetlight glitter, we suddenly emerged from the last valley onto a small plateau that led down into Proctorsville—and our destination, the Golden Stage Inn, a large, insistent, white wooden structure with traditional Vermont determination to remain on the landscape for even more years than it had achieved to date. Arrival. Greetings by innkeepers Tom and Wende. A brief 'sniff' around. Dump the luggage. A warm and sympathetic invitation for a late soup and sandwich. By the end of the sandwich (which really was concluded in the kitchen) we knew we had more than arrived. The food from breakfast to dinner was pleasurable, imaginative, certainly more than satisfying, and on occasion distinguished. Where else could one witness 'polished' plates returned to the kitchen after a healthy portion of Mandarin pork served to an ethnically varied mix of household guests."

—*Richard Sharpe*

Open all year, except April.

8 rooms, 2 with private bath.

Rates $25 single, $35 double, including breakfast. Special winter rates, 3- and 5-day ski rates, MAP rates and rates for children under 12.

Credit cards: Master Charge, Visa.

Copper-topped bar, fireplaces, gardens.

Saxtons River

Saxtons River Inn
Main Street
Saxtons River, Vermont   05154
Telephone: (802) 869-2110

"The inn sits squarely in the center of a small town lying in the shallow valley west of Bellows Falls on the road to Grafton. The town is relatively secluded, architecturally charming and virtually unspoilt. Being happily at some remove from the nearest ski area, the town has avoided the excesses of American Tyrolean-style architecture and the associated commercial banalities that invariably plague such resorts. Rockingham, a twenty-minute drive to the north, boasts a magnificent 18th-century meetinghouse that stands in solitary grandeur on a hilltop overlooking a sloping, grassy cemetery, some of whose slate gravestones bear wondrous primitive designs.

"The inn was renovated in 1973 by the Campbell family. They wisely chose to retain the character of the building. Each bedroom is decorated in individual style with taste and panache and a rare attention to detail. The bar and dining room have their own distinctive treatments, and the breakfast room is filled with plants and morning sunlight. A house across the street has additional bedrooms. The food offered is interesting without being pretentious. The menu is comfortingly brief, though frequently changed, and is accompanied by a modest wine list. Special mention should be made of the homemade soups and the marvelous homemade gâteaux." —*David Arnold*

Open all year, except for January and Mondays through Wednesdays in February and March.
20 rooms, 12 with private bath.
Rates $15 single, $20–$35 double, $45–$55 suites, including continental breakfast.
No credit cards.
Copper bar, inn store, outdoor dining.
French spoken.

South Londonderry

The Londonderry Inn
Route 100
South Londonderry, Vermont   05155
Telephone: (802) 824-5226

"On a hillside overlooking the West River and the town of South Londonderry is the magnificent Londonderry Inn. The inn has a large, clean, spring-fed pool, regulation-size racquet

ball courts, horseback riding and fishing nearby. It is close to major ski slopes and many small towns to interest history and antique buffs. The inn has its own bakery across the road, which provides very tasty breads and pastries. A horse-drawn cart makes its rounds of the surrounding small towns with these goodies. The spacious dining room is tastefully furnished and serves good food. A fine wine list and delicious desserts are available. We had lunch on the flagstone patio with a breath-taking view of Magic Mountain. Once a week in summer there is a cookout around the pool featuring chicken ribs and corn on the cob. Once a month there is a seafood cookout with lobsters, clams and such. Each Sunday there is a buffet in the dining room."
—James Beattie

Open all year, except for April and November.
28 rooms, all with private bath.
Rates $25–$40; family rooms, suites, chalet $50–$120 (sleeping up to 6). Higher on weekends. Special midweek packages.
Credit cards: Master Charge, Visa.
Lounge, paddle tennis courts, pool, specialty nights in dining room.

South Woodstock

The Kedron Valley Inn
Route 106
South Woodstock, Vermont   05071
Telephone: (802) 457-1473

"The oldest part of this country inn was built in 1822. It has been added to and modernized through the years. There are six fireplaces, a Franklin stove, two parlor stoves (they all work) plus hidden modern features that add to the comfort. Paul and Barbara Kendall are the owners and innkeepers, and they pay attention to making their guests comfortable. They have a wonderful chef, who uses real whipped cream in large quantities. Fine fish comes in from Boston. The inn is five miles from Woodstock, a most interesting place, and three and a half miles from a good golf course. There are stables with thirty horses, and good riding trails all around. The inn has a pond for swimming and a nice porch with rocking chairs. There are winter sleigh rides—and a real country store across the street. Pleasant walking trails wind through the countryside. The little village of South Woodstock has old Vermont houses and is full of charm."
—H. Thomas Hallowell, Jr.

Open all year.
34 rooms, 30 with private bath.
Rates $8–$34 single, $18–$44 double.

Credit cards: Master Charge, Visa.
Cross-country skiing, horse-drawn sleighs, paddle tennis, skating, pond.

_____*Stowe*

Andersen's Lodge
Route 108
Stowe, Vermont   05672
Telephone: (802) 253-7336

"Andersen's Lodge on the mountain road in Stowe was purchased from the Andersens about six years ago by a charming Tyrolean couple, Trude and Dietmar Heiss. The profits from the past have enabled the couple to expand the place and add a heated swimming pool. Rooms are cozy and gemütlich, but it is the food that is the inn's chief attraction. While Trude tends to the business of booking, running and cleaning the inn, Dietmar practices his New York-polished skills as a four-star chef. Aside from the Topnotch up the mountain road, there are few restaurants in the area to match Dietmar's accomplishments. Schnitzels and roasts are served piping hot, graced with exquisite sauces; pastries and breads are home-baked. Be sure to bring your own bottle of wine, as the inn (at last report) has not yet obtained a license to serve alcoholic beverages. But don't bring the wine from New York or Boston; stock up at considerable saving at the IGA grocery store in the village. An extra bottle of fine German white wine for your hosts will be much appreciated as a gratuity."   —*Michael W. Glueck*

Open June to October, December to April.
17 rooms, 16 with private bath.
Rates $18–$27 double per person, including two meals. Slightly lower rates in summer. European plan also available.
Credit cards: American Express, Master Charge, Visa.
Set-up bar, pool, game room.
German spoken.

Edson Hill Manor
RFD 1, Edson Hill Road
Stowe, Vermont   05672
Telephone: (802) 253-7371

This small inn, originally a private home in 500 acres, is well off the main highway and surrounded by the Green Mountains. There is now a cross-country ski center there with rental equipment and instructors and a network of trails through the woods. In summer the trails are used for horseback riding and the ski center becomes the stable.

"The best phrase to describe this inn is 'simple elegance.' There are working fireplaces, wooden beams, lots of brass, Oriental rugs and wildflower arrangements in the living room. We like to stand around the fire and talk before dinner, and they have ice buckets filled with ice that you can take up to your room with you." *—Mrs. Yetta G. Samford, Jr.*

Open from mid-June to the end of October, and from mid-December to mid-April.

16 rooms, 9 with private bath.

Rates $38–$52, including breakfast and dinner. Special family rates and ski and riding packages.

No credit cards.

Bar, cross-country ski touring center, fishing pond with boat, riding stables, swimming pool.

The Green Mountain Inn
Stowe, Vermont 05672
Telephone: (802) 253-7301

"Stowe was once a tiny village tucked into a broad valley six miles from Mt. Mansfield. Connected to the Montreal-New York railroad line at Waterbury, Stowe produced lumber, dairy products, wood turnings, maple syrup and sap. Then in the late 1930s, skiing came to the area and Stowe became the ski capital of the East. About forty years ago, Parker Perry bought the Green Mountain Inn, which dated back to 1833, and proceeded to modernize it in the right places (firm mattresses, for example), leaving its inherent charm in the other right places. With his wife, Dottie, Parker created a mecca for lovers of good food and lodging—not only among skiers, but also among the fall foliage and summer tennis tourists as well. Dottie's dried flowers abound in the public rooms. (I always have to sniff to be sure they are not fresh.) Old New England furniture and marvelous local watercolors by Blodgett create a delightful aura of repose, highlighted on a quiet afternoon by the tick-tock of the Regulator clock on the office wall. The Perrys' restaurant is the finest in Vermont, I think. No fried foods ever (except doughnuts); New England apple pie, prime meats and the delights of fresh vegetables prepared farm style and beautifully served by pleasant ladies who speak Vermontese. As Michelin would say: 'Definitely worth a (long) detour.' "
—Professor John R. Wiley

"This is one of the classic small inns of America. From time to time I did my evening broadcast from there, and regard it as my second home."   —*Lowell Thomas*

Open all year, except for November and May.
63 rooms, all with private bath.
Rates $36 single, $34 double per person, including breakfast and
    dinner. Special weekly rates and ski packages.
No credit cards.
Bar, skiing, swimming, whip collection.

West Dover

The Inn at Sawmill Farm
Crosstown Road, Route 100
West Dover, Vermont   05356
Telephone: (802) 464-8131

"We discovered the inn by asking a famous French chef where he went on his days off. We were not disappointed. Sawmill Farm is the creation of a multitalented family. In a previous life Rod Williams was an architect—he still keeps his hand in it—and his wife, Ione, was an interior decorator. They took an old farmhouse and its outbuildings and created a hostelry of unique character. Each of the rooms is different. A tremendous old brick fireplace dominates a large sitting room, magnificent in its proportions yet rustic in its appointments. A lordly chime clock, such as once dominated the old Wanamaker's in New York, adds a rich sonorous note to the tranquility. We have left till last Brill Williams, son of Ione and Rod, who has made of the kitchen a bastion of dedicated gastronomy. He no doubt learned a great deal from his mother, a fine cook in her own right, but he has gone on in his professional training to become an accomplished chef de cuisine."   —*Dr. Bernard Berkowitz*

"If you never again wish to see plastic 'glasses,' paper tapes across a topless john, a cardboard cone advertising the location of the coffee shop, a foamex ice bucket or those infuriating clothes hangers that fight back—and win, then Sawmill is for you. Step instead into a world of scented candles, brick fireplaces, beautiful antiques and beds that are sybaritic. Bathroom mirrors are framed in gold, walls are done in contemporary florals. The springhouse suite has a kitchen and dressing room, done in handsome print. No phones, no ice machine, no noise. In the spring peepers sing from the pond, in winter the dry crunch of powder snow—these are the only sounds that will assault your ears, other than the Sunday bells that toll from the church across the hill. The house dogs, golden labs named Ginger and Crystal, race through the lawns, chasing sticks."

—Miriam H. Finucane

Closed November 15 to December 12.
20 rooms, all with private bath.
Rates $60–$75 single, $80–$100 double, including breakfast and dinner.
No credit cards.
Bar, lounge, pool, trout pond, skiing and golf nearby.
French and Spanish spoken.

_____*Weston*

The Inn at Weston
Route 100
Box 56
Weston, Vermont   05161
Telephone: (802) 824-5804

"There are so many things that make this inn a special place. Two of the most important ones are the innkeepers, Stu and Sue Douglas. Another is the fantastic food. Stu prepares a breakfast that is so hearty one should really skip lunch. The pancakes are especially delicious, a house recipe served with Vermont maple syrup. Sue is in charge of dinners. Her specialties are the soups and salads. In summer all the salads are made of vegetables fresh from the garden. The breads and desserts are all homemade. Vegetarian dishes are available on request. The area is a haven for people like us who feel the need to flee the city periodically to recharge their batteries. There are many ski areas for both cross-country and downhill enthusiasts. During the spring, summer and fall there is hiking, fishing, canoeing and biking. The quiet country roads are great for joggers, too."   *—Pamela Myers and Ruth Dickey*

Open from Memorial Day weekend to the end of October and from December 15 to Easter.
13 rooms, 7 with private bath.
Rates $26–$28, including breakfast; 10 percent discount Sunday to Friday.
No credit cards.
Game room, pub.
French spoken.

Turn to the back of this book for pages inviting *your* comments.

_____*Wilmington*

Nutmeg Inn
Route 9
P.O. Box 818
Wilmington, Vermont   05363
Telephone: (802) 464-3351

"Coddled by the foothills of the Green Mountains, a stone's throw from the shopper's delight of Wilmington, the inn is quite centrally located for the summer Marlboro Music Festival, for winter skiing and for the fall foliage season. No place in the world can compare with southern Vermont for foliage, and perhaps no place is more spectacular in the fall. Add the Bach Festival at Marlboro every Columbus Day weekend, and you have an unbeatable combination. The area is also a skier's fantasy fulfilled, with six ski areas in easy reach. Wilmington is chock full of wonderful craft shops, many of which feature first-class New England textiles, ceramics, woodworking and more esoteric originals.

"The Nutmeg Inn is suffused with the gentle warmth of its proprietors, Joan and Rich Combes, a transplanted Long Island couple who thrive on and share the tranquility of southern Vermont. The rooms are modest, comfortable and immaculately kept. The service is always willing, friendly, efficient but never intrusive. The atmosphere is very informal and, most pleasing to us, homelike, with none of the pretentiousness of some of the older inns. That includes the reasonable prices. The Combes know the area intimately and are marvelous help in setting up a day's activities. During the off-season, the Combes serve only breakfast, but a full and satisfying one. The area abounds in truly fine restaurants."

—*Alison and Jerome Rogoff;*
also recommended by Douglas and Kim Hall

Open all year except Thanksgiving and the last two weeks of April
 and the first two weeks of May.
9 rooms, 4 with private bath.
Rates $18 single, $20–$24 double in summer and fall. Special winter
 rates include breakfast and dinner. Weekly rates in summer and
 fall; family and group rates available all year. Rates for students
 and senior citizens.
No credit cards.
BYOB bar.

Part Two

Mid-Atlantic

Delaware
District of Columbia
Maryland
New Jersey
New York
Pennsylvania
Virginia
West Virginia

Delaware

Wilmington

Hotel duPont
11th and Market Streets
Wilmington, Delaware   19899
Telephone: (302) 656-8121

"On the outside it looks like an office building, which it is in part, but inside the Hotel duPont there is an air of spaciousness, elegance and hospitality. The high-ceilinged lobby is designed as a place for people to meet, and the dining areas range from the formal Green Room with tall windows looking out on the city's central square, through the more intimate Christina Room, to the Brandywine Room, reminiscent of a gentleman's club. Unique to the Hotel duPont are the paintings in its public rooms, originals by N. C. Wyeth, his son Andrew, and his grandsons Jamie and A. N., as well as by other members of the famous Brandywine School. Most of the Wyeth-family pieces are in the Christina Room, while the balance of the hotel's collection of several hundred works of art, most of them by distinguished area artists, is displayed throughout the building. The Gold Ballroom, richly decorated as its name implies, is the setting for special functions. Also in the building is the Playhouse, a 1,250-seat theater." —*Dorothy Walker Greer*

Open all year.
300 rooms, all with private bath.
Rates $35–$58 single, $49.50–$58.50 double, $116 suites.
Credit cards: American Express, Carte Blanche, Diners Club, Master Charge, Visa.
2 bars.
Chinese, Danish, Dutch, French, German, Greek, Italian, Japanese, Korean, Lithuanian, Norwegian, Polish, Russian, Spanish, Swedish and Vietnamese spoken.

District of
Columbia

Washington, D.C.

The Gralyn
1745 N Street, N.W.
Washington, D.C.   20036
Telephone: (202) 785-1515

"This street was once full of fine private homes. Presidents and their families lived here; Robert Todd Lincoln had a home here; several Roosevelts lived here. But by the time the Depression came along, many of the homes had been sold and Number 1745 had become the Persian embassy. It was in World War II that the 1870 four-story Georgian building with a pink awning became a mid-city inn. With the war on, there was a shortage of places to stay in the capital, and Allied groups were some of the first guests. It remains a favorite place for the British to stay—in fact, the owner said that her inn was 'better known in London than in Washington.' The rooms range from an oak-paneled one with a massive carved bed to a plainly furnished basement suite. Breakfast is served in a room with organdy curtains, four tables and mismatched tablecloths. The lobby is furnished with Victorian, Oriental and other unexpected pieces. If you sit down to read some of the plentiful supply of magazines, the desk clerk is likely to offer a soft drink." —*Peggy Payne*

Open all year.
34 rooms, all with private bath.
Rates $20–$40. Breakfast.
French and Japanese spoken.

The Jefferson Hotel
1200 16th Street, N.W.
Washington, D.C.   20036
Telephone: (202) 347-4704

"The Jefferson Hotel—just a few blocks from the White House—is the kind of elegantly tacky hotel that reporters weary of the plastic and formica of Holiday Inns and Quality Courts take to like editors to headlines. There is real, honest-to-God furniture in the Jefferson. Bookcases (with glass doors) filled with good reading (that is, if you like 'Little Women,' 'Silas Marner' and the like). Some rooms have a small kitchenette where you can warm coffee and cook eggs. If you are very lucky, you get a room with a canopied bed with enough gauze to make Rhett Butler feel at home. It is centrally located (the hotel, not the bed) and has a nice home feeling.

"Then there is the legacy of Nettie Karpin, who ran the place (and left several years ago). Nettie is married to Fred Karpin, the bridge expert of the *Washington Post,* and she had a soft spot for reporters. The hotel was never too full for Nettie to find room for a passing newspaper person. She'd squeeze you in somehow. She was enormously kind." —*Doug Robinson*

Open all year.
125 rooms, all with private bath.
Rates $47–$52 single, $52–$57 double. Monthly rates available.
Credit cards: American Express, Diners Club, Master Charge, Visa.
Bar.
French spoken.

The Tabbard Inn
1739 N Street, N.W.
Washington, D.C.   20036
Telephone: (202) 785-1277

"When you call for a reservation at the Tabbard Inn, ask for Room 3. For one thing, it has a private bath, and not all the Tabbard's rooms do. What makes it charming, though, is a huge bay window overlooking a row of 19th-century town houses. In fact, the inn is a 19th-century town house itself, or rather three of them side by side. The rooms are furnished with comfortable hand-me-downs (one of them even has a piano!) and you get the feeling that if a piece of furniture breaks it would be unthinkable to replace it with anything new. The bookshelves in the rooms are furnished with collections of books and magazines left behind by previous guests. The living room of one of the houses has been converted into what may be the most comfortable hotel lobby in the United States. Directly behind it is a sunny dining room overlooking a garden. It's where every overnight guest is served what they call a 'continental breakfast,' but is in reality an American breakfast, with eggs and fruit added to the traditional croissant. Lunch, brunch and dinner are also available in this room, and it has a twenty-four-hour bar. The Tabbard has all the air of a country inn, yet it's a short walk from the White House, one block from the Metro and surrounded by Hiltons and Holiday Inns."

—*Bill Harris*

"First impressions of the Tabbard Inn are promising: no malarkey or heel-clicking at the reception desk, but a cheerful welcome from mostly young staff give one the feeling they enjoy their work. Second impressions were slightly less encouraging: the downstairs bathroom was very down at heel, without even a lock to the door. Carpets in the corridors badly needed vacuuming. And our room was *not* good enough for a self-respecting hotel: e.g., springs broken on the one upholstered chair, with the stuffing coming through the part one sits on; one bare light bulb and the other bedside light with its lampshade broken; no stopper for bath or basin. It took an hour for them to produce a bath stopper, and the basin still lacked a stopper when we left after three days. Our son's room was altogether better. We may have been unlucky, but Room 44 ought not to have been let to us in its run-down condition—and it wasn't too clean either.

"The inn is well known among those visiting Washington who prefer a small friendly establishment in the city center. It is booked up most of the time, and perhaps is too popular for its own good. It used to be very much cheaper, I was told, but its prices are now less competitive. In general, I felt it was trading too much on its reputation, and needs to put its house a little more in order."   —*Hilary Rubinstein*

Open all year.
38 rooms, 19 with private bath.
Rates $21–$51 single, $38–$63 double, including continental breakfast.
No credit cards.
Bar.
Chinese, French, Japanese, Portuguese and Spanish spoken.

Maryland

Oxford

The Robert Morris Inn
Oxford, Maryland 21654
Telephone: (301) 226-5111

"We came upon it as most people must have been coming upon it for centuries: along the tree-shaded main street leading to the ferry slip. There it stands, the Robert Morris, at the edge of the water, full of dignity and age. A couple of days at this inn go far in recreating the comfortable and graceful colonial style for which the Eastern Shore is so well remembered. The inn was built as a home early in the 18th century by ship's carpenters using hand-hewn beams, wooden pegged paneling and ships' nails. In 1730 an English trading company bought it as a residence for Robert Morris, its representative in the area. Morris died in 1750 after wadding from a ship's gun being fired in his honor struck him. His son, Robert Morris, Jr., became a partner in a Philadelphia law firm and a well-to-do man who used his entire savings to help finance the Continental Army in the Revolutionary War.

"Murals in the inn's dining room were made of wallpaper samples carried by manufacturers' salesmen 135 years ago, the tavern's slate floor is from Vermont and art works throughout the building come from local painters and crafts people. The inn still has old stairs to climb, floors that aren't quite straight and windows not quite symmetrical—and the shared bathrooms are as idiosyncratic in design as those in a comparable British inn. Our room had a trundle bed, and a view from a small gabled window of the little ferry docking and on its way back across the Chesapeake inlet called the Tred Avon River. Outside the inn, Oxford is a waterside town made for walking—as is St. Michaels, another memorable village not far away."   —*B. C.*

Open all year, except Christmas Day.
32 rooms, 19 with private bath.
Rates $20–$54.
Credit cards: American Express, Master Charge, Visa.
Bar.

The Chalfonte Hotel,
Cape May

New Jersey

Cape May

The Chalfonte Hotel
Howard and Sewell Streets
Cape May, New Jersey   08204
Telephone: (609) 884-8934

"Cape May has been designated a National Landmark and the Chalfonte Hotel is one of the reasons. It is Cape May's only hotel in continuous operation every summer since it was built in 1876. Many of the families have been vacationing there almost as long—children, grandchildren and great-grandchildren. But newcomers are welcome. There is a 'Brigadoon' quality here. Guests who return after several years find everything is much the same. The same great cooks turn out the same great meals. Management changes only gradually; waitresses, bellboys, night watchmen, desk clerks become guests and, on occasion, vice versa. The exterior of the three-story white frame hotel is Victorian gingerbread with beautiful porches lined with rockers. The interior is plain and unpretentious. Some people find it too stark, but most of the rooms have at least one piece of the original furniture. The Chalfonte is good for parents and children. Children under six are encouraged to go to the children's dining room where they can have fun and be looked after while their parents have cocktails and dinner. Older children who want to eat earlier and get to skeeball on the boardwalk can eat there too."   —*Merrinelle Sullivan*

"The Chalfonte is my summer dream house and has been ever since I can remember. It is a wonderful place for children, because of the beach and other activities. Mothers love it too because of the safe and gradual water that allows them to enjoy the beach also. A five-year-old (a faithful Chalfonte-goer since the age of one) said of the children's dining room: 'I like it there, the waitresses are nice, the food is yummy and I meet new kids.' "   —*Amanda Sullivan (age 12)*

"Often, in a gathering of self-styled world travelers, the question rises: 'Where do you go for the hot summer months and where do you stay?' My reply is that I have, for the past thirty years, gone to the Chalfonte, now being superbly run by two young women. It is really a way of life, or a state of mind, if you prefer. It is not the type of place to be classified with the more elaborate hotel chains. Rather it might be likened to a true boardinghouse with a front porch full of rocking chairs, which seem to be filled every hour of the day. Old heirloom furniture fills the downstairs lobby and writing room and an air of serenity hovers over it all. If Southern-style cooking is to your liking, it does not take too long to get to know the many dishes—batter bread, fried chicken and kidney stew on Sundays—all these with the various hot breads. Perhaps the Chalfonte is the last of its kind. The little town of Cape May is never-never land; one soon finds that it is so pleasant just to stay on and on, hoping that *mañana* will never come. In recent years many have come to enjoy the golden days of early autumn that follow Labor Day."   —*Duff Merrick; also recommended by Ron Campbell and Marion S. Wescott*

Open from Memorial Day to mid-September.
102 rooms, 11 with private bath.
Rates $24–$27 single, $44–$48 double, $52–$57 with bath, including breakfast and dinner. Special weekly and family rates.
No credit cards.
Cocktail lounge, patio, playroom.

The Mainstay Inn
635 Columbia Avenue
Cape May, New Jersey   08204
Telephone: (609) 884-8690

"Cape May, which claims to be our country's oldest seashore resort, is not the usual commercial location with flashy motels and boardwalk amusements. Cape May is Victorian and Federal homes, streets shaded by sycamore trees, a leisurely Southern feeling, band concerts and walking tours. Along the oceanfront there is a blacktop promenade, built to withstand the northeasters and hurricanes better than the old boardwalk, which fell in the storm of 1962. There are a number of modern motels at either end of the town for those who require a private bath and TV. As for me, Cape May's charm is in the many guest cottages, old hotels and inns where visitors share a bath down the hall and rock on a spacious porch with other guests. The Mainstay Inn is the gem of the town. Built in the mid-1800s, it is a Victorian mansion of Italianate style. It was first called Jackson's Club House, built to be a gambling house for Southern gentlemen.

"In the summer a light breakfast (juice, cereal, Sue's freshly baked goodies, coffee and tea) is served on the veranda. Afternoon iced tea with mint from the garden is served to guests and those who come for the daily tour of the mansion. In the cooler months, a full breakfast is served in the formal dining room.

"Other delights I have experienced are croquet games in the shady side yard, relaxing in porch swings and rocking chairs. One can observe people strolling by, stopping to stare at the beautiful old inn: You can tell that they wish that they were staying there too. Inside, the house is full of beautiful antiques. Guests may sit in the parlor, play cards or checkers or read the books about old Cape May. There was even a time when the men and women had separate hours to go on the beach. A crowning touch is the cupola. It is reached by climbing a ladder stair from the upstairs hall. It is a spot to retreat to with a good book. But on a lazy summer afternoon you may find that you're napping or just enjoying the four-sided view of the town and the sea. It's also a nice spot when the moon is full."

—*Jessie Daniels; also recommended by John and Marion Castellucci, Ted and Eleanor Peter and Barbara and John Raup*

Open from April through October. Also weekends in March and November.
9 rooms, 2 with private bath.
Rates $28–$35, including breakfast and afternoon tea. Special weekly rate—10 percent off for Sunday to Sunday.
Only breakfast and afternoon tea served.
No credit cards.

All innkeepers appreciate reservations in advance; some require them.

Washington Inn
801 Washington Street
Cape May, New Jersey   08204
Telephone: (609) 884-5697

"A lovely old house built in 1856, it has cozily decorated guest rooms. My favorite has a four-poster bed and a large bath with tub to soak in. Breakfast is served on a screened-in porch, and dinner is served either on the porch or in the dining room. The food is excellent with just the right-size servings. My husband liked his rice pudding so much he once ate it seven nights in a row. The inn has just had a change of ownership, however, so there may be some changes."   —*Mary Jo Impalli*

Open from March 1 to January 1.
6 rooms, all with private bath.
Rates $28 single, $25 double per person, including breakfast and dinner.
Special weekly rates and rates with continental breakfast only.
Credit cards: Visa.
French spoken.
Limousine service for pickup.

Frenchtown

Frenchtown National Hotel
29-31 Race Street
Frenchtown, New Jersey   08825
Telephone: (201) 996-4871

"Frenchtown is one of those working river towns on the Delaware. It is quiet, minds its own business, is slightly down-at-the-heels in an attractive way and is close enough to New York to see people line up on the sidewalk for the direct bus service to Manhattan. It is easy to explore the Pennsylvania side of the river here and to miss some of the New Jersey towns such as this one and Milford. Like most of the river towns it has its hotel built in 1840 and dating back to the era of canal building. Mainly because of almost indestructibly thick walls, it has survived what, by all accounts, has been a rough history. At times it was a quiet meeting point for the town, at other times it was jazzed up with the introduction of a cabaret. It is now in one of its quieter periods, with the owner determined to restore its calmness and to concentrate on good eating. The main barroom is rather bare, but it has a handsome carved mirror behind the bar. The restaurant, with its pictures of ducks on the walls, specializes in Greek foods, such as sish kebab and moussaka. Its baked stuffed clams are also a source of pride to the owner. Upstairs the modest rooms have polished wood floors and could, with skillful handling and imagination, become interesting bedrooms. The views are nothing startling, as the hotel is away from the river."   —*David Wigg*

Open all year.
15 rooms, 1 with private bath.
Rates $10 single, $15 double. Special weekly rates.
Credit cards: American Express, Master Charge.
Bar.
Greek spoken.

Lambertville

Lambertville House
32 Bridge Street
Lambertville, New Jersey   08530
Telephone: (609) 397-0202

" 'In the wayside inn,' wrote Harriet Martineau, the English writer who visited Jacksonian America in 1834 to report what she saw, 'the disagreeable practice of rocking in the chair is seen in its excess. In the inn parlour are three or four rocking-chairs in which sit ladies who are vibrating in different directions, and at various velocities, so as to try the head of a stranger almost as severely as the tobacco-chewer his stomach. How this lazy and ungraceful indulgence ever became general, I cannot imagine, but the nation seems so wedded to it, that I see little chance of its being forsaken.'

"Despite these sharp and sniffy words, Americans, who put much store in movement, remained wedded to the rocking chair, a restful and admirable piece of furniture, which Europeans came to adopt. Even the editor of the *Times* of London presides over editorial conferences quietly moving to and fro in a rocking chair.

"All along the grillwork-decorated front porch of the Lambertville House are red rocking chairs facing, unfortunately, the main street of the town with all its traffic. But, together with flowering window boxes, they add the right touch to a hotel that is smart and always busy. Lambertville is just across the Delaware River from the more popular town of New Hope, Pennsylvania, and has none of the latter's charm, but a walk across the bridge into New Jersey is certainly worth it.

"Opened as a stage house in 1812, the hotel has very little atmosphere left of earlier times—it has decided to go for modern comforts, with a quiet, cool old English bar, which has an electronic game in it—the one jarring piece of furniture. On the wall is a photograph of the flood of 1955—a catastrophe about which the residents of the Delaware Valley constantly talk. The menu is extensive and there is a lunch special priced at $3.95, which on the day I was there consisted of sautéed chicken livers, corn on the cob, a salad, homemade bread and beverage. There are thirty-two rooms, some of which are small but attractive inasmuch as they have slightly sloping floors and four-poster beds or beds with iron frames. The management likes to stress the age of this hotel. The register has signatures such as 'Andrew Johnson, President U.S.A.' and 'U. S. Grant, Lieut. Gen., U.S.A. 1866,' and Edward VII of Britain stayed here before he became king, but this, compared with many inns on the Pennsylvania side of the river, is a working hotel—mainly a center for the commercial life of the town."   —*David Wigg*

Open all year, except Christmas Day.
32 rooms, 5 with private bath.
Rates $14–$18 single, $14–$27 double.
Credit cards: American Express, Master Charge, Visa.
Bar.

Princeton

The Peacock Inn
20 Bayard Lane (Route 206)
Princeton, New Jersey   08540
Telephone: (609) 924-1707

This is a favorite place for many who come to stay in this university town: Bertrand Russell, Albert Einstein and F. Scott Fitzgerald have been among its guests. A handsome white building set back among bushes and trees off the busy road, it does not trumpet the fact that it is a hotel. There is only a small, neat sign. The building first appeared on the tax rolls in 1775; it became an inn in 1912. The owners are Agnes and Chuck Swain, the latter a peaceful man who writes poetry about his inn and about the power and the suffocation of love.

"The inn is close to the university and the Nassau Street shops and restaurants. There is an English pub and a restaurant that serves good onion soup and excellent fish. You have to walk around the corner for breakfast, but there is lunch and dinner every day but Sunday."   —*Polly S. Kahn*

Open all year.
17 rooms, 8 with private bath.

Rates $16–$24 single, $20–$30 double.
Credit cards: American Express, Diners Club, Master Charge, Visa.
Bar open during dining hours.

Red Bank

Molly Pitcher Inn
Route 35
Red Bank, New Jersey   07701
Telephone: (201) 747-2500

"In the summer of 1978, the 200th anniversary of the Battle of
Monmouth was celebrated in Freehold, where Molly Pitcher
served water to the exhausted troops and took over the firing of
a cannon when her husband was wounded. In the same year the
inn named for her celebrated its 50th anniversary. The inn has
been greatly enlarged and improved with excellent docking facilities, an outdoor swimming pool and plenty of parking space.
You enter a large lobby, then go on to formal and informal
dining rooms, a huge bar overlooking the river and many small
rooms for private parties. The inn can boast the most spectacular view of the Shrewsbury River—called the Navesink on
maps, but known to old-timers as the North Shrewsbury. In the
summer the river is dotted with sails, and in winter, ice condi-
tions permitting, ice boats and skaters take over. If you are not
strictly an old salt, the inn is within a short distance of Monmouth Park, the Freehold Raceway and even the Meadow-
lands."   —*Margaret E. Rullman*

"You can drive to the inn in only an hour from New York (in
off-peak hours). One hour and you are in real countryside with
foxes, raccoons and possums. It's a fine place to stop if you are
driving south to Trenton or Philadelphia and want to stay a
night away from the big cities. The inn has good food, including elk, venison, rabbit and pheasant in season. The wine list
contains a selection of forty to fifty labels from Californian to
French, German and even the occasional Spanish wine. The
decor is successfully 'historical,' with a collection of Toby jugs
and china pieces in the front hall."   —*Dr. J. S. Courtney-Pratt*

Open all year.
149 rooms, 107 with private bath.
Rates $20–$27 single, $24–$50 double.
Credit cards: American Express, Diners Club, Master Charge, Visa.
Bar, outdoor pool.
French and German spoken.

Greenville Arms,
Greenville

New York

Ancram

Oliver House
Ancram, New York   12502
Telephone: (518) 329-1166

"Some two hours north of New York City in the rolling farmlands of Columbia County, Oliver House is part of the Ancram Restoration, worthy project of John Peter Hayden and Donald Chapin, who are managing to reclaim much of the town's past. The inn has only five guest rooms, a circumstance that keeps things on the human scale. All of the rooms are comfortable (we have slept in most of them at one time or another), and there is no tipping permitted. The parlor, with its overstuffed furniture and crackling fire, invites the traveler to unwind while waiting for the announcement that dinner is ready. There are delicious homemade breads and soups, a very civilized salad, a selection of two to three quite satisfying entrees and the superb temptations of the dessert cart. A variety of carefully chosen operatic pieces accompany the meal. At the moment the inn does not have a liquor license, but guests are welcome to bring their own (there is a liquor shop close by in the town). The inn provides ice and glasses to those who want a drink before or after dinner, and will chill or decant one's dinner wine. In addition to Oliver House, the Ancram Restoration includes a charming 19th-century opera house (well worth attending in the evening or touring during the day), an atheneum that shows films, a second guesthouse and a church."

—*Mr. and Mrs. William E. Power*

Open all year.
5 rooms, none with private bath.
Rate $26.50, including breakfast of coffee and homemade nut breads.
No credit cards.

_____*Auburn*

Springside Inn
41 West Lake Road
Auburn, New York   13021
Telephone: (315) 252-7247

A Dutch Reformed Church pastor, the Rev. Samuel Robbins Brown, opened a school in 1851 to "avoid the evils necessarily attendant upon large and promiscuous assemblages of the young." When it became a private residence, tradition holds that the building was used as part of the Underground Railroad for runaway slaves during the Civil War. A summer theater was started here in 1970—the opening show was *The Fantasticks*, and Broadway musicals and comedies such as *Hello, Dolly!*, *Man of La Mancha, Cabaret* and *Applause* continue to play five nights a week, Wednesday to Sunday, through July and August.

"Situated close by Owasco Lake, the inn is comfortable and competently run to make you feel welcome—and is obviously well appreciated in the Finger Lakes region for the fine food, judging by the many weekend dinner guests. The Weekend Fling proved to be an ideal way to spend from Friday night to Sunday afternoon. There are pleasant drives and walks around the lake, or you can shop in the nearby towns of Auburn and Syracuse."   —*Peter and Barbara Liehr*

Open all year.
7 rooms, 3 with private bath.
Rates $14.98 single, $19.26 double, including continental breakfast.
   Special Weekend Fling for Two, $95.
Credit cards: Master Charge, Visa.
Bar, cross-country skiing, duck pond, hiking trails, pool, summer dinner theater.
Greek and Italian spoken.

Canaan

The Inn at the Shaker Mill Farm
Canaan, New York   12029
Telephone: (518) 794-9345

"When we arrive at the Mill, peace descends. The New York week falls away like an outmoded skin. There is calm beauty in everything, from the simple but well-equipped bedrooms and the great circular fireplace round which one takes tea or a pre-dinner drink, to the glory of the meadows and woods outside and the gentle sounds of Bach or Purcell. There is a lot of lovely walking here, in places where no highways ever have been. Food is sinfully good. One often has to choose between imaginative hors d'oeuvres—served round the fireplace before dinner—and dinner itself, because there are just too many good things to eat. In winter the marvelous trails and roads become cross-country ski trails. There are also, very close by, a number of first-rate commercial slopes. A natural pond for swimming in summer and early fall is on the grounds.

"Other inns may have more sumptuous facilities or larger grounds—but what makes this one unique is the personality of its owner-host, Ingram Paperny. It was he who transformed the precious shell of an old Shaker mill into a living space of both functional and old-fashioned comfort. He combines craftsmanship with sophisticated taste, and intellectual curiosity (he holds a higher degree in political science) with interest in people and a warm affection for his guests, who often become his long-term friends. This is one of the reasons that a steady core of often unusual people regularly return to the inn. They know that, in an ambiance of social ease, they will meet old friends and perhaps make some new ones."   —_Dr. Ernest and Evelyn Angel_

Open all year.
12 rooms, 10 with private bath.
Rates $20, including breakfast. Special weekend rates with meals.
No credit cards.
Bar, sauna.
French, German, Italian and Spanish spoken.

Details of special features offered by an inn or hotel vary according to information supplied by the hotels themselves. The absence here of a recreational amenity, a bar or a restaurant doesn't necessarily mean one of these doesn't exist. Ask the innkeeper when booking your room.

_____*Castile*

Glen Iris Inn
Letchworth State Park
Castile, New York   14427
Telephone: (716) 493-2622

"The Glen Iris Inn is an extraordinarily charming inn situated in Letchworth State Park at Castile. It was the former home of William P. Letchworth, a businessman who became involved in his later years with philanthropic work. He spotted this former temperance tavern, which had been built in the late 1820s, and converted it into his country home in 1859. Letchworth State Park has been called the Grand Canyon of the East. However, in many ways it is more spectacular, in that the natural wilderness is so accessible. With twenty rooms, the accommodations are good, particularly the Cherry Suite, which is done in the original cherry of the mansion and has a balcony with French-leaded glass doors that open out directly over the Middle Falls. This room has always been our favorite. The quality of the food has always been good, with particular emphasis on prime ribs, lamb chops and lobster tails. The wine list is adequate to good and sometimes there are some very interesting finds with some fine vintages.

"It should be noted that the autumn season is the most magnificent time in which to see Glen Iris, when the trees are resplendent. You must book several months in advance for any of the suites, and dinner reservations for weekends must be made several days in advance since travelers come from as far as Rochester and Buffalo simply for a fine dinner."
— *James and Patricia Vazzana; also recommended by Lola Rothman*

Open from Easter to the first Sunday in November.
20 rooms, all with private bath.
Rates $22–$27 double.
Credit cards: American Express, Master Charge, Visa.
Located in Letchworth State Park near Portageville—Route 19A and 436.

Rates quoted were the latest available. But they may not reflect unexpected increases or local and state taxes. Be sure to verify when you book.

Cazenovia

Lincklaen House
79 Albany Street
Cazenovia, New York   13035
Telephone: (315) 655-3461

"Cazenovia Lake is one of the loveliest of the many lakes in central New York. At the southern tip of the lake is Cazenovia, a village with personality—part resort, part college town, part rural community. And in the heart of the village is the Lincklaen House, built as a hotel in 1835 and still admirably fulfilling that function. The name comes from John Lincklaen, a land agent for the Holland Land Company, who bought the land in the 1790s and founded Cazenovia. All sleeping rooms are on the second and third floors, so the lack of an elevator and the probable absence of any bellhop is not too discouraging. There are small rooms, large rooms—in fact if there are any two just alike, I haven't found them. The elderly plumbing has asthmatic wheezes, but it works; the rooms are clean and the beds are comfortable. There is no chrome and plastic uniformity; these rooms have individuality.

"The real charm of this hostelry is twofold: the friendly, willing service of the staff, and the comfortable, attractive public rooms. In the graciously furnished main dining room, high ceilinged and with a huge fireplace, excellent food is served for lunch and dinner. The adjoining Terrace Room, bright and cheerful, has a fine breakfast menu. The fenced-in outdoor patio with its greenery is an ideal spot for reading, cards or just plain loafing on a summer afternoon; surpassed, however, by the comfort and charm of the East Room, with its own large fireplace, during winter evenings. The old-fashioned tavern, tucked into an out-of-the-way corner, is a popular but rarely crowded watering spot. Helen Tobin and her associates have well maintained the spirit of the old hotel: Lincklaen House itself seems to say, 'Welcome, traveler. Enter, relax and rest. I'll take care of you.' "   *—Roger B. Cobb; also recommended by Jeanne and Bob Glass*

Open all year.
24 rooms, 22 with private bath.
Rates $24 single, $30 double, $35 suite.
Credit cards: Master Charge, Visa.
Bar, courtyard dining.
French spoken.

All innkeepers appreciate reservations in advance; some require them.

Clarence

Asa Ransom House
10529 Main Street
Clarence, New York   14031
Telephone: (716) 759-2315

"How nice it is to find an Asa Ransom House in the midst of the motels in the Buffalo area. From arrival to departure the hospitality extended by Bob and Judy Lenz is unmatched. There are two dining rooms, the larger of which is reserved for the nonsmokers. Hurray! The menu always has some unusual items to offer. The food is superbly prepared, using fresh ingredients and as few additives as possible. Service excellent. A continental breakfast is included in the price of the room, and what a masterpiece it is. The restaurant is not open to the public for breakfast, so one can fairly well set his own time to eat. Bob serves freshly baked bread or pastry, several kinds of fresh fruit and juices, a quiche, and of course coffee, tea or what have you. Not to be missed is the Clarence Community Park just a block or two up the street. This is a delightful area of trees, large grassy areas, a lagoon complete with ducks, geese and boys fishing, two tennis courts, flowers—a real treasure. The flowers were in large masses and phenomenal."

—*Charles L. Newberry*

"A warm greeting made us soon forget the chill of a rainy fall afternoon arrival. Upstairs there are four rooms in the inn, each prettier than the other—furnished with beautiful antiques and decorated with unbelievable charm and good taste. We chose to stay in the Gold Room with its iron and brass beds, a beautiful old writing desk, comfortable chairs and a spacious, ultramodern, immaculate bathroom. A knock at the door soon after our arrival brought a bowl of fruit with the innkeeper's best wishes. Dinner in the evening must be country cooking at its finest, with the touch of a master chef in the kitchen. There are homemade soups, fresh vegetables, crisp green salads with just the right dressings, home-baked breads, a choice of entrees to suit any taste, and always a daily specialty. A nice touch, we thought, was the offer of the innkeeper to serve smaller portions to guests with smaller appetites at a reduced price."

—*Martha and Carl Anderson*

"The waitresses, dressed in long skirts, old-fashioned blouses and pert little caps, all truly enjoy serving the house specialties. Their enthusiasm spreads to all the guests, as they ladle out the soup of the day from a little brown kettle. We love the fresh flowers from the garden and the dry arrangements placed here and there. We have often seen the innkeepers scoot out of the herb garden to select something special to adorn our plates. We can never depart without a visit to the Sunshine Square gift shop, just off the library room. Something decidedly different for that special gift for a friend: a unique selection of cards, herb teas, dolls and loaves of their delicious homemade fruit breads. Our interest in antiques is more than satisfied when we walk to the little shops not far from the inn."

—*Mr. and Mrs. Clarence A. Brittell*

Closed first 3 weeks in February.
4 rooms, all with private bath.
Rates $24–$32, including breakfast.
No credit cards.
Bar, library, gift shop, herb garden, nonsmokers' dining room.
French and German spoken.

Clinton

Clinton House
21 West Park Row
Clinton, New York   13323
Telephone: (315) 853-5555

"The former Alexander Hamilton Inn has been completely redone inside. There are five large, airy and light bedrooms, a pleasant bar and sitting room–lounge downstairs. Food is excellent and reservations are best for dinner. The inn is located at one end of the village green and evokes a tranquil country-village feeling. Parents of Hamilton College students like to stay here, as do alumni when they return to the Hill. This part of New York State is bucolic, with many important historical spots close by. In twenty minutes you can be in the foothills of the Adirondack Mountains—a region of lovely valleys, rivers and hills."   —*Mr. and Mrs. G. H. Dalton*

Open all year, except Christmas Day.
5 rooms, all with private bath.
Rates $30 single or double, including coffee and juice.
Credit cards: Master Charge, Visa.
Bar.
Italian and Spanish spoken.

Do you know a hotel in your state that we have overlooked? Write *now*.

Elka Park

The Redcoat's Return
Dale Lane
Elka Park, New York   12427
Telephone: (518) 589-6379

"In the heart of New York's Catskill Mountains, England's flag flies beneath the Stars and Stripes at this charming inn atop Mt. Platte Clove near Tannersville. It appears to be an old-fashioned farmhouse. But Peg and Tom Wright have transformed this turn-of-the-century summer retreat into a British bed 'n' breakfast inn. The colorful carved signboard on the lawn tips guests to both the creativity and sense of humor of the innkeepers. On one side of the sign is a Redcoat; on the other, an English pub maid. Of course, they are profiles of the Wrights. After sipping arrival tea, guests are warmly welcomed to individually decorated quarters. Thirteen upstairs bedrooms, many with private baths, are papered, curtained and quilted, offering a spot to read, write or rest. Inviting corners throughout the inn beckon guests to park with a book. Besides several fine paintings and a set of Hogarth prints on the sitting room walls, the Wrights own a magnificent book collection. It lines an entire wall of the elegant dining room, where the food is all prepared by Tom, whose culinary credentials include London's Dorchester and the Cunard Line. While small, the menu includes curries, shrimp maison, escalopes of veal, frog legs Provençale and steak and kidney pie. Tom's cold avocado soup to launch the meal, and his sherry trifle to end it, are special.

"Guests may hike one of several fine trails nearby: Jimmy Dolan's Notch, Indian Head or Devil's Kitchen Leanto each offer breathtaking views of the Hudson Valley. Other guests choose to golf, swim, ride or play tennis. The artists' community of Woodstock, at the mountain's base, offers streets lined with galleries and pottery and craft shops."   —Liz Einstein

Open all year, except from mid-April to mid-May.
13 rooms, 7 with private bath.
Rates $22–$25 single, $32–$36 double, including breakfast.
Credit cards: American Express, Master Charge, Visa.
Bar, fireplace, lounge.

If you would like to amend, update or disagree with any entry, write *now*.

_Garrison

Bird and Bottle Inn
Route 9
Garrison, New York   10524
Telephone: (914) 424-3000

"New Yorkers often fail to appreciate that less than an hour's drive from the city lies some extraordinarily beautiful countryside, dotted with quaint towns that hold innumerable delights for the tourist. On the outskirts of one such town, Garrison, stands the Bird and Bottle Inn, a lemon yellow, colonial structure with impeccable black and white trim. The grounds are beautiful and well kept; taking a peaceful stroll early one evening, we spotted several deer grazing in a meadow. We are long-time country inn enthusiasts and have had many memorable experiences at inns all over the country. Our stay at the Bird and Bottle Inn ranks easily among our most pleasant. We were truly overwhelmed by the warmth and hospitality of the staff— quietly inconspicuous but always available and faultless in their service—and by the owners, Tom and Nancy Noonan. They have just recently opened a few rooms for lodging and we were fortunate to be among their first overnight guests. Our room, with its big stone fireplace, was spacious, comfortable and beautifully decorated. Before dinner we sipped drinks in the small, rustic bar. The _prix fixe_ dinners we enjoyed were pure culinary hedonism. There are two sittings each evening; don't be afraid to choose the first, as you will never be rushed. The fixed price (quite reasonable) includes a delicious full-course meal, and the choices are numerous including some specialties of the chef. An amusing anecdote might best illustrate the atmosphere of the inn. As we were having dinner, we overheard a young couple at the next table. They had just finished their meal and were appalled at discovering that they had no cash, credit cards or checks with them. Their embarrassment and anxiety were swiftly and calmly dispelled by the maître d', who—without a trace of annoyance—kindly offered to bill them. They left looking sheepish but very grateful.

"During the day, we explored some of the nearby sites of interest: the town of Cold Spring, with its antique shops, craft stores and art galleries; Hyde Park, Franklin D. Roosevelt's estate; West Point; the Boscobel mansion and Bear Mountain State Park. On the morning of our departure, over Sunday brunch in the smaller dining room—complete with the _New York Times_—Tom and Nancy apologized that they had been unable to spend more time with us. Nancy explained that there would be a wedding held at the inn that afternoon and she was busy with the arrangements. When we last saw her, she was fixing flowers and ribbons to the bridge that spans a small stream that gurgles through the property."

—*Donna and Stephen Herman*

Open all year, except Christmas Day and Mondays and Tuesdays from November 1 to June 1.
5 rooms, all with private bath.
Rates from $45–$55, $75 suite, including continental breakfast.
Credit cards: American Express, Master Charge, Visa.
Bar, terrace dining.
French, German and Spanish spoken.

Greenville

Greenville Arms
Greenville, New York   12083
Telephone: (518) 966-5219

"It is nice to realize as you come into Greenville that it is ideally located: a pleasant back-road drive to Albany and its many attractions; Saratoga, the racetrack in August, and many, many delightful day trips. Greenville is of course at its best in the summer. A short drive or walk in any direction brings you in touch with the natural wonders of the northern Catskill Mountains. Fall and spring offer the splendors of the changing seasons and winter is lively: There are many famous ski runs nearby.

"And of course the best thing about Greenville and its environs is the Greenville Arms, which was built as a home in the 1890s by William Vanderbilt. There is always a sense of quiet and rest. Ruth Stevens's greeting immediately makes you welcome. The rooms and especially the dining rooms are furnished in lovely and time-worn early American antiques, enhanced by paintings of mostly local scenes by local well-known artists. Fireplaces with old burnished copper accessories enhance the public rooms. The grounds are surprisingly spacious and beautifully landscaped, with a swimming pool ringed by majestic pine trees."

—*Mr. and Mrs. George Arancio*

Open all year.
20 rooms, 14 with private bath, from May 1 to November 1. 11 rooms from November 1 to May 1.
Rates $25–$28 single, $36–$52 double, including breakfast and dinner. European plan also available. Special weekly rates.
No credit cards.
Lawn games, library.

Hillsdale

L'Hostellerie Bressane
Hillsdale, New York   12529
Telephone: (518) 325-3412

"Whether it's remembered as the Dutch Hearth Inn or known by its new name, L'Hostellerie Bressane, one can expect the same country elegance visit after visit. Those unfamiliar with the bucolic environs of Columbia County might locate Chef and Madame Morel's inn by its proximity to Tanglewood. For me, the finest orchestration in the area is to be found in the dining room, not the Shed. My preference is for a leisurely meal with chicken liver soufflé, pea soup with sorrel and poached salmon in champagne sauce. For the selection of wine, I yield to my wife. Such a meal and my wife make the entire evening for me. I have observed, however, that Madame Morel and the staff pace the meal appropriately for those who also feel the need for Tanglewood or the Berkshire ski slopes. What is a recommendation without a comparison? In a frame of reference encompassing Lyons and New York City, Jean Morel excels. Choose your own standards and make your own comparisons."   —_Dr. James T. Corkins_

Closed for either February and March or March and April.
5 rooms, none with private bath.
Rate $23.
No credit cards.
Bar, fireplaces.
French spoken.

New Paltz

Mohonk Mountain House
Lake Mohonk
New Paltz, New York   12561
Telephone: (914) 255-1000

"Mohonk Mountain House, near New Paltz, is an ideal retreat for nonswinging New Yorkers. It is less than two hours from Manhattan by car or bus. It's a huge, rambling place with over 300 rooms, most of which have private baths and fireplaces with beautiful carved mantelpieces. The rooms are furnished with oak dressers and rocking chairs and are simple and comfortable. Each room has a small porch. The public rooms are spacious and inviting, with grand pianos, Victorian sofas and stuffed chairs, huge fireplaces and gently worn carpets. The building itself is an architectural conglomeration of at least four distinct styles. The oldest part was built in 1870 by Albert and Alfred Smiley, twins and Quaker schoolteachers. Once a twelve-room structure, it now is seven floors high and one-eighth of a mile long. The hotel sits in 2,500 wooded acres laced with hiking trails, from simple walking paths to the rock-climbing kind. There is horseback riding, excellent tennis courts, a putting green and a beautiful glacial lake for swimming and ice skating. There's a surrey for summer jaunts and sleigh riding when there is snow. Evening activities are old-fashioned, with occasional movies, slow dancing or variety shows. There are weeks or weekends of special events such as astronomy, nature, chamber music or jogging. Be warned: there is no bar or cocktail lounge, but ice is available for the rooms and drinks are served in the large dining room. Food is country American with generous portions and excellent soups, breads and desserts."   —*Patricia Berens*

Open all year.
305 rooms, 210 with private bath.
Rates $32–$66 single, $30–$55 double, including three meals.
Special 3-night packages including weekends, and special midweek ski-tourer package. Special family rates in the summer.
Credit cards: Master Charge, Visa.
Cross-country skiing, hiking, horse-drawn sleigh rides, ice skating, riding in winter. Boating, croquet, fishing, golf, haywagon rides, lawn bowling, putting, riding, shuffleboard, softball, swimming, tennis in summer.

_____*New York*

The Algonquin
59 West 44th Street
New York, New York   10036
Telephone: (212) 840-6800

"The Algonquin's reputation blossomed in the 1920s when its Round Table became a sort of clubhouse for New York's reigning literary wits—Dorothy Parker, Robert Benchley, George S. Kaufman—many of whom worked for the *New Yorker* across the street. In 1977 the magazine threw a seventy-fifth birthday party for the hotel and a few writers were on hand, but lately the hotel's clientele has become more theatrical—Laurence Olivier, Yves Montand, Jeanne Moreau. (We were recently audience to a matchless Peter Ustinov pantomime as he sucked in his considerable girth to allow 'ladies first' off the elevator. Ustinov is a favorite with the staff, reportedly dealing with all the bellhops and waiters in their various mother tongues.)

"Europeans love the Algonquin for the personal service, the musty dowdiness, reminiscent of so many continental hotels. In fact, much of the Algonquin's antiquity is facade. A few years back owner Ben Bodne and his son-in-law/manager Andrew Anspach spent over a million dollars fixing it up. They just didn't tell anyone. Wing chairs from the lobby-lounge (a bee-hive of a cocktail party every evening from five to seven) were secretly smuggled out for reupholstering and the carpets were replaced in the dead of night to avoid worrying regulars about 'renovations.' The cranky elevator is, in fact, rather new. It's just that Mr. Bodne likes operators, hates pushbuttons. About the only changes anyone noticed were the redecorating of the Rose Room (by Oliver Smith, who designed *My Fair Lady*) and the introduction of Cardgards—an electric door-opening system far more secure than keys with room numbers and mail-back tags.

"The Algonquin works hard at being an unchanging 'home' for its clients. It took us four visits to notice that we always had, not just the same floor location, but the same *room* every time. The reservations desk keeps files. Other guests' cards note 'two single beds pushed together' or 'thermos of milk and bowl for cat.' Food in the Oak Room and the Rose Room remains maddeningly inconsistent, just like home."

—*Mechtild Hoppenrath and Charles Oberdorf*

Open all year.
200 rooms, all with private bath.
Rates $46–$52 single, $51–$60 double, suites $95.
Credit cards: American Express, Carte Blanche, Diners Club, Master Charge, Visa.
French, German, Swedish and Spanish spoken.

The Alrae
37 East 64th Street
New York, New York   10021
Telephone: (212) 744-0200

"I found the Alrae one spring day on foot and in panic. I had just come to New York for the first time in several years, and checked into the hotel that had served as home base during my period as *Look*'s man in South America and, later, Europe. The passenger elevator wasn't running, my old room had been decorated out of all its small-hotel charm, the shower would scald, I was told, unless you knew how to use it and the price had risen 150 percent since my last visit. Someone had told me about a quiet, well-run, fairly-priced *and* attractive hotel in the Sixties—couldn't remember the name and didn't know the street. But I'd worked with fewer clues than those before, and I was highly motivated. Whether the Alrae was the hotel my informant had in mind I never learned, but it was there that my search ended. The hotel is on the north side of a tree-lined street, between Madison and Park. It *is* quiet, well-run and attractive, and at the time it was fairly priced. My two-room suite cost me $5 more a day than the wretched single I had abandoned, and it came complete with the rudiments of a kitchenette. Alas, time marches on, and the $55 a day I paid for the suite will now get you no more than a single. Doubles are $65, two-room suites $90–$100. Suites in the back are less expensive, and also less noisy. Room service is—or was—expensive but not ridiculous. That strange language you'll hear in the elevators is Portuguese; the Alrae is extremely popular with Brazilians."

—*Leonard Gross*

Open all year.
246 rooms.
Rates $55 single, $65 double, $90–$100 suites.
Credit cards: American Express, Diners Club, Master Charge, Visa.
Arabic, French, German, Portuguese, Russian and Spanish spoken.

The Stanhope
995 Fifth Avenue
New York, New York   10028
Telephone: (212) 288-5800

"Deposit your scuffed shoes outside the door of your room at the Stanhope. They will not only be there next morning, you will be able to see your face in them. It is all part of 'luxurious living in the continental manner' at the quietly classy hotel superbly located opposite the Metropolitan Museum of Art, overlooking Central Park.

"The Stanhope coat of arms, castle and griffin, is elegantly displayed in the richly paneled lobby and repeated on stationery, china and other appurtenances. A bell captain from the northern most city in the south of Ireland gives the impression that he has been waiting a lifetime to look after you. He and the rooms are friendly, he in a charming brogue, they in warm colors with handsome chests of drawers, comfortable writing desks and people-sized bathtubs (hooray!). And you need not be an engineer to operate the sink, shower and tub hot and cold water faucets. They are simple and old-fashioned, unlike the intricate and newfangled hardware that can chill or par-broil the naked body slow to figure out the mechanics.

"The heated bathrooms boast fluffy floor mats (there's another in one of your three closets), the medicine chests are roomy, the lamps plentiful and your own door chimes announce guests. The housekeeping, valet, front desk and room service staff are all a pushbutton away and tend to your comfort with gracious competence. They will notorize your papers, walk your dog and obtain splendid theater seats on merely minutes' notice.

"Dine in the elegantly intimate Rembrandt Room and drink in the casual Cluny Bar, draped in MacPherson plaid and named for Cluny MacPherson (who else?), a mid-19th-century Scottish clan chieftain. In clement weather the sidewalk Café du Parc is open for cocktails and lunch.

"Small wonder that the Stanhope attracts such clientele as the Aga Khan and Princess Grace. The late actor and art collector Edward G. Robinson maintained a suite and when diva Maria Callas checked in during her last world concert tour, she stayed for three months."   —*Edna Buchanan*

Open all year.
274 rooms, all with private bath.
Rates $60–$75 single, $70–$85 double.
Credit Cards: American Express, Diners Club, Master Charge, Visa.
Chinese, French, German, Italian and Spanish spoken.

Speculator

Zeiser's
Speculator, New York   12164
Telephone: (518) 548-7021

"I really believe you should include Zeiser's in Speculator, New York. It is owned and operated by John and Genevieve Zeiser (and Ludwig, the cat). The operation is housed in what used to be the Annex of the Sturges House, which was built in 1858 by David Sturges, back when the crossroads near the hotel was called Newton's Corners. The Zeisers have been in business here for twenty-three years. There is an attractive bar, lunch areas—including a long screened porch in season—and a handsome formal dining room, with lighting, napery, silverware and table settings beyond reproach. Every part of the operation is spotlessly clean. There is no American plan. You are expected to find your breakfast elsewhere in the village. There is no room service for drinks or food. The food is excellent, tending toward the German. The wine cellar is heavy on good Moselles. Mr. Z, a tidy and formal man, reigns at the bar. His no-nonsense attitude has given the bar the flavor of a good, small private club. Service is swift and courteous, and one would go a long, long way to find a better dry martini. Or more civilized conversation at a bar. Mr. Z is a host!

"Speculator, incidentally, is in Hamilton County, which is in the middle of the Adirondack Park Preserve and is the most sparsely settled county in New York State. It is reputed to have more black bears than people. The crossroads a couple of hundred feet from Zeiser's is the intersection of Route 8, which begins way down at Deposit, N.Y., on the Pennsylvania border and ends at Hague, N.Y., on the northwest shore of Lake George, and Route 30 which begins, or ends, down at Harvard and Shinhopple, N.Y., near the Pennsylvania border, and ends, or begins, at Trout River on the Quebec border.

"Lest this sound too obscure, let me say that Zeiser's is 42 miles from Gloversville, 61 from Utica, 75 from Schenectady, 90 from Albany, 94 from Troy and 109 from Syracuse. The most handsome way of driving up to Speculator is to exit the Thruway at exit 29, Canajoharie, and drive north on Route 10 to Route 8, and turn right on 8 to Speculator, twelve miles farther. The last seventeen miles of Route 10, before it intersects Route 8, is known locally as the Arietta Road. When it was repaved a few years ago, the Park Authority did not consent to the usual 'straightening.' So there are sixty-five curves in those hilly miles, beautifully graded, a feast in autumn, but special at any time of year. Speculator is lakes and camping in summer, hunting in the fall, skiing in the winter.

"Room reservations are a must, and dinner reservations almost as necessary. This past year, the Zeisers had a Bavarian festival with tent, music, fantastic German food, superb beer on draft and the best zither player I have ever heard anywhere, an engaging chap named Toni Noichl."   —*John D. MacDonald*

Open all year.
6 rooms, all with private bath.
Rates $9.50 single, $18.50 double.
Credit cards: American Express.
Bar.
German spoken.

Stony Brook

Three Village Inn
Dock Road
Stony Brook, New York   11790
Telephone: (516) 751-0555

"An ideal inn for a weekend escape for those high-powered professionals who need R&R in a quiet, 18th-century setting not too far from the city (60 miles from Times Square) but a world away. It's across the road from Stony Brook harbor and a few steps from the restored colonial village. There are museums as well as tennis courts and a golf course nearby, but walking is *the* thing—this part of Long Island is especially delightful in spring and fall. Many people come from New York and even New Jersey for lunch or dinner—the Sandbar is snug on a winter day and the drinks are good. I have spent one night a week there in term time for almost ten years, have made genuine friendships and worked my way through the super dessert menu from apple crisp to lemon fromage—mmm good."

—*Roderick J. Minogue*

Open all year.
24 rooms.
Rates $20–$30 single, $30–$40 double.
Credit cards: American Express, Master Charge, Visa.
Bar.
French, German and Spanish spoken.

Pennsylvania

Buck Hill Falls

Buck Hill Inn
Buck Hill Falls, Pennsylvania   18323
Telephone: (717) 595-7441

"I first explored this wonderful old resort by way of the back-stairs when, as a college student in Pennsylvania, I got a summer waitress job there almost twenty years ago. Buck Hill was then still its old Quaker self, a haven of quiet gentility set in 6,-000 acres of woods and hills. Quaker equality meant that we, the help, were free to roam and enjoy (with only a few exceptions) the whole wonderful place, from the quiet Sunday Meeting room—where Browning was quoted at such eloquent length one First Day that time hung there suspended among the hills—to the tennis courts and the nightly lectures and travelogues. I went back recently for a visit. 'That Quaker stuff's all gone now,' the young woman at the bar (a bar: at Buck Hill!) said cheerfully. And so it is, along with the funky old reception desk and the hushed dining room: Oh, how we once burnished the silver and polished the service plates! Where once there was poached fish eaten in silence there was now a buffet luncheon laid out to feed a crowd of noisy conventioneers with name tags. A little sorry I had tried to come back, I went for a walk again, and thought about what the years had done to Buck Hill. In the dark, wide lobbies, the old furniture was still there; a pianist was idly fingering the piano in the old Meeting room. On the porch elderly regulars still sat peacefully in chairs looking over the equally peaceful hills that rolled away into the distance. What is an inn like this to do? Once one of a handful of turn-of-the-century grand resorts in Pennsylvania's Pocono Mountains, frequented by the rich, the intellectual, the 'refined,' it now lives in a very different world. Until the summer throngs return, I decided, Buck Hill has to hang in there any way it can. And that's what it is trying—under new management—to do. It still has the marvelous old golf course and tennis club, to which an indoor pool, a skating rink and skiing—among other things—have been added. At sunset it is still a marvelous pile of stone set among the wooded hills. Those of us who knew it when, wish it well."   —B. C.

Open all year.
350 rooms.
Rates $73 single, $52 double per person, including two meals. Children and third person in room half price.
All major credit cards accepted.
4 cocktail lounges, 27 holes of golf, 2 putting greens, outdoor and indoor pools, horseback riding, paddle tennis, sailing, skiing.
Limousine service will pick up guests at Mt. Pocono bus depot.

Centre Bridge

Centre Bridge Inn
River Road
New Hope, Pennsylvania   18938
Telephone: (215) 862-2048

"Some unlikely people get the urge to own an inn. Among them was Robert Cobun, a TWA pilot who spends a lot of time in the capitals of Europe but likes his little corner of Bucks County, Pennsylvania, best. Several years ago he bought and restored this inn, with its checkered history. The handsome building is perched on the canalside, with a wide view of the Delaware River beyond. The bar and public dining room open on a canal-bank terrace where parties arriving by barge from nearby New Hope disembark for a waterside party. Mr. Cobun is furnishing his inn with antiques: He says his goal is a canopy bed in every room."   —B.C.

Open all year.
8 rooms, all with private bath.

Rates $30–$35.
Credit cards: American Express, Carte Blanche, Master Charge,
Visa.
Outdoor dining.

_____*Lititz*

General Sutter Inn
14 East Main Street
On the Square
Lititz, Pennsylvania   17543
Telephone: (717) 626-2115

"Founded by members of the Moravian Church more than 200
years ago, Lititz retains the dignity and charm of that early set-
tlement. An active historical society, long before it was fashionable, plus a real sense of civic pride has aided in the
preservation of the town, and today many of the original buildings, including the Moravian Church, are still in use. Among
those early buildings is an inn about 225 years old on the town
square. Named for General Sutter, on whose land the California gold rush began and who later, as the story has it, died a
poor man in Lititz, the General Sutter Inn combines the past
with today's 'necessary' conveniences. The rooms are clean and
spacious and the staff is friendly, helpful and informed. Ask the
evening desk clerk for directions and she is likely to help you
plan your entire stay in the Lancaster area with candid observations on what to see and visit. The kitchen, presided over by
Jim Constantine, the owner, offers a wide selection ranging
from the informal coffee shop to the gourmet dining rooms.
The writer strongly recommends, as he did on one recent snowy
evening, sitting down to a delicious steak, chosen and prepared
to your taste by Jim, with house potatoes and a big salad followed by an after-dinner cordial or coffee in front of the fire in
the lobby. If one is planning to visit the many historical places
and attractions in Lancaster County, and likes the charm of a
delightful, friendly small town and does not feel a strong, com-
pelling need to stay in the stereotype lodgings, then Lititz and
the General Sutter will be a delightful stay."

—*Richard M. Cloney*

Open all year, except Christmas Day and New Year's Eve.
14 rooms, 12 with private bath.
Rates $16 single, $24–$32 double. Special weekly and monthly rates.
Credit cards: American Express, Master Charge, Visa.
Cocktail lounge, outside patio.
Greek spoken.

Lumberville

Black Bass Hotel
Route 32
Lumberville, Pennsylvania   18933
Telephone: (215) 297-5770

"Few places in the overbuilt, overpaved development area that passes for the Mid-Atlantic states could be so overlooked and free of ruin as the riverside stretch of Pennsylvania's Bucks County that straddles the winding, two-lane River Road—also known as Route 32. Along River Road with the Delaware River and the Pennsylvania Canal running beside it, hotels and taverns have been in existence since fifty years or more before the American Revolution. The first of them marked ferry points across the wide river; they were later joined by newer hotels that followed the building (in the 1820s) of the canal. Together they served bargemen, farmers bringing grain to the mills and travelers on their way between cities linked by the waterways or reached by one of the river's ferries. Several of these old hotels—through up years and down—never stopped serving the traveler and the local community alike. One of the oldest of them is the Black Bass.

"Clinging to the road like a wayside inn of Europe, the Black Bass (built in the 1740s) displays the wrought-iron ornamentation outside that marked the river towns. Inside it is a jumble of old wood, fireplaces, comforting bars (one with a pewter bar top from Maxim's) and seven wonderful richly furnished old rooms with names like 'Grover Cleveland,' 'Victoria' and 'Vendôme.' There is also a suite overlooking the river. The Black Bass has been a weekend escape for New Yorkers and Philadelphians for years: It's not unusual to have to book a room a year ahead for a holiday weekend. Its dining rooms, too—one a porch stretching along the canal bank and river— are popular, and packed as a local pub on Saturday nights."

—B. C.

Open all year.
7 rooms, 1 suite.
Rates $35, $75 for the suite, including continental breakfast.
Credit cards: American Express, Diners Club, Master Charge, Visa.
Several bars.

All innkeepers appreciate reservations in advance; some require them.

1740 House
River Road
Lumberville, Pennsylvania 18933
Telephone: (215) 297-5661

"Prepare yourself for Harry Nessler. If all innkeepers are characters, this is one writ large. 'We only serve the things I like here,' he told me on my first visit to 1740 House. 'And we only cook them the way I like them.' There are rumors (nay, legends) about how he preselects his guests for a lot of quirky (though strictly legal) reasons. But when he hung out his sign (a fine screen print by artist Allen Saalburg, by the way), he adopted as his motto: 'If you can't be a houseguest in Bucks County, be ours.' And he meant it.

"Harry Nessler and his wife stumbled into innkeeping—he had been in real estate in New York City—when they bought a summer home and discovered that the real estate office, on the bank of the Delaware, was for sale, too. He'd always wanted to be an innkeeper, so he bought the place. A couple of core buildings in his now strung-out inn are very old (one room has a stone-walled bathroom that goes well back into the 18th century), the rest were skillfully added with no violence done to Lumberville's lazy, lovely main street—well, its only street, actually. The 1740 House now has twenty-four rooms, a private dining room for hotel guests, with a comfortable parlor and library. Harry won't have a bar: He doesn't want the crowds to roll in off the streets and cramp his guests. He serves a very satisfying breakfast in his brick-floored dining room along the canal bank. If you're lucky, you'll catch him padding through his domain early in the morning in his lounge slippers (dogs at heel), feeling talkative." —B. C.

Open all year.
24 rooms, all with private bath.
Rates $35–$40, including buffet breakfast.
No credit cards.
No bar, but set-ups provided.
Swimming pool, boats for use on the canal.

Where are the good little hotels in Boston? Philadelphia? Omaha? Dallas? If you have found one, don't keep it a secret. Write *now*.

Mendenhall

Mendenhall Inn
Kennett Pike
Mendenhall, Pennsylvania   19357
Telephone: (215) 388-1181

"This old inn has a long and interesting history. It is on the Kennett Pike in the village of Mendenhall, near the Delaware State line and close to suburban Wilmington. The rooms are comfortable, located on three floors in the rear of the main building and thus insulated against the noise of rather heavy traffic on the busy Kennett Pike. It is an ideal base for sight-seeing in beautiful, rolling hill country. Nearby are Longwood Gardens, Winterthur Gardens and Museum, the Brandywine Museum at Chadd's Ford, Pa. (Andrew Wyeth country) and places of cultural and historic importance in Wilmington, New Castle, Odessa and Dover. The restaurant is outstanding, featuring continental and American cuisine. It is comfortable, food is well-prepared, attractively and promptly served. The experienced 'eater-out' will find the prices in line with better restaurants in the larger cities, another way of saying they are not cheap—with wine, a couple would pay $25 to $40 for dinner."   —*Willis Warnell*

Open all year.
16 rooms, all with private bath.
Rates $18 single, $28 double, $50 suite. Children under 12 free.
Credit cards: American Express, Diners Club, Master Charge, Visa.
Bar.

Myerstown

Tulpehocken Manor Inn and Plantation
Route 422
RD 2
Myerstown, Pennsylvania   17067
Telephone: (717) 866-4926

"Only four months after I had immigrated to the United States, my landlords in Lancaster, Esther Nissly and James Henry, invited me to tour the Amish country that surrounds the town. This trip, it turned out, had another purpose for Jim and Esther, besides showing me how a dedicated group of people live in the 20th century with traditions and tools of several hundred years ago. Jim had always wanted to own a farm, and

Esther was very fond of old stone mansions. They had heard that a plantation called Tulpehocken Manor was for sale.

"The mansion, built in 1769 as an eight-room home and enlarged in 1883 to a twenty-seven-room Victorian manor, stood there among high trees, waiting to be restored to new life. It was surrounded by 150 acres of farmland, with grassy pastures and cornfields yielding fodder for over sixty black Angus. A creek, which at the time of the American struggle for independence was a shipping canal, made the property even more pleasant. Jim and Esther saw their dreams come true, and shortly after bought the place.

"Today Tulpehocken Manor is an unusual combination of inn, museum, home and farm. On occasion it is also a meeting place for craftsmen showing off their art, or a rally point for antique car buffs. The recreated historic Hanover Rifle Battalion made Tulpehocken its headquarters, and the lucky visitor can sometimes see a Sunday afternoon maneuver, inspect the old, front-loaded rifles and admire the uniforms. Beside the main manor house, there are several old stone buildings erected in the early 1700s and converted into cozy apartments of various styles and sizes. Almost any need for an overnight or longer accommodation can be met. But the main mansion is, of course, the focal point. Tools of early settlers are displayed. Locally made and imported historical furniture can be seen, and different periods of architecture studied. Woodwork, especially on the arched doorways, and stained-glass windows catch the eye.

"To sleep at Tulpehocken is not just getting a night's rest. It is an experience into the past. In case you are interested in the historical details, try to engage Jim in a conversation. But don't ask too many questions or you may be sitting up well past midnight, fascinated by the stories of your host."

—*Wolfgang Kutter*

"Tulpehocken Manor appealed to us because of the warm, and informative, welcome extended to us by the owners. It was like visiting a family who lived in one of the most beautiful historic homes Pennsylvania had to offer. For us New Zealanders, Tulpehocken was the highlight in hospitality and lodgings at a reasonable price of our trip through the United States."

—*N. D. R. and J. L. Stirrat*

Open all year.
20 rooms, several cottages. 7 rooms with private bath.
Rates $25–$30; cottage (4 to 6 people) $50–$75.
No meals.
No credit cards.

If you would like to amend, update or disagree with any entry, write *now*.

New Hope

The Inn at Phillips Mill
North River Road
New Hope, Pennsylvania   18938
Telephone: (215) 862-9919 or 2984

"Phillips Mill is little more than a bend in the road near the better-known town of New Hope. It is still a center for artists, with an annual show in the mill itself—a 1756 stone building that, with the similar structures around it, gives the tiny cluster the look of a Cotswold hamlet. The inn started life as a barn in the middle of the 18th century and did time as a girls' school before becoming, consecutively, a tea shop, a restaurant and now an inn. Its small dining rooms are beautifully decorated to enhance the dark wood and stone of the building. Ceilings are low, fireplaces blaze: the whole atmosphere gives off a welcome, especially in winter. There are only four rooms, and one suite here. Like all the inns along the Delaware River and the canal that parallels it, this small hostelry is close to miles of towpath walks—the canal flows for more than fifty miles and its banks are state parkland now."   —_B. C._

Open all year except for three weeks in early January.
4 rooms, 1 suite, all with private bath.
Rates $28, suite $38.
No credit cards.
French spoken.

Logan Inn
10 West Ferry Street
New Hope, Pennsylvania   18938
Telephone: (215) 862-5134

"New Hope was once little more than a ferry slip on the Old York Road linking pre-Revolutionary Philadelphia with New York. It later became a mill town of some prosperity. But it was the discovery of New Hope early in this century by artists and literati that gave the town a special flavor and a certain notoriety: a kind of country retreat for the Algonquin set, the home of artists and writers and the site of the Bucks County Playhouse. Get hold of Carl Lutz, who, with Arthur Sanders (both ex-New Yorkers), runs the inn, and persuade him to tell a few stories about New Hope's golden years and the crazy people who passed through his hotel trailing the glitter of Broadway and Hollywood.

"New Hope has changed much over the last decade or two with the introduction of more commerce, which elbowed some of the craft shops aside and draws dreadful crowds. But the town is working hard to hold the line—and to restore its quiet and brassy/classy/haute bohémienne ambiance. Carl Lutz knows all about that, too. He's New Hope's mayor. The Logan Inn is something of a flagship for his cause—it has endured for more than 250 years. The rooms upstairs have been restored and furnished with some Lutz family antiques. There is also a small stone cottage in the garden for guests. The bar is a gem, full of wonderful paraphernalia. And the glass-walled garden room is a delight for dining year round."   —B. C.

Open all year, except Thanksgiving, Christmas and New Year's Day, and from January 15 to February 15.
10 rooms, 1 stone cottage; 8 rooms with private bath.
Rates $25–$35.
Credit cards: Master Charge, Visa.
Bar.
French and German spoken.

_____Orefield

Guthsville Hotel
RD 1
Orefield, Pennsylvania   18069
Telephone: (215) 395-2122

"The hotel occupies the most visible corner of the only cross-roads in the village of Guthsville where it is surrounded by a small collection of the graces of Pennsylvania country architecture—flaking common brick, stucco, puddingstone, clapboard, lacy ironwork, scalloped porch supports, fat chimneys, stained glass and beaded curtains in the windows. The foundation was laid in the 1790s, and it has been open as a hotel ever since except for six months in 1900 when it was restored. The charm is 'of the period' without making a thing of it. People obviously come here to eat and drink and talk. John O'Hara would have felt at home in the bar. Across the hall from the bar is a large cabinet with several dozen nameplate shaving mugs. That is the only display that distracts from the principal business of a restaurant, but then a local history of the area suggests there was once a barbershop next door. The hotel has seven newly renovated rooms.

"At lunch on our first visit we enjoyed better than average sandwiches while our guide sipped soup and tea. We understood his waiting game when he ordered dessert. It was a kind of German layer cake with a thickness of chocolate mousse be-

tween the layers to drive the most confirmed ascetic to glut-
tony—that victimless mortal sin. We took the next opportunity
to go for dinner with little on our minds save that cake. The
platters of seafood we saw and inhaled as they were being delivered to the twenty or so tables beguiled us, and we decided to
make a meal of it. We had no regrets other than renouncing a
second dessert, for the choice is as broad as the consequences.
The wine list, however, is more limited than a Pennsylvania
State Store."   —*John Ravage*

Open all year, except Christmas Day and New Year's Day.
7 rooms, none with private bath.
Rates $35 single, $75 double, including breakfast. Special weekend
   rates.
Credit cards: American Express, Master Charge, Visa.
French spoken.

Riegelsville

Riegelsville Hotel
10-12 Delaware Road
Riegelsville, Pennsylvania   18077
Telephone: (215) 749-2092

"The more popular Delaware River inns are farther south in
Lumberville and New Hope, but Riegelsville also has its river
inn. Not in the same league as the Black Bass or Logan Inn,
certainly, but far less expensive, and in business mainly for the
people of the town rather than for the tourists who come to the
area for canoeing on the canal and the river, or walking along
the towpath. It tends to be missed by visitors because, while the
other inns are on the river road itself, the Riegelsville Hotel is
one block off Route 611, tucked discreetly round a corner. Opposite it is a narrow, delicate bridge across the wide river, built
in 1905, so fragile-looking it appears as if it might sway in the
wind. Large vehicles are not allowed over it and guards sit im-
portantly at each end to make absolutely certain. The hotel,
which dates from 1828, is being restored by Fran and Harry
Cregar, and they have made an excellent job of the dining
room, where they have exposed the stone walls, wooden beams
and fireplaces. It is now quiet and elegant. Harry, a host with a
nice sense of humor, will bring out his wallet and show you
photographs of what the room looked like before they started
work on it. The lunch I had—fish chowder, baked chicken and
coffee—was very good and extremely inexpensive, about $8 for
two people. In the evening, the prices range from about $8 to
$11 for the entrees, but I had a generous plate of steamed clams
for $2.50 sitting up at the bar one evening, listening to a young

man playing the piano with an extremely light touch. On Sundays, in winter the brunch will leave you stuffed for days. Harry will show you with pride the stained-glass windows in the bar, fashioned by his son—a skill that is rapidly becoming a cult in many parts of America. The Cregars live on the second floor and rent out a few basic rooms on the third floor."

—David Wigg

Open all year except for Christmas Day and New Year's Day.
12 rooms, 4 with private bath.
Rates $14–$20 double.
Credit cards: Master Charge, Visa.
Bar.

Scenery Hill

Century Inn
Scenery Hill, Pennsylvania 15360
Telephone: (412) 945-6600 or 5180

"Whenever we have business in the Pittsburgh area, we plan to stay at the Century Inn, in the quaint town of Scenery Hill. Generally arriving in the early evening, we can always find soft lights glowing in our room, making us feel so welcome. Having stayed in several of the available rooms, we haven't been able to settle on a favorite, although we do enjoy one of the front rooms, which has a lovely couch for added comfort when we want to read quietly in our room or plan the next day's activities. Our favorite room for dining is the 'keeping-room.' We have often enjoyed breakfast in the pleasant room overlooking the back yard, where we have savored a favorite at Scenery Hill—the scrumptious waffles, which are also available on the dinner menu."   *—Mr. and Mrs. Clarence A. Brittell*

Open mid-March to mid-December.
5 rooms, all with private bath.
Rates $17 single, $22 double.
No credit cards.
Service bar.

American hotels and inns generally list rates by the room, assuming one person in a single, two in a double. Extra people in rooms normally incur extra charges. Where rates are quoted per person per day, at least one meal is probably included under a modified American plan (MAP). A full American plan would mean three meals are included.

Shartlesville

Haag's Hotel
Main Street
Shartlesville, Pennsylvania   19554
Telephone: (215) 488-6692

"This is the place to sample traditional Pennsylvania Dutch food. Haag's is famous for its vast, family-style meals, and people come from miles around, particularly on a Sunday, to gorge themselves. The meals include twenty different dishes—you are invited to eat as much as you can from the white bowls set out all over the table in front of you. It is easy to forget one or two dishes on the perimeter as you skim from one to the next. A typical dinner might include chicken, ham or beef, gravy, potato filling, sweet potatoes, lima beans, chick peas, dried corn, garden peas, pickled beets, pepper cabbage, chowchow, chicken salad, olives, pickles, celery, mustard beans, piccalilli, applesauce, tapioca pudding, dried apricots, old-fashioned homemade sugar cookies, home-baked pies (lemon sponge or shoofly), ice cream, bread, milk, tea and coffee.

"The dining room seats 250 people and is, as you would expect in Pennsylvania Dutch country, plain and practical (like the hotel rooms), although for some reason there is an incongruous, grotesque mock grotto on one side, with plastic flowers, plastic ferns and stuffed birds. Many of the ingredients for the meals come from the family's adjoining 125-acre farm and you can look into the kitchen from the sidewalk to watch the frenzy of activity, as the family and local staff prepare the food on old gas and coal-fired stoves.

"The town of Shartlesville, founded in 1765 and named for a Revolutionary War hero, Colonel Peter Shartle, is not very pretty—at least the main street is not. An example of roadside America with all its faults. But people tend to come here for the bluegrass music (the town is at the foot of the Blue Mountains) and to buy up those old family bits and pieces that were once thrown out, but are now becoming valuable antiques."

—*David Wigg*

Open all year, except Christmas Day.
6 rooms, 4 with private bath.
Rates $6.36 single, $9.54 double.
No credit cards.
Bar, field for recreation.
German and Pennsylvania Dutch spoken.

Virginia

Chincoteague

Refuge Motor Inn
P.O. Box 173
Chincoteague, Virginia   23336
Telephone: (804) 336-5511

"Yes, it is a motor inn. And yes (especially by the yardstick of
the Eastern Shore), it is new. But without the Refuge, I can't
imagine ever doing more in the town of Chincoteague than
eating seafood and passing on through to the Assateague National Seashore wildlife refuge. It was on such a 'through trip'
that I first spotted the Refuge Motor Inn, nestled off the road
just before the entrance to the wildlife preserve. Next year we
went back to stay. The inn's weathered wood camouflages
rooms of modern motel decor. But each of these is open to the
woods and grasslands around, and it is possible to glimpse seabirds or wild ponies (and some tame ones) from the rooms and
quiet grounds of the inn. The protected seashore with its good
sandy beach—a short drive or longer walk across a small
bridge, past a lighthouse and along a road winding through
marshlands where the famed Chincoteague ponies and thousands of other wild things live, run, swim and fly—is spacious
and unspoiled. The inn has somehow captured the same
spirit." —*B. C.*

Open all year.
68 rooms, all with private bath.
Rates $30–$32 double, Memorial Day to September 15. Lower at
   other times. Up to 2 children under 12 free in room with parents.
No meals served.
Credit cards: American Express, Master Charge, Visa.
Pool, outdoor cooking.

Front Royal

Constant Spring Inn
413 South Royal Avenue
Front Royal, Virginia   22630
Telephone: (703) 635-7010

"After arriving at the inn, only a quarter of a mile from the
Skyline Drive, we settled our belongings in our room and
walked to the restaurant at the foot of the hill, also owned by
the innkeeper. Our meal, served family style, was meat loaf,
potatoes, six vegetables and rolls, all for $3.95 a person. When
we returned to the inn later, the innkeeper's mother met us and
asked us if we wanted lemonade out on the porch. As we sat on
the large rockers on the enormous porch, Ms. Iden started telling us about how the house, over fifty years old, had been converted to an inn. The view of the mountains was so beautiful
and her stories so interesting that we didn't think of the time
until we were ready to retire about midnight."
—Bette A. Dufraine

Open all year, except Christmas Day.
7 rooms, all with private bath.
Rates $14 single, $16 double, $24–$34 suites.
No credit cards.
Canoeing, fishing, skiing, near Shenandoah National Park.

Leesburg

Laurel Brigade Inn
20 West Market Street
Leesburg, Virginia   22075
Telephone: (703) 777-1010

"With only a few overnight accommodations, this stone town
house is primarily a dining establishment. It was here that the
Marquis de Lafayette was entertained by President James
Monroe in 1825; and, in many ways, it still seems like 1825 at
this inn. The antique furnishings are immaculately clean and

polished. The large staircase leading to the upstairs overnight rooms is smooth to the touch from so many years of dusting and waxing. The main dining room, one wall of which is all pane-glass doors, looks out over a beautifully manicured and maintained back yard. The opposite side of this house is protected by an English garden, and the entire inn fronts right on one of the main streets in this historic northern Virginia town. The overnight accommodations on the second floor—there are five in all—are roomy, restful and very quiet. The second floor hallway is wide and airy and everywhere is the sense of cleanliness and order. This is a great stopping-off place en route from Washington, D.C., to other parts of Virginia. And the nicest thing of all about this relatively unknown little jewel of a place is that you have the feeling you are actually in your own home, having dinner, and then slipping unnoticed, and happily, upstairs for a real night's sleep."   *—Rikki Stapleton*

Closed in January.
5 rooms, all with private bath.
Rates $9.36 single, $14.56 double.
Service bar only.

Lexington

The Alexander Withrow House
3 West Washington Street
Lexington, Virginia   24450
Telephone: (703) 463-2044

"Lexington is a delightful town—old houses, quaint streets and Southern charm. While there we stayed at the Alexander Withrow House—a restored 1789 house near the campus of Washington and Lee University. Our suite, No. 3, was a gem to find after a long journey—the multiwindowed sitting room had antique sideboard, comfortable wing-back chairs and original oil paintings, while the bedroom had a reading nook by the window. You enter this through a piazza, which overlooks a small bricked courtyard, into a hall with Oriental rugs. Try the doughnuts in the little coffee shop around the corner—this is the way doughnuts should taste. We took two dozen home with us, but I'm afraid they never made the journey to Pittsburgh—we ate most of them on the way."   *—Mrs. Edward Sverdrut;*
also recommended by Rikki Stapleton

Open all year.
7 rooms, all with private bath.
Rates $30–$40 per person.
No meals served.
No credit cards.

Middleburg

The Red Fox Tavern
Middleburg, Virginia   22117
Telephone: (703) 687-6301

"The Red Fox is only fifty minutes from downtown Washington, D.C., and twenty-five minutes from Dulles Airport. But once I'm at its front door, light years seem to separate this peaceful, wonderful place from bustling metropolitan areas. The inn, a four-storied fieldstone structure built around 1728, is right on the main street of a town filled with lots of lovely old-fashioned shops, making it a browser's delight. There are several good local restaurants, but much of the town's activity seems to center around the Red Fox Tavern. The Night Fox Pub in back of the tavern is a great spot for drinks in the evening. In warm weather there is an outdoor patio for drinking and dining.

"The main part of the inn has been completely renovated in the last few years, but everything has been done to preserve its look and sense of times past. The downstairs is primarily a dining room and bar, all woody and filled with pewter. The lunch and dinner menus feature some local yummies like bourbon apple pie. The real beamed ceilings and white stone fireplace in the main dining room make eating here a cozy pleasure. Upstairs there's the J. E. B. Stuart room. Built around several huge fireplaces, this room is filled with couches and chairs meant for relaxing, reading, chatting and having a drink or afternoon tea or coffee. There is always the smell of wood burning and recently waxed floors.

"Several rooms, some including sitting areas, are available for overnight stays. The rooms are decorated to the period, most with canopy beds so high you almost need a stool to crawl into them. Every bedroom has its own fireplace with a hearty supply of firewood.

"All around Middleburg there are horse farms and riding, for this is the center of Virginia's horse country: Everywhere there is talk of horses and hunts and race meets."   —*Rikki Stapleton*

Open all year.
6 rooms, 2 units in annex, most with private bath.
Rates $35–$55.
Credit cards: American Express, Visa.
French and Spanish spoken.

Turn to the back of this book for pages inviting *your* comments.

Middletown

Wayside Inn
7783 Main Street
Middletown, Virginia   22645
Telephone: (703) 869-1797

"The Wayside Inn sits comfortably in the northern end of the Shenandoah Valley in Middletown. For the traveler, it offers easy access, in a matter of minutes, from the modern pace of Interstate 81 to the quiet charm of the 1700s. Entry to the dining areas is through a parlor furnished with period pieces. I still don't know how many different rooms there are in which one may eat, but I know which are my two favorites. The 'Slave Kitchen' lends itself to a cozy meal with no more than four tables in the room. (Be sure to ask for a seat by the old fireplace in which, of course, the food was cooked in years past.) The Senseney Room, too, has a fireplace, but of much more grandeur. It is stone and is the focal point of this much larger room—ideal for parties and large dinners. The menu displays a variety of Southern meals which are served by pleasant waitresses dressed in colonial style. Guests should choose to stay for the night in one of the rooms upstairs and wonder if it is the one that George Washington slept in or, perhaps, the one once occupied by the Lyndon Johnson family.

"The most exciting time for visitors is the first weekend of May. This coincides with the Apple Blossom Festival held yearly in nearby Winchester, the Apple Capital, and only a twenty-minute ride from the inn. As a native of the area, my favorite season at the Wayside is Christmas. Old-time decorations are hung in the Williamsburg manner and there is a contest for handmade Christmas tree ornaments. The entries are placed in a display case in the lobby at the main entrance until the contest is over, at which time each ornament takes its place on the tree."   —_Mary Henkel_

Open all year.
21 rooms, all with private bath.
Rates $18 single, $24 double. Special 3-day rates.
Credit cards: American Express, Master Charge, Visa.

If you would like to amend, update or disagree with any entry, write _now_.

Monterey

Monterey Hotel
Main Street
Monterey, Virginia   24465
Telephone: (703) 468-2290

"There is a whole way of living in the mountain areas of Virginia that is quite unlike any other life-style. The mountain way of Virginia is a pristine, casual, hearty life, focusing primarily on the sport in season and relying on friends and neighbors for conversation and company. Set in a mountain area known all around as Virginia's Little Switzerland, the Monterey Hotel fits right in with this kind of getting together. It is a long, low, almost rambling clapboard structure sitting rather casually on this town's Main Street. It is an inviting place, and before you know it you are feeling like a lifelong resident. After a short time you, too, are looking for the hunters and skiers to return with their endless tales of woe and adventure. There is an immense front porch with more than enough rocking chairs. The entrance foyer is woody and large, dominated by a wide graceful staircase. All the furnishings are antique, and everywhere there are old-fashioned lanterns and photographs. The kitchen is presided over by an Icelandic cook who seems to know even more about Southern cooking than did my Virginia-born-and-bred grandmother. Most of the overnight rooms are on the second floor; the third floor serves as living and business space for the staff. The hotel has just been refurbished by its new owner, Mrs. Chenault, who likes doing whatever she can to make you feel treasured, from picking fresh flowers for your bedside table to dashing out for a bottle of celebratory champagne at the not-too-nearby liquor store. (The county is dry.) The guest rooms, neither elegant nor fancy, are wonderfully cozy and comfortable. Many of the rooms look out to the nearby Allegheny Mountains. There is a small-town, old-world, lazy feeling at this grand hotel. This is a place where visitors and locals mix with ease, where dogs and children are welcome and where local musicians stop off and play before calling it a day. The hotel is only about thirty-five miles from Hot Springs, one of Virginia's largest ski areas. In the spring, trout fishing abounds—starting at noon on the first Saturday in April. The Monterey Hotel was built in 1904 and has been named a national historic landmark."   —_Rikki Stapleton_

Open all year.
29 rooms, all with private bath.
Rates $15 single, $20 double.

No credit cards.
Wine and beer served.
Arabic, French and the Scandinavian languages spoken.

Natural Bridge

Natural Bridge Hotel
Natural Bridge, Virginia   24578
Telephone: (703) 291-2121

"If you travel through the Shenandoah Valley on the Blue
Ridge Parkway, there is a charming old hotel to consider for an
overnight stay. This is a grand hotel with some of the most
tastefully decorated guest rooms I have ever encountered. The
service was polite and very attentive. The dining room was popular with those passing through, though the food was not outstanding. The hotel is named for the natural stone bridge that
spans the river valley—a building has been constructed for
people to view the bridge, and of course there is a charge."
—*Philip Fretz*

Open all year.
125 rooms, all with private bath.
Rates $16–$22 single, $20–$26 double, $50–$78 suites.
Credit cards: American Express, Master Charge, Visa.
Heated pool, tennis.
German spoken.

Warm Springs

The Inn at Gristmill Square
Box 359
Warm Springs, Virginia   24484
Telephone: (703) 839-2231

"Warm Springs is in a lovely part of Virginia. The countryside
is beautiful, and there are interesting places to visit on every
side. We have now been to Gristmill Square twice, once in the
spring and once in the fall: We think those times of year would
be particularly appealing to any visitor. Gristmill Square is a
small restoration project and the inn itself is small and quite
self-sufficient. We valued both features. It was nice to find we
were among no more than a handful of guests. And we liked the
quiet, peaceful atmosphere: We've stayed in such noisy, un-

pleasant places through the years. The staff did everything possible to make us and our family feel at home. Their warmth and friendliness were outstanding, and it was especially enjoyable to have the owner, Philip Hirsh, and his wife, Catherine, at the next table during dinner one evening. They are delightful people, and even a short conversation reveals how much of themselves they have invested in the inn. The rooms could hardly be more attractive. Taste and imagination have played an important part in the development/restoration/expansion of this small group of old buildings. Everywhere were interesting touches to delight the eye and provide additional comfort. Our suite of rooms had a washer/dryer combination and a small, but remarkably complete kitchen alcove. We made little use of either, preferring, where meals were concerned, to eat in the Waterwheel Restaurant, just across the courtyard. There the food is superb, and, believe me, that is no idle compliment! Moreover, the converted mill, where meals are served, is full of atmosphere and charm. In the evening, a folk singer moves among the guests, receiving requests. That, too, is a lovely touch which our young children particularly appreciated."

—*The Reverend William Hill Brown III;
also recommended by Geraldine S. Comley*

Open all year, except March 1–14.
11 rooms, all with private bath.
Rates $37–$46 single, $42–$53 double, including continental breakfast.
Credit cards: American Express, Master Charge, Visa.
Bar, pool, tennis courts, gallery, country store.
German spoken.

_____*Williamsburg*

The Cedars
616 Jamestown Road
Williamsburg, Virginia   23185
Telephone: (804) 229-3591

"Situated directly across the street from Phi Beta Kappa Hall, College of William and Mary, the Cedars is a handsome brick home with large comfortable rooms for tourists. Part of what makes the Cedars special is Rose Harris, the genial owner, who has the knack of making her guests feel at home. If a visitor needs any information about Williamsburg or environs, Mrs. Harris is the resident expert. The atmosphere at the Cedars is one of freshness, hominess and quaintness in keeping with Williamsburg. The furnishings in each room are antique and many

rooms have four-poster canopy beds. The Cedars offers a welcome relief from the stale sameness of motels together with a location within a short walking distance of Colonial Williamsburg."
—*Ann M. Peterson*

Open all year.
7 rooms, 5 with private bath. One cottage sleeping 6.
Rates $16–$18 single, $20–$22 double, $55 cottage. Special weekly and off-season rates January through March. 10 percent discount for senior citizens and students.
No meals.
No credit cards.

West Virginia

Lewisburg

General Lewis Motor Inn
301 East Washington Street
Lewisburg, West Virginia   24901
Telephone: (304) 645-2600

"This is a charming old-fashioned inn in the heart of the county seat of Greenbrier County, beautiful farm country where you will find Morlunda Farm, one of the top Hereford breeding farms in the country. The climate is very pleasant with cool nights and warm days from April through November. Lewisburg is 2,300 feet above sea level. It is an old historical town full of lovely homes with spacious, well-kept grounds. The country is traversed by the lively Greenbrier River, a truly clean river where swimming, fishing and canoeing are most enjoyable. The General Lewis Inn is named for Andrew Lewis, who gathered a force of frontiersmen and won one of the first battles of the American Revolution at Point Pleasant on the Ohio in 1774. The inn has antique furniture with four-poster beds and old-fashioned, comfortable chairs. Windsor chairs predominate throughout. The General Lewis has an excellent dining room. There are special touches, such as the relish tray, family-style service and hot breads. The lobby is full of relics. Take time to browse in Memory Hall."   —*S. Cooper Dawson, Jr.*

Open all year.
26 rooms, all with private bath.
Rates $18 single, $24 double.
Credit cards: American Express, Master Charge, Visa.

_____*Sisterville*

The Wells Inn
316 Charles Street
Sisterville, West Virginia   26175
Telephone: (304) 652-3111

"Sisterville is a rural town fifty miles south of Wheeling and thirty-eight miles north of Parkersburg. It is nestled in the wide floodplain of the Ohio River. During the turn of the century, Sisterville lived through an oil and gas industry boom. As the industry grew, the town and its attendant services expanded and out of this growth came the Wells Inn.

"Established in 1895, the inn became a favorite overnight stop for weary travelers going north and south on the Ohio River steamboats. Entertainers and people of importance dwelled in its Victorian elegance and rested before another long day of travel. The inn continued to be a bustle of activity until the oil and gas industry began to falter, and traffic on the Ohio River waterways became less congested. After the industrial decline the hotel became much less prominent. Now the signs of age are apparent, but the inn remains well kept with beautifully decorated rooms and excellent dining facilities, which are primary attractions to residents of the surrounding area. Being a native West Virginian, my most enjoyable hours at the inn were spent dwelling upon the nostalgia of those early-20th-century years."   —*Larry G. Bayles*

Open all year.
36 rooms, all with private bath.
Rates $15–$24 single, $24–$28 double.
Credit cards: American Express, Carte Blanche, Diners Club, Master Charge, Visa.

Part Three

South

Alabama

Mobile

Malaga Inn
359 Church Street
Mobile, Alabama   36602
Telephone: (205) 438-4701

"The Malaga Inn, in the historic downtown district of old Mobile, has been lovingly created from two splendid 1850s town houses joined around a quiet patio garden. Each of the forty-one rooms has been furnished with a great deal of individuality. All rooms have private bath and color television. Guests are warmly welcomed by name. The tiny, dark bar is often frequented by local artists and theatrical personalities who may be performing at the Civic Auditorium behind the inn. Meals are usually well prepared and courteously served. The Malaga is the answer in Mobile for those who wish to stay away from the large, carbon-copy, impersonal hotels and motels that abound in most large cities in the United States."

—*Robert Hochhauser*

Open all year.
41 rooms, all with private bath.
Rates $28 single, $34 double, $80 suite.
Credit cards: all major cards.
Bar, pool.

Florida

St. Augustine

St. Francis Inn
279 St. George Street
St. Augustine, Florida   32084
Telephone: (904) 824-6068

"One of the most picturesque towns in all of Florida is historic St. Augustine, 'America's Oldest City.' Alive with history, there stand, side by side, originals and restorations. In the midst of the quiet and quaint neighborhood known as the Old Spanish Quarter, there is the charming St. Francis Inn. As you enter the Spanish courtyard, there are tropical plants in lush profusion, a fountain complete with goldfish and water lilies. The inn's rooms are furnished in antiques and are extremely comfortable—cheerful and breezy in summer and warm in winter. One can hear echoes of the hoofbeats of the carriage horses passing along the brick streets." —*Faun C. Garrett*

"I happened to spend a week in the inn during an off-tourist season. I picked it because I did not want to stop in the regular commercial-type hotel or motel. While it is true that the rates were somewhat cheaper than the national chains, that was by no means my major consideration. Having done a great deal of traveling in Europe where there were once not too many commercial motels, I had come to prefer the intimate quality of the family-run inn. At the St. Francis I was permitted the run of the downstairs living room, furnished with marvelous and valuable antiques. I came away with the feeling that the inn was my home away from home, in the best sense of the expression. The section of town in which the St. Francis is located is historic, well kept and quiet, and yet within a few minutes' walk of the main part of the city. The whole area exudes charm and warmth, and while it is perhaps just a little on the conservative

side, only the best values and customs have been conserved."
—*Professor William J. Beck*

"A Spanish iron gate squeaks at your arrival. St. Francis himself, in stone, greets each traveler. A two-story cozy cottage—available to visiting families—and double-decker verandas spread the entire length of the inn border this oasis. Through the east garden gate awaits a spotless, sparkling swimming pool. As you enter the centuries-old, thick red-paneled door, you find yourself enfolded in an environment in tune with what our grandsires loved. I have enjoyed being quartered on both upper floors, as well as several exterior sides. One would have been at home here during past centuries with Spanish explorers, French settlers, English governors and Indians. This circumnavigator has found nothing like it in any of seventeen countries from north of the Arctic Circle to the foot of South America's Angel Falls. Totally done over, but not spoiled with overmodernization. Many rooms include the surprise of miniature refrigerators and compact cooking facilities affording breakfast in bed or midnight snacks.

"So smitten were we by this triple-storied, twin-centuried inn that we have given weekend stays as nuptial gifts to two special bridal couples. What modern motel would still be there to greet their descendants?" —*Dorothy Wms. Davis-Dodge*

Open all year.
3 rooms, 4 suites, 1 cottage, all with private bath, several with kitchenettes.
Rates $15–$50. Weekly and monthly rates available.
No credit cards.
Swimming pool.

Would you be so kind as to share discoveries you may have made of charming, well-run places to stay in Europe? Please write to *Europe's Wonderful Little Hotels and Inns,* c/o Thomas Congdon Books, E.P. Dutton, 2 Park Avenue, New York, N.Y. 10016. (By the way, a new and greatly expanded edition of this splendid guide is now available at your bookseller's.)

Georgia

Savannah

The John Wesley Hotel
Abercorn and Congress Streets
P.O. Box 9056
Savannah, Georgia   31402
Telephone: (912) 232-7121

"Methodists and Girl Scouts will feel particularly at home in this narrow, six-story hotel on shady Reynolds Square. The John Wesley, the oldest operating hotel in the city, is part of a national Methodist landmark; it also has a floor decorated for Girl Scouts—Savannah was the birthplace of Juliette Gordon Low. The hotel seems not only homey, but also a touch homemade. It gives the impression that the woodwork painting may have been a family's Saturday project. The beds offer character-building firmness. Downstairs the flower-patterned lobby carpet looks like old-fashioned needlepoint.

"John Wesley, the founder of Methodism, had a parsonage on this site, but that building was destroyed in the early 19th century. The present hotel was built in 1913. The reason it is so skinny is that it was designed to be built on only half of one of the trust lots left for churches and public buildings in an early city plan. The lobby, with intricate plasterwork ceiling, is just as it was when the building opened as the Hotel Collins; only the large front windows have been added. After World War Two the hotel deteriorated. In the 1970s, Bill and Peg Barutio bought the place and have worked continuously at restoration." —_Peggy Payne_

Open all year.
38 rooms, all with private bath.
Rates $22–$30. Group rates for minimum booking of 20 rooms.
Credit cards: American Express, Master Charge, Visa.
French spoken.

*Old Talbott Tavern,
Bardstown*

Kentucky

Bardstown

Old Talbott Tavern
107 West Stephen Foster Avenue
Bardstown, Kentucky   40004
Telephone: (502) 348-3494

This historic tavern has been in continuous operation since 1779. The post roads from all directions passed by, making it an important stopping place for stagecoaches. Naturally, stories of famous guests are part of the personality of the place—an exiled Louis Philippe whiling away time in an upstairs room in 1800; Abraham Lincoln's family staying there while a trial was in progress to settle the ownership of a farm.

"I've always enjoyed the meals, from one of the best Thanksgiving dinners ever many years ago to that country ham last fall. And I love my big old bed in '14'—the room number a concession to progress. The furnishings *are* the Old Talbott and, yes, the fire in the old fireplace, the link (for me) between the warmth of yesterday's Talbott and the warmth of the Talbott of today." —*Herbert Pender, Jr.*

Open all year, except Christmas Day.
5 rooms, all with private bath.

Rates $16 single, $20 double.
Credit cards: American Express, Master Charge, Visa.
Bar.

_____*Berea*

Boone Tavern Hotel
Berea, Kentucky   40403
Telephone: (606) 986-9358

"Berea College provides educational opportunity to the isolated young people of the mountains. Eighty percent of the college's students are natives of the southern Appalachian region. For sixty years all the college's students have shared in a labor program, working ten hours a week to help defray their bills. For countless young mountain people, this program has made the difference between a college education and no college at all. The students who run Boone Tavern are part of this work program. Each room in the hotel is furnished with handcrafted pieces made in the college's woodcraft shops. Crafts of the southern Appalachian highlands are to be found in the shops of Boone Tavern Square. The inventory comes from recognized production centers and from individual artists and crafts people—potters, jewelers, painters, carvers, quilters, sculptors, weavers, dollmakers, blacksmiths, chairmakers, printmakers and dulcimer craftsmen.

"Boone Tavern's dining room is nationally acclaimed for its consistently excellent and interesting regional food. It is not difficult to choose even a restricted diet from the varied menus—and 'no tipping' is the rule. Greatly appreciated is the pure white table linen. The tavern's overnight guests find individualized rooms, with windows that open to let in the fresh mountain air. Spotless baths are supplied with an abundance of linen, including the old familiar huckaback hand towels."

—*Alice and E. G. Getman*

"The tavern is a delight both to the eye and the mouth. This lovely old inn is run by Berea College and completely operated by the students from kitchen to dining room to room service. These young people are on work scholarships with the college, a requirement for admittance, and will be glad to direct you to a most beautiful campus nearby. The crafts and woodworking of Berea are internationally known and respected."

—*Senator Wendell H. Ford*

Open all year.
59 rooms, all with private bath.
Rates $10–$17 single, $17–$30 double.
Credit cards: Restaurant accepts Master Charge and Visa.
German spoken.

Harrodsburg

Beaumont Inn
Harrodsburg, Kentucky   40330
Telephone: (606) 734-3381

"At Beaumont Inn Southern cooking at its best awaits the tourist who can beat local citizens to the table. This restaurant has facilities for overnight lodging in a stately old inn that was built in 1845 as a girls' college and became an inn in 1919. The menu features mouth-watering Kentucky country ham, Kentucky fried chicken that even the Colonel would admire and tasty corn pudding. A marvelous gift shop with a variety of selections is another part of the treat."   *—Senator Wendell H. Ford*

Closed from December 1 to March 1.
27 rooms, all with private bath.
Rates $20–$25 single, $30–$44 double, including continental breakfast. Special group rates.
Credit cards: Master Charge, Visa.
Swimming pool.

The Inn at Pleasant Hill
Route 4
Harrodsburg, Kentucky   40330
Telephone: (606) 734-5411

"This inn is just possibly the best-kept secret in America: Southern hospitality, Southern cooking and American scenery at its loveliest. Set amidst the rolling hills of Kentucky, a Shaker community was restored as it appeared before the Civil War. The architecture is a tribute to the Shakers' functional simplicity. The meals served in the Trustees' House under the direction of Elizabeth Kremer are superb. The breakfast buffet is a specialty. Accommodations are available throughout the village, in structures faithfully restored down to the reproduction furniture and wall-to-wall hanging wooden pegs. Most often we request lodging in the 1839 Trustees' House, with its lovely, twin spiral staircases reaching to the third floor. Each building is a museum in itself, although the Center Family House serves as the principal Pleasant Hill museum. There is as much or as little to do here as you desire. After strolling through the village and watching crafts people at work, you might walk a mile or so down to the Kentucky River. Or you might look again at the Shaker cemetery: there most headstones are marked only with worn initials, true to the Shaker way."
—Joanne and Nick Apple; also recommended
by Mr. and Mrs. Myrl Schnake

"Here you can find some of the most delicious victuals—home grown right in view on the grounds—that you could ever put in your mouth. And you can feel the spirit at the same time. The dining room is in one of the buildings that make up the restored village (hence the locally popular name of Shakertown). Browsing around the grounds, the visitor learns the heritage of the Shakers, views some of their unequaled carpentry—beautiful for its simplicity of line—and sees skillfully accomplished crafts. Located in the Palisades, Pleasant Hill's environs are in the heart of one of Kentucky's most scenic areas and near the Lexington Bluegrass region."   —*Senator Wendell H. Ford*

Open all year, except Christmas Day.
61 rooms, all with private bath.
Rates $15–$19 single, $23–$32 double.
No credit cards.

Louisiana

New Orleans

Lamothe House
621 Esplanade Avenue
New Orleans, Louisiana   70116
Telephone: (504) 947-1161

The house was built about 1800 by a wealthy sugar planter
called Jean Lamothe, a Frenchman seeking a safe place for his
family after an upheaval in Santo Domingo. It became a guesthouse in the 1950s and most of the rooms are furnished with
antiques. Some have canopied beds and armoires.

"As I walked along Royal Street in New Orleans, I came to a
tree-lined avenue—Esplanade—and found a delightful inn
called the Lamothe House. Walking through the entrance hall,
you are confronted at the end of the hall with a three-storied,
balconied patio with a fishpond and lots of plants. Ascending
the curved stair you are warmly welcomed by the innkeeper,
Mimi Langguth, or one of her associates. A visit to the French
Quarter of New Orleans is much enhanced with a visit to this
charming inn."   —*James K. Mellow*

"To stay at Lamothe House for the first time is to experience a
perfect blending of the old and new—the very best in furnish-

ings and atmosphere in the tradition of the Old South and the modern conveniences of the 1970s. On arrival we were greeted by the houseman who showed us through a spacious hallway lined with beautiful antiques. Your room may be in the main house or facing the garden in the rear. A continental breakfast is served in the dining room on the second floor."

—*Mr. and Mrs. William Croxen; also recommended*
by Bill Bailey Carter

Closed from July 15 to September 1.
14 rooms, all with private bath.
Rates $33–$35 double, suites $41–$43, including breakfast.
No other meals.
Credit cards: American Express, Master Charge, Visa.

Maison de Ville
727 Toulouse Street
New Orleans, Louisiana   70130
Telephone: (504) 561-5858

"It is easy to overlook the small wooden sign at 727 Toulouse Street designating the Maison de Ville. Maybe that is as it should be. When you step inside, it is even easier to overlook that you are in a hotel. The building was a home from early in the 19th century until the late 1930s. The conversion to a well-maintained hotel offering modern comforts has been achieved without any changes in appearance. Furnishings in the public areas and the rooms are authentic to private homes in New Orleans early in the 19th century. But best of all, every person on the staff extends such a genuine warmth and interest in you that you can't help but feel that you are a fortunate guest in a very hospitable home. A pleasant custom is the complimentary service of tea or sherry during the afternoon and a fine port in the evening. The courtyard, with a delightful fountain in the center and flanked by the former slave quarters that have been converted to guest rooms, is a delightful spot for your complimentary continental breakfast, your afternoon tea or evening port.

"The sightseer could not find a more convenient location. A half-block to the left and you are in the fine shopping area of Royal Street. A half-block to the right and you are in the heart of the Bourbon Street 'night' life, which is really in full swing around the clock. Some of the best restaurants in New Orleans are within three blocks. By all means, ask one of the charming young ladies at the reception desk to make your reservations. They seem to be on a first-name basis with all of the reservationists and always get you a good table."

—*John B. Parramore, Jr.*

"We were sitting in the patio one evening when the sounds of a calliope came to us from the street. Realizing it was the *Mississippi Queen*'s departure, we ran down to the wharf—a matter of a few moments—and saw the lighted vessel getting ready. So, at the Maison de Ville, you can be in another time and be within moments of the excitement of the French Quarter and the city itself.

"A large part of this excitement is the excellence of the restaurants and here the variety is exceptional. Across from the Maison de Ville is a pub called Molly's, on Toulouse, which we enjoy for its barbecue and beans. More elegant, and infinitely fine, is the food available at a restaurant in Gretna, across the river, LeRuth's, but reservations are needed long in advance. We have actually made ours months ahead of time and thoroughly delighted in the service and cuisine. Also a favorite is the Caribbean Room at the Hotel Pontchartrain, an excellent restaurant. And the oysters Mosca at the Elmwood Plantation are a fine experience. Try Crozier's as well."

—*Art and Susan Bachrach*

Open all year.
21 rooms, all with private bath.
Rates $50 single to $75 double; cottages $150–$250. Breakfast included.
No credit cards.
Swimming pool.
French and Spanish spoken.

Olivier Guest House Hotel
828 Toulouse Street
New Orleans, Louisiana   70112
Telephone: (504) 525-8456

"The Olivier Guest House Hotel is in the heart of the Old French Quarter, the original Franco-Spanish city of the Creoles. Most French Quarter tourist attractions, restaurants, clubs, antique and gift shops, and historic sites such as St. Louis Cathedral, Jackson Square, Cabildo Museum, the Jazz Museum, Pontalba Apartments, the Mississippi River and the French Market, are within a four-block walking distance.

"The hotel has forty rooms and suites—some with kitchenettes furnished with electric range and refrigerator. All rooms have air-conditioning, television, telephone and private baths. Also, it has a lovely patio and swimming pool, and parking facilities are just around the corner from the hotel entrance. The major part of the building consists of the renovated Olivier family mansion with the old slave quarters in the back. It was built in 1836 as the town house for the widow of Nicolas G. Olivier, a wealthy plantation owner."

—John and Jeannette Holt

Open all year.
40 rooms, all with private bath.
Rates $30–$52. Suites $65 and up.
No meals served.
Credit cards: American Express, Diners Club, Master Charge, Visa.
Pool, two patios.

St. Francisville

The Cottage Plantation
Route 5, Box 425
St. Francisville, Louisiana   70775
Telephone: (504) 635-3674

"Just thirty-five miles up the road and the Mississippi from Baton Rouge, and sitting deep in its 500 acres, is this historic plantation. The entire area up the Mississippi is filled with history, and the Cottage is part of it. The annual Audubon Pilgrimage in nearby old St. Francisville includes this home, where Andrew Jackson and his men stayed en route to Natchez from the Battle of New Orleans. The treat for guests is in the fine antique furnishings and the truly plantation-sized breakfast served in the beautiful old dining room on fine silver and china. Hanging moss from giant live oak branches envelops the Cottage's entire front gallery (one of the longest in the South). At night the silence can be 'heard.' "

—Charles L. Hoke; also recommended by
Genevieve and Morrell Feltus Trimble

Open all year, except Christmas Day.
6 rooms, 5 with private bath.
Rates $20 single, $35 double, including breakfast.
Only breakfast served.
No credit cards.
Antique shop, swimming pool, tours of house and grounds.

Propinquity
P.O. Box 814, Royal Street
St. Francisville, Louisiana   70775
Telephone: (504) 635-6855

"St. Francisville is one of the most charming old towns in the South, quiet and sleepy. The majority of the old homes are occupied, and if the owners wish to show their houses to the public they place an 'Open' sign on the building. As tourists go along the quaint, narrow streets they are welcome to visit any home with the 'Open' sign. This is how we found Propinquity. The house is of Spanish design, built high with two porches across the southeast exposure to catch the breeze. This had been Mrs. Seif's childhood home, but through the years it has seen many changes. The Seifs have now restored it to its original condition, except for a few modern conveniences such as air-conditioning and an all-electric kitchen."

—Mr. and Mrs. Ralph E. Heasley

"We had the entire upstairs to ourselves—a huge sitting room adjoining an equally spacious bedroom and modern bath. Our breakfast order was taken before we retired and served in the sitting room in the morning by Mr. Seif. Breakfast consisted of toast with homemade fig jam, tea or coffee, freshly squeezed orange juice, a small bowl of grits and a sample of jam cake, which is a specialty of the house. We were treated royally. It was one of the highlights of our trip—a wonderful experience."

—Marguerite Wood

Open all year, except Christmas Day and New Year's Day.
1 suite with private bath.
Rate $30, including continental breakfast.
No credit cards.

Mississippi

Mendenhall

Mendenhall Hotel
P.O. Box 6
Mendenhall, Mississippi   39114
Telephone: (601) 847-3113

"When I first came to Mendenhall to teach school, it was my pleasure to find room and board for two years in this family-owned, third-generation hotel. The atmosphere was always cordial, and many interesting and important people came to eat—and some to stay. The large front porch has plenty of rocking chairs and a good view of Main Street—Mendenhall is the county seat of Simpson County and the courthouse is just up the street at the top of the hill. The food is Southern country-style, made from scratch. There is always plenty of fried chicken, cornbread, muffins, hot biscuits, sausage, vegetables, salads and desserts. Often you can also find chicken pie, special homemade casseroles and home-baked caramel or chocolate pie. The food is served on three large lazy Susan tables: You spin the top, take a dish off and serve yourself. No one goes away hungry. A sign on the wall says, 'Eat till it ouches you.' Mendenhall citizens are proud of the hotel. It is always interesting to read the guest register and see if a famous person has been by—the governor? or a movie star?"

—*Mrs. Ben Shivers; also recommended by I. M. Nichols*

Open all year, except New Year's Day, July 4, Labor Day and Christmas Day.
13 rooms, 11 with private bath.
Rates $9.45–$16.80.
Credit cards: Visa.

_____ *Natchez*

The Burn
712 North Union Street
Natchez, Mississippi   39120
Telephone: (601) 445-8566

"Natchez was a legend in its own time, the queen of the Mississippi River for over a century, known for the grandeur on the bluff and the bawdy under the hill, the meeting place of dukes and thieves. Today, her attractions are more visible than ever before, and one of the most prominent is The Burn, on a quiet residential street within walking distance of many points of interest. Nestled on a rise of manicured lawn in the shade of majestic oaks and pines, The Burn is to all appearances a small cottage. Inside, one sees the error of the first impression, for the house is large and beautifully appointed with antiques of varying periods enhancing the circa 1835 structure. The guesthouse has four lovely bedrooms, wonderfully private and relaxingly soundproof, furnished with canopied beds. The garden and grounds could entice even a recluse out to laze by the pool or walk the hidden paths. Yet the greatest pleasure of Natchez and The Burn is the warm hospitality of Mr. and Mrs. Buzz Harper, the hosts."

—*Valette Randall*

"The Burn, meaning 'the brook,' was given its name by its Scottish builder nearly 150 years ago. It survived the Civil War and years of neglect until it was purchased and beautifully restored in 1978 by the Harpers. It is now lovelier and certainly more comfortable than at any time in its history. What makes The Burn unique in this city of antebellum homes is that you don't have to admire its antiques from behind a velvet rope.

"When you are shown to your room in the house or nearby garçonnière, you will find a beautifully draped four-poster bed, perhaps one carved in New Orleans by Prudent Mallard. You will find a fireplace with candelabras, comfortable velvet or tapestry chairs, real flowers on your Empire table and every lamp an antique gem. You are free to stroll on the Aubusson carpets, to marvel at the Harpers' collection of fine French porcelain or to sit on a brocade sofa carved by John Belter to study a fine old piano. You are surrounded by Sèvres, Meissen, Old Paris and Waterford. If your visit is during the Pilgrimage, the ladies of the house will be wearing period costumes. Your morning coffee will be brought to you in a silver coffeepot and your linen napkin in an antique silver ring."

—*Mrs. William J. Simmons*

"We enjoyed a beautiful evening at The Burn when a Wisconsin tour group was being entertained with a candlelight tour, a concert, singing and refreshments. All of the Old South was there. 'Dixie' was stirringly sung, and the handsome liveried butler sang many delightful songs of the South. As if to tie our history back together, an elderly Wisconsin grandfather exclaimed that this night would be something 'to tell my grandchildren about.' "
—*Charles L. Hoke; also recommended by Bill Bailey Carter*

Open all year.
4 rooms, all with private bath.
Rates $45 single, $50 double, including breakfast.
No credit cards.
Pool and tours of house.

American hotels and inns generally list rates by the room, assuming one person in a single, two in a double. Extra people in rooms normally incur extra charges. Where rates are quoted per person per day, at least one meal is probably included under a modified American plan (MAP). A full American plan would mean three meals are included.

North Carolina

Bryson City

Hemlock Inn
Bryson City, North Carolina   28713
Telephone: (704) 488-9820

"The excitement of springtime in the mountains is enhanced by a visit to this inn just outside Bryson City on the southern edge of the Great Smoky Mountains National Park. In May the guests may be wildflower enthusiasts; family groups come in the summer, and in the fall couples come to see the autumn colors. The inn is owned and operated by John and Ella Jo Shell, who had had no previous experience in innkeeping when they acquired the inn in 1969. Ella Jo takes care of the food, while John oversees all other aspects of the operation. They like what they are doing, and their guests become friends. When asked how she felt about running an inn, Ella Jo replied: 'Why, it's just like having company all the time.'

"All the rooms are attractively furnished, some with beautiful antiques. The food is superior, with lots of fried chicken, country ham, fresh vegetables and yummy desserts. Meals are served family style at six large round tables. Guests assemble promptly and remain standing while John gives a blessing: His prayers are short, earnest and eloquent.

"One can hibernate here: just eat, sleep, rock on the porch, read and rest, walk around the wooded grounds. Within fifty miles of the inn are the National Park, Nantahala Forest, Nantahala Gorge, Joyce Kilmer Memorial Forest, Fontana, Cherokee, Gatlinburg, the Blue Ridge Parkway, Asheville,

Waynesville, Hendersonville, Brevard—beautiful mountain country with many waterfalls, hiking trails and picnic areas."
—*Willis Warnell*

"We have been acquainted with Hemlock Inn for more than a dozen years, and have not missed a year spending at least a weekend there. The charm that lures a devoted clientele back year after year almost defies description. The setting—isolated on the side of a mountain with spectacular views in two directions—bestows a calming influence. The building is no architectural gem, but rather a simple one-story brown, board-and-batten structure that belongs to the land. Rooms are without the usual television set, radio, clock or telephone. Air-conditioning is the cross-ventilation provided by gloriously unpolluted mountain breezes that can get nippy in early spring or fall, relieved by electric wall heaters.

"Only five miles from the inn is a Cherokee reservation, but be careful to avoid the profusion of souvenir shops selling 'made in Japan' junk. One can drive over the ridge of the Smokies to Gatlinburg to shop for mountain crafts—pottery, quilts, wood carvings. It's an easy drive to Asheville through picturesque mountain scenery to see the Biltmore House, called the largest private residence ever built in America. Near Franklin, twenty-five miles south, you can join rock hounds digging for rubies and sapphires." —*John C. Roesel*

Open early May to early November.
25 rooms, all with private bath.
Rates $40 single, $50 double including two meals.
No credit cards.

Burnsville

Nu-Wray Inn
Burnsville, North Carolina   28714
Telephone: (704) 682-2329

"The hams are still parboiled on a wood stove at this big house on the town square of Burnsville. The inn opened in an eight-bedroom log house on this mountain green in 1831 or 1832. It now has thirty-five bedrooms, built around that original building. The home-cured ham is served every morning, when the breakfast bell rings, along with grits, red-eye gravy, eggs, biscuits and honey. At dinner there's likely to be ham again, with fried chicken, corn pudding, watermelon-rind pickles, candied yams and turnip greens. The food is unmistakably Southern. And the style is relaxed. The main room offers a big stone fireplace and armchairs. There are sofas in the halls where a guest can curl up with a book. Sitting rooms are filled with antique china and curious odds and ends to pick up and wonder about. The wallpaper is in grandmotherly patterns and the ceilings of the rooms slant at odd angles. For warm nights, there are big porches. This inn is more of a place for socializing than for escape. At night you can hear voices and traffic from the green, people gather in front of the fireplace and the meals are served family style at long tables. The Wray family is still in charge. Manager Rush Wray says he was born into innkeeping. 'It's like circus life,' he said. The third generation of some of the same families are coming to the inn." *—Peggy Payne*

Closed from January 1 to May 1.
35 rooms, 15 with private bath.
Rates $15 single, $20–$25 double. Special weekly rates.
No credit cards.
Hiking, summer playhouse.

Chapel Hill

Carolina Inn
Box 1110
Chapel Hill, North Carolina   27514
Telephone: (919) 933-2001

"One of the finest places to stay in the Research Triangle area of Raleigh, Durham and Chapel Hill is the Carolina Inn. Established in 1924 by a local philanthropist who had made good on Wall Street, the inn was donated to its next-door neighbor, the University of North Carolina, in 1935. A plaque recognizing the benefactor is prominently displayed in the main lobby. And profits from the inn's operation now go to the university's library endowment. The inn resembles a large country house: red brick with dark-green shutters flanking tall windows, and porches with wrought-iron rockers under high white porticos. The main lobby abounds in soft, plump sofas and wing chairs—a spacious living room. The dining room is muraled and has a high ceiling. (While the main dining area is closed in the summer, the cafeteria is conveniently open all year.) Hallways too are muraled—in fact, I once watched in awe for almost an hour as a muralist put finishing strokes to a new creation. Tapestries, wood carvings and plants are also numerous. Lodging in the comfortable rooms is convenient. The inn is a thirty-minute drive from the Raleigh-Durham airport through beautiful, modern Research Triangle Park where the highest concentration of Ph.D.'s and engineers in the country live and work for research centers of large companies. Situated just one block from the main business district on Franklin

Street, the inn is in easy walking distance of the entire UNC campus and the central town. Nearby are an art center, planetarium, library, hospital, theater, stadium, music hall, botanical garden and historic campus landmarks. Sports facilities are available at the university though golfers should not hesitate to venture an hour's drive to Pinehurst and its unequaled golf course."   —*Mark H. Mirkin*

Open all year.
143 rooms, all with private bath.
Rates $15–$22 single, $18–$28 double.
Credit cards: American Express, Master Charge, Visa.
French, German and Spanish spoken.

Raleigh

The Velvet Cloak Inn
1505 Hillsborough Street
Raleigh, North Carolina   27605
Telephone: (919) 828-0333

"The only true inn left in the capital city, the Velvet Cloak Inn is a distinctive Southern institution among countless chain motels. When you enter the small but neatly functional lobby, you see a wooden statue of Sir Walter Raleigh laying his cloak down over a puddle so Queen Elizabeth might avoid getting wet—hence the name of the inn. The plush red velvet theme of the cloak is carried throughout. Even some of the staff wear colonial costumes of red velvet. There are two dining rooms. The Club of the Eight Lords is a dinner club, while the Charter Room off the main lobby is for breakfast and lunch. High-backed Chippendale chairs, traditional colonial decor and ornate chandelier lighting provide a relaxed atmosphere. Sunday buffet-champagne brunch is offered during the spring months.

"The centrally located pool is enclosed in a Plexiglas cage for winter swimming. Surrounding it are large green tropical plants, and at night gas torches make a nice effect. Each bedroom has a large bay window with shutters and a colonial lamp outside; inside they are spacious, freshly painted and meticulously clean. Each morning, the local newspaper is delivered at no charge to every guest's room with breakfast."
                                                  —*Mark H. Mirkin*

Open all year.
172 rooms, all with private bath.
Rates $29–$31 single, $36–$38 double.
Credit cards: American Express, Carte Blanche, Diners Club, Master Charge, Visa.
Bar, pool.

Battery Carriage House, Charleston

South Carolina

Charleston

Battery Carriage House
20 South Battery
Charleston, South Carolina   29401
Telephone: (803) 723-9881

Charleston is, by wide acclaim, among the most gracious of cities. The home of 17th-century aristocrats and a bustling port, it became a town of elegant houses, fine churches and imposing public buildings set among winding streets and luxurious gardens. A number of the houses and gardens are open to the public in the spring and early summer months. Boat tours in the harbor offer a view of the mansions lining Charleston's famous Battery.

"The little brass plate by the wrought-iron gate is the only way to tell from the outside that this five-story mansion behind four-story palms is an inn. Battery Carriage House opened to guests only a couple of years ago. The 1845 house is the home of Mr. and Mrs. Frank G. Gay, Jr., who have restored the ground floor and the carriage house in back for guest rooms. Mr. Gay, who serves sherry to arriving guests in his small living room-like office, says he's trying to operate the house as a small European-style inn. Personal attention seems to be an important part of the service.

"A breakfast of coffee, juice and cheesecake is brought to your room or served to you in the walled garden dripping with wisteria. Furnishings in the inn are in 18th-century styles. The rooms, with canopied beds, look like the sort you usually view from behind a velvet rope. They are, however, equipped with kitchenettes, television and a bottle of chilled wine. There is a little pool on the second floor of the house. Bicycles are left leaning against a wall downstairs, available for guests' use."

—Peggy Payne

Open all year.
10 rooms, all with private bath.
Rates $44–$53, including breakfast.
Credit cards: American Express, Master Charge, Visa.
French spoken.

Mrs. Carr's Guest House
Two Meeting Street
Charleston, South Carolina   29401
Telephone: (803) 723-7322

"On the corner of South Battery and Meeting Street is Mrs. Carr's late Victorian rooming house. This is the waterfront edge of Charleston's historic district. On this corner, carriage drivers sometimes wait with horses for riders to take a buggy tour of the old part of the city. Behind the big trees of the yard, the light is dim in the lower rooms of the guesthouse. The 1892 building has an almost spooky feel inside. It's a quiet place. The downstairs is dominated by a massive stairway and leaded-glass windows. The doors are locked at 10 P.M., but guests can use a key. The original owners, faced with financial trouble, hung out the guest sign in the 1930s. In 1944, Mrs. J. H. Carr bought the house. Out front is White Point Gardens, shaded by live oaks, where thirty-nine pirates were hanged in the harbor breeze in 1717. Now there are monuments and joggers and big trees here. All of old Charleston is in walking distance."

—Peggy Payne

Open all year.
17 rooms, 4 with private bath.
Rate $20.
No meals.
No credit cards.

Rates quoted were the latest available. But they may not reflect unexpected increases or local and state taxes. Be sure to verify when you book.

Tennessee

Gatlinburg

Mountain View Hotel
500 Parkway
Box 727
Gatlinburg, Tennessee   37738
Telephone: (615) 436-4132

"It seems proper to use a double negative in saying you can't hardly find hotels anymore with rocking chairs on a wide veranda and a huge, friendly fireplace in the lobby. But you find these reminders of a simpler past at the Mountain View Hotel, which sits almost as a guardian of the entrance to the Great Smoky Mountains National Park at Gatlinburg. There's a natural homespun friendliness about the rambling old hostelry where the owners and help are all native mountain people. But I must admit that most of all I like those breakfasts of fried country ham (the sweet, sugar-cured kind), eggs to order, hot biscuits fresh from the oven, grits, honey and preserves. How can anyone be grumpy after such a breakfast? Incidentally, when you hear anyone refer to 'the far in the farplace' you'll know that person is speaking with a true mountain accent."—
Don Whitehead

Open all year.
80 rooms in main lodge, 40 in adjoining motor hotel.
Rates $22–$34.
Credit cards: American Express, Diners Club, Master Charge, Visa.

Part
Four

_____

Midwest

Illinois
Indiana
Iowa
Michigan
Minnesota
Missouri
Nebraska
Ohio
Wisconsin

Hotel Nauvoo,
Nauvoo

Illinois

Chicago

The Whitehall Hotel
105 East Delaware Place
Chicago, Illinois   60611
Telephone: (312) 944-6300

"Clearly designed to satisfy the sybarite accustomed to the comforts of the finest hostelries, the Whitehall employs a charming French-trained concierge, Ahlyce Kaplan, who'll do her damnedest to get you scarce tickets to the Chicago Symphony (some say it's the best in the world) or the Chicago Bears (who boast the solo performances of Walter Payton). Nearby attractions include: shopping on the 'Magnificent Mile,' with a new branch of Marshall Field's department store and elegant boutiques of every genre; the somewhat robust night life of Rush Street, and a few outstanding restaurants, notably Le Perroquet. One of a string of fine sand beaches is steps away at Oak Street. No room abuts an elevator shaft and thick drapery and other devices are used to buffer the big-city noises. The tiny lobby (the only public lounge) offers tight screening of the coming and going of guests and visitors—a security feature that is welcomed by celebrities who stay there. There is economical (maximum $4.25 per twenty-four hours) parking in a city-owned garage next door. Or, you may order the Whitehall's chauffeured limousine to take you around ($20 per hour, two hour minimum). Don't forget to announce any unusual beverage preferences so that the limousine's rolling bar will be stocked with ingredients for your Mai Tai or whatever.

"The Whitehall's minimum accommodation is a room with a king-size bed and enough floor space to do your yoga exercises. For a few dollars more you can have an executive room which offers all of the basic amenities—here that includes color television, two phones, a refrigerator and even a bathroom scale—plus a permanent wall separating the bed from a comfortable sitting area where TV may be watched or meals taken in privacy. I know an executive from New York who personally supplements her $60-maximum hotel expense account to enjoy the luxury of an executive room. The Whitehall is crowned by the price-is-no-object accommodations on the top four of twenty-one floors. The ultimate (maximum of $300 per day) is one of four large apartments, each with special decor—Oriental rugs in the Churchill, Breuer chairs in the Contemporary. The most charming of these may be the Terrace Suite, which wraps around three exposures of the building. The large terrace—commanding a vista of Lake Michigan and awesome views of the urban sprawl with jewel-like strings of lights defining the traffic arteries for miles in the distance—adjoins an intimate and sumptuously furnished dining room. The kitchen may be fitted with cutlery, crockery and crystal and the large refrigerator stocked with meal makings. During a five-week theatrical engagement, Katharine Hepburn enjoyed her own cooking in the Terrace Suite. The living room has books on the shelves, eight-track cassettes for the stereo and large, living greenery. The bedroom has all the goodies of the simpler sleeping quarters, including the small refrigerator (so you won't have to walk the length of the suite to the kitchen for your nightcap) plus a bidet and third TV in the bath (so you won't miss the morning news while shaving).

"In all, a luxurious island in a city of surprises."

—*Camille J. Cook*

Open all year.
226 rooms, all with private bath.
Rates $69–$100; suites $100–$300.
Credit cards: American Express, Carte Blanche, Diners Club, Master Charge, Visa.
Bar, private dining room for guests and dining club members.
French, German, Greek, Italian, and Spanish spoken.

Do you know a hotel in your state that we have overlooked? Write *now*.

Galena

DeSoto Hotel
230 South Main Street
Galena, Illinois   61036
Telephone: (815) 777-9208

Galena, a town of 4,000 souls in the far northwest corner of Illinois, seems to drop its visitors into a kind of time warp. It has changed little in the past hundred years, thanks to a combination of economic and historical factors that conspired to leave the old lead-mining town and one-time home of Ulysses S. Grant pretty much as it was. The town is tucked away in a rugged, almost mountainous area with long slopes and staggering views. It was the richest town in Illinois back in 1845 and the town's aristocrats built spacious airy mansions in a rich variety of styles—Federal, Queen Anne, Second Empire, Italian villa, Gothic Revival, Greek Revival. There were verandas and uncommon amounts of New Orleans grillwork. Once the mines ran out and the miners moved on to California for gold, the town fell into a virtual slumber and became a historical oddity. Not only have most of its old houses and buildings remained intact, but several have been converted into guesthouses of enormous charm.

"Downtown, there is the 1855 DeSoto Hotel, with fifty rooms. It is the genuine old-time hotel, still going strong. It wears signs of age, but rather well. It is old and dusty, but one of its best features is the dining room, the Great Galena Tea Company, all brick with wide board floors and oak farmhouse tables and chairs, authentic—and none of them matching. The room has overhead paddle fans, macrame hangings, lots of plantings and a $2.95 Sunday brunch that includes eggs Benedict and a help-yourself buffet of homemade pastries, fruit and juice. Lincoln once was a guest at the hotel. It has changed little since, save for the electricity."   —_Jerry Klein_

Open all year.
50 rooms, 7 with private bath.
Rates $8–$12 single, $17–$19 double.
No credit cards.
Bar, skiing.

If you would like to amend, update or disagree with any entry, write _now_.

Ryan Mansion
Highway 20 West
Galena, Illinois   61036
Telephone: (815) 777-2043

"Just north of Galena is the hundred-year-old Ryan Mansion with twenty-four rooms and ten fireplaces of Italian marble, many of them inoperable. The mansion has etched-glass front doors and trappings from the era when lavish carriages rolled up the gravel drive. There are a few enormous rooms for rent. A motel with pool is adjacent. Unfortunately, so is a nightclub that features stupefyingly loud music on weekends."

—Jerry Klein

Open April through November.
24 rooms, 7 with private bath.
Rates $11 single, $17 double.
No credit cards.
No meals.

Stillman Manor
513 Bouthillier
Galena, Illinois   61036
Telephone: (815) 777-0557

"The Stillman Manor, near the U. S. Grant Home, was built in 1858 and is operated today as a guesthouse and restaurant by Erik and Marilyn Jensen. It was once an old people's home, but has been carefully restored. There are six rooms for rent, all furnished with antiques from a century and more ago, and some of the rooms have gas fireplaces. There is a small, sunny pub at the rear, reminiscent of a European country inn, and two dining rooms, one elegant and formal and the other, in the basement, with its own wine cellar. There is a rooftop balcony, or widow's walk, with a grand view of the town and the area."

—Jerry Klein

Open all year.
6 rooms, all with private bath.
Rates $28–$31.50.
Credit cards: Master Charge.
2 bars.

Turn to the back of this book for pages inviting *your* comments.

Victorian Mansion
301 S. High Street
Galena, Illinois   61036
Telephone: (815) 777-0675

"The Victorian Mansion Guest House was once the home of a lead miner, Augustus Estey. U. S. Grant was a guest at a party there. The house sits on two and a half acres and owners Charles and Linda Primrose have restored six of the rooms— which are open all year—and are working on more. They are authentic, high-ceilinged rooms, many with brass beds. There is no television, not even a radio, and the bathroom is down the hall. 'We have lots of artistic people as guests,' Mrs. Primrose says. 'They don't mind sharing the plumbing.' There are sinks in the rooms, however."   —*Jerry Klein*

Open all year.
6 rooms, 1 with private bath.
Rates $16–$24.
No credit cards.

Nauvoo

Hotel Nauvoo
Mulholland Street
Nauvoo, Illinois   62354
Telephone: (217) 453-2211

"Each year when the trees begin to glow with autumn color, my husband and I travel to the little river town of Nauvoo, high on the bluffs overlooking the Mississippi River. The serene relaxation we enjoy when most of the summer tourists and campers have gone would not be possible without the old Hotel Nauvoo. The hotel looks like the gracious private residence it was in 1841. The architecture is pure Mormon. The rooms of the hotel are large and airy. Paintings by Lane Newberry adorn various rooms. The furniture is not fancy, and there is no room service or recreation room—but there is real comfort and serenity. Few people are aware of the historic treasures found in the once-prosperous river towns in the Nauvoo area. Almost abandoned, they are collectors' items. On the Iowa side there is the old Vernon schoolhouse, restored by an artist and family. On the Illinois side is Hamilton, a place for fossil or geode hunting, and Warsaw, where one can still get an old-fashioned chocolate soda. Sometimes a pleasant afternoon can be spent at a farm auction. We always return home with a supply of Nauvoo wine, blue cheese and wheat bread—and memories—to sustain us till the next October."   *—Jeanne Purdom*

Open from April 1 to November 1.
14 rooms, 4 with private bath.
Rates $14.50 single, $18.50 double.
No credit cards.

Indiana

New Harmony

The New Harmony Inn
North Street
New Harmony, Indiana   47631
Telephone: (812) 682-4491

"New Harmony is the site of two marvelously motivated communal efforts (the Lutheran Separatists and the Owenites) which, though they failed partially, contributed much to the lore of the westward movement of our country. The inn is a modern structure that, while it is most efficient, embodies a sense of relaxation and home. The rooms are spacious (most with fireplaces), furnished with custom-made, beautifully simple and comfortable furniture—not motel contemporary. There is a small lake on the premises, and a separate building houses a pool. You register in a separate structure, the Entry House, which includes a common room—a sort of salon where groups converse. Most unusual and totally moving spiritually is a small chapel included in the Entry House. Immediately adjacent to the inn is the Red Geranium restaurant, serving lunch and dinner, which in my opinion are the best meals in all Indiana. A short walk away is the Shadblow restaurant, modern but quaint, serving a simpler menu."   *—Paul A. Welbon*

Open all year.
45 rooms, all with private bath.

Rates $25 single, $30 double, including continental breakfast. Lower
   rates from November 15 to March 31.
Only breakfast served.
Credit cards: American Express, Carte Blanche, Diners Club, Master Charge, Visa.

Iowa

Homestead

Die Heimat
Homestead, Iowa   52236
Telephone: (319) 622-3937

Heimat means homestead in German, and Homestead, Iowa,
was a small railhead village that became the seventh and last of
the Amana Colonies, settlements founded by religious pilgrims
of German, Swiss and Alsatian background who came to Iowa
in the mid-19th century. This inn was built in 1858 as a communal kitchen. It remained one until 1932, when the religious
Amana organization regrouped as a secular corporation. The
building then became a boarding and apartment house. In 1964
four Amana men bought the house and made it Die Heimat
Motor Hotel. In 1975 the inn was taken over by Jim and Barbara Loyd, who now run their small hotel in a very personal
fashion. From Die Heimat tourists can visit the restorations and
shops and restaurants of the Amana Colonies. There are also
Amana museums and working industries to visit, including a
hearth bakery, a woolen mill, a furniture and clock shop and a
smokehouse.

"Die Heimat is the only hotel in the Amana Colonies proper. It
is easy to locate, but on a quiet street. It is a restored inn furnished with lots of Amana furniture and is charming inside and
out. The host-owners always make a guest feel at home. We
love it and highly recommend it."
                                        —*Captain and Mrs. James Blum*

Open all year.
18 rooms, all with private bath.
Rates $15–$17 single, $17.50–$26 double.
No credit cards.
Continental breakfast only served.
Small beer room.

_____*Keosauqua*

Hotel Manning
Keosauqua, Iowa   52565
Telephone: (319) 293-3232

"Hotel Manning, on the bank of the Des Moines River, was constructed in 1839 as a general store to serve early travelers in southeastern Iowa. Later a second story was added and the impressive old red-brick building served as one of the first hotels for people traveling the Des Moines by steamboat. Pillared and porticoed, it is known as a classic example of 'steamboat Gothic' architecture. A rathskeller bar has been added, with the original sandstone foundation walls exposed. Upstairs guest rooms are furnished in authentic antiques but with all the modern conveniences, and prices are a real bargain. Motel accommodation also is available for the less adventuresome."

—Mary Ovrom

Open all year, except public holidays.
24 rooms, 20 with private bath.
Rates $8–$12 single, $11–$15 double.
No credit cards.
Bar.

Michigan

Farmington Hills

Botsford Inn
28000 Grand River
Farmington Hills, Michigan   48024
Telephone: (313) 474-4800

"Botsford Inn is in Farmington Hills, a suburb of Detroit and easily accessible at Grand River and the base line of Michigan, Eight Mile Road. Built in 1836, it was a popular stopping place for drovers, farmers and travelers to and from Detroit. Dances were held on the 'spring dance floor,' which is still a part of the inn. Henry Ford attended many of these dances with his future wife; he purchased the inn from the Botsford family in 1924 and restored it, furnishing it with many antiques and artifacts from his extensive collection. Still in the downstairs parlor is a square piano once owned by General Custer's sister, and there is a buffet from General Lee's home. In 1951, after Mr. Ford's death, the Anhuts purchased the property. John Anhut has made two additions to the original inn, and has converted the coach house into an attractive area available for banquets, receptions and meetings. There is an early American garden created by Mrs. Ford, a pleasant patio and a walled-in swimming pool. The dining room specializes in authentic

American dishes, and the Sunday-morning brunch is a popular local tradition. The inn is surrounded by an extensive lawn in which is set an official State of Michigan historical marker telling the inn's history."   *—Kathryn Briggs; also recommended by Victor G. Hanson*

Open all year.
60 rooms, all with private bath.
Rates $22–$28 single, $24–$32 double.
Credit cards: American Express, Master Charge, Visa.
Bar, recreational area.
German spoken.

Mackinac Island

Iroquois-on-the-Beach Resort Hotel
Mackinac Island, Michigan   49757
Telephone: (906) 847-3321

"The hotel was built in 1902 as a private home and converted into a guesthouse in 1904. It is located on the water overlooking the beautiful straits of Mackinac. A very peaceful setting, yet not far from the town, riding stables and historical points of interest. Their dining room (The Carriage House) is all glass; the view and the food are superb. The sundeck above the dining room has an excellent view of the many freighters and ocean-going ships that pass daily. They only serve lunch and dinner but for hotel guests they have a room service breakfast of homemade blueberry muffins, coffee, juice and such.

"There are many annual events that keep the island busy, such as the lilac festival in June and the Mackinac sailboat races in July. Aside from special events, all historical sites are open as of Memorial Day and the carriage tours start as early as May 15. Automobiles are not allowed on the island, so the most popular modes of transport are the horse-drawn carriage and the bicycle."   *—Becki Barnwell*

Open May 15 to October 15.
33 rooms, all with private bath.
Rates $45–$68 double.
Credit cards: Master Charge, Visa.
Bar, sundeck.
French and Spanish spoken.

Turn to the back of this book for pages inviting *your* comments.

Marshall

National House
102 South Parkview
Marshall, Michigan   49068
Telephone: (616) 781-7374

"On the town square of Marshall stands a two-story brick building with large windows that beckons the traveler to come in. The door opens to reveal a wood-plank floor with old benches, crocks filled with flower arrangements and a huge fireplace with a crackling fire. Each room in this inn is named after a prominent person from the Michigan area. Opening one door, there is a room that is Victorian to the massive bed, the dresser with marble top and the washstand with a bowl and pitcher. The feeling of being in the Victorian age is all about you. In the 'country room,' the metal bed, quilt and country oak dresser and blanket chest return a guest to the era of the brave homesteaders. The National House is habit-forming. We now find excuses to make the trip to Marshall just to stay there."
—*Shirley and Syd Waggoner*

"The inn was built in 1835 and, after having many owners, the two-story Federal-style building was restored by Mr. and Mrs. Norman Kinney and Mr. and Mrs. Harold Minick in 1976. It has been recognized as an official state historic site, and a marker detailing its history is on the front. A former slave is among the figures from local history for whom the inn's rooms are named. The only meal served here is a complimentary continental breakfast. Lunches and dinners are available at Win Schuler's restaurant a few blocks away. The inn is across the street from the Historical Society's Honolulu House, and many of the town's well-kept 1,200 pre-1900 homes are within walking distance. Marshall, called the world's biggest 'show-off town,' holds a historic homes tour on a weekend in September. It attracts thousands."   —*Kathryn Briggs; also recommended by M. E. Houran*

Open all year, except Christmas Eve and Christmas Day.
14 rooms, 11 with private bath.
Rates $23–$42 single, $26–$52 double, including continental breakfast. Only breakfast served.
No credit cards.

If you would like to amend, update or disagree with any entry, write *now*.

_____*Onekama*

Portage Point Inn
Onekama, Michigan   49675
Telephone: (616) 889-4222

"We have been enjoying this lovely inn for eighteen years—so have our children and now our grandchildren. It is a family resort: something for everyone. We oldsters enjoy the dinner dancing, the bingo, the shuffleboard and other games, the surprise parties and the food in the bright, attractive dining room. We enjoy looking for Petoskey stones along the Lake Michigan beach, and hiking all around the inn. Another plus is going to the discount stores in Manistee, where one can buy the famous Glen of Michigan and Jack Winter clothing at greatly reduced prices." —*Wanda Dillon*

Open June 15 to Labor Day.
82 rooms and 10 cottages. 40 rooms with private bath.
Weekly rates $252–$302 single, $197–$222 per person double, including three meals.
No credit cards.
Bar, swimming pool.

_Minnesota

New Prague

Schumacher's New Prague Hotel
212 West Main Street
New Prague, Minnesota 56071
Telephone: (612) 758-2133

In this community with its largely Czechoslovak and German heritage, John and Nancy Schumacher have restored this 1898 hotel. Each of the twelve rooms, named after the twelve months of the year, has hand-painted Bavarian folk art, goosedown pillows and comforters. Above the entrance of each room is a glass medallion from Munich with the name of the month: "Januar," "Februar," "Marz". . . .

"We spent our honeymoon here in the April room with its king-size circular bed with a mirrored headboard. The doors to the rooms that had not been rented were left open, so we could see what each one of them was like. We thought the hotel was terrific because we found it very European. The stairway was decorated with flowers and the small dining room was always full. We had veal and there were fresh fruit and vegetables and everything was homemade. It was certainly comparable to first-class hotels in France and Italy. The town itself is small and ordinary—a typical farming town."

> —*John A. Austin and Melita Toon; also recommended by Dale E. Barlage*

Open all year, except December 24, 25, 26.
12 rooms, all with private bath.
Rates $30 single, $40–$50 double. Special weekly rates and weekday packages.
No credit cards.
Bar, billiards.
Czech spoken.

_____*Sauk Centre*

Palmer House Hotel
Sauk Centre, Minnesota   56378
Telephone: (612) 352-3431

Sauk Centre, at the southern end of Big Sauk Lake, was the childhood home of Sinclair Lewis, who was later to satirize small-town America in *Main Street.* Sauk Centre became his Gopher Prairie. Later in life, he mellowed: Among his lesser-known books is *Work of Art,* which praised a small-hotel keeper. When Lewis died in Rome, his ashes were returned to his birthplace. Both the Lewis home and a center devoted to the works of the United States' first Nobel prize-winning novelist are open to the public in the summer.

"In his early life Sinclair Lewis had worked at the Palmer House, so there is much there to recall his book *Main Street.* In the hotel are two private party rooms—the Kennicott and the Minniemashie—both reminiscent of Lewis characters. The Palmer House was bought several years ago by two young men who had tired of the rush of metropolitan living. The hotel, which had been closed for some years following the previous owner's death, has been restored as it was in the early 1900s, when Lewis worked there as a boy.

"I checked into the hotel quite by chance. I found no elegant decor or impressive decoration as one finds in many hotels today, but I soon felt I had stepped into the past, and the lack of luxury was immediately overcome by the warm hospitality that prevailed. Frequently, fabulous eight-course dinners are served —and all other meals are good."   —*Pauline Wilcox*

"I lived in the Palmer House for eight months, and I found it as charming and friendly an atmosphere as you can imagine. The cafe is as up-to-date as you'll find anywhere, yet dinners and special events are served with elegance. The lake, two blocks north of the hotel, provides many recreational activities."

—*Patricia Hansen*

Open all year.
37 rooms, 5 with private bath.
Rates $7–$10 single, $9–$12 double. Weekly and monthly rates available.
No credit cards.
Skiing, tennis, water sports nearby.
German spoken.

_____*Stillwater*

Lowell Inn
102 North Second Street
Stillwater, Minnesota   55082
Telephone: (612) 439-1100

"The inn is a very special place to stay for that very special weekend. My husband and I have spent ten anniversary weekends, not to mention a honeymoon, here. Each room is furnished differently. No blaring TV will interrupt your rest. Last time we stayed, there weren't any radios, either. Stillwater, the 'birthplace of Minnesota,' is a beautiful little town north of St. Paul on the historic St. Croix River. It is loaded with antique shops; but don't get the idea that it is just another tourist town—it has a long history and is proud of it.

"The Lowell Inn's lobby has generously overstuffed furniture arranged in comfortable groupings for conversation and cocktails while waiting for a table in the dining rooms. The Washington Room is white linen, silver and china. The Garden Room is stone floor, wrought-iron tables and a natural spring waterfall. But the third is the best of all. There is no menu, just fondue, served with escargots, salad, dessert and a carefully selected wine. All this set in a room with exquisite Swiss wood carvings. The service is the best I have found in the state."

—*Margaret A. Levey; also recommended
by Judy and Marinus Van Putten*

Open all year, except Christmas Day.
20 rooms, all with private bath.
Rates $29–$69.
Credit cards: American Express, Master Charge, Visa.
German spoken.

Do you know a hotel in your state that we have overlooked? Write *now*.

_____*Wabasha*

Anderson House
333 West Main Street
Wabasha, Minnesota   55981
Telephone: (612) 565-4003

"Established in 1856, the Anderson is Minnesota's oldest continuously operating hotel. It has recently been designated an historical landmark by the federal government—and received a proper plaque placed there by the governor of Minnesota. Except for a few years, it has always been operated by the Anderson family. Two daughters of the Andersons—Mrs. Ebner and Mrs. McCaffrey, eighty-nine and ninety-one years old respectively—still live in a house adjacent to the hotel and keep a watchful eye on the operation. The present operators are a daughter and grandson who have had extensive experience in nationally known hotels and resorts. They have wisely kept the hotel in its original state—bedrooms with gorgeous antique furniture over a hundred years old. One room is called The Mayo because doctors from the Mayo Clinic, forty miles away, frequently stayed there. The kitchen has been completely modernized. The food is regarded as 'home cooking' and is known for hundreds of miles around. Busloads of guests come for lunch and dinner—or stay a few days. The budget-minded will find the dining room prices much to their liking. Pastries are made at the hotel, as are relishes, jams and jellies. Each meal is a delight.

"Furthermore, Wabasha—population 2,300—is a very important city historically. It is seventy miles southeast of the Twin Cities, on the Mississippi River, which divides Minnesota and Wisconsin, and on the direct highway from Minneapolis to Chicago via Redwing, Winona, La Crosse and Milwaukee. A bridge spans the Mississippi at Wabasha, so that one can drive on an equally fine highway to Chicago on the other side of the river. In the 1820s Wabasha (or Wapasha, named for a Sioux Indian chief) was an important fur-trading center. The unit of exchange was the Muskrat (5 cents). The Grace Memorial Episcopal Church, given to the town by wealthy lumber people, is probably the most beautiful church in the world in a town this size. Designed by a famous New York architect and possessing gorgeous Tiffany windows, the church is now about ninety years old, and in perfect condition. The *Delta Queen* and its new counterpart, the *Mississippi Queen,* make regular stops at Wabasha as they travel to St. Paul and Minneapolis.

"I get quite garrulous when Wabasha is mentioned. But being past eighty-five, that is a characteristic of my generation.

My late wife and I had a home on the riverbank in Wabasha during the time I was chief of internal medicine at Mayo for thirty-five years. After my retirement we lived there for seven years before moving to California. In our lives together, we were able to travel many times to many places. But I still believe that Wabasha is the most charming place of all."

—*Dr. Harold C. Habein*

Open all year, except Christmas Day.

51 rooms, 32 with private bath.

Rates $14.50–$22.50 single, $18.50–$26 double. Suite $28, cottage $25. 10 percent discount for senior citizens. Special midweek and weekend packages.

Credit cards: Master Charge, Visa.

Farm, outdoor cooking.

Portuguese spoken.

Missouri

St. Louis

Forest Park Hotel
4910 West Pine Boulevard
St. Louis, Missouri   63108
Telephone: (314) 361-3500

"The hotel has the atmosphere of a small, quiet place and the convenience of a large establishment. Its location is ideal, away from the downtown area and within a section of the city that offers the best cultural, culinary and scenic advantages. Forest Park itself is close by. The hotel is a good deal larger than it appears from the outside, yet smaller than one assumes from its spacious lobby. The decor is a pleasant French provincial in blue and gold, with many prints (Parisian scenes, Picassos and, alas, the inevitable Keanes). The rooms are large by American urban standards, and the rates relatively low. There is free, secure parking across the street from the entrance. A new restaurant has recently opened in the hotel. It competes, of course, with a good assortment of French, Italian and seafood restaurants in the area."   —*Shari and Berni Benstock*

Open all year.
225 rooms, all with private bath.
Rates $20–$30 single, $28–$35 double.
Credit cards: American Express, Carte Blanche, Diners Club, Master Charge, Visa.
Bar, outdoor swimming pool.
German and Spanish spoken.

Nebraska

Belgrade

Bel Horst Inn
Belgrade, Nebraska   68623
Telephone: (308) 357-1094

"Nestled in the Cedar River Valley of central Nebraska is Belgrade, a quaint and picturesque village with a unique attraction—the Bel Horst Inn. Built in 1907 as the Andrews Hotel, it was used by cattlemen and railroad men, but it became a victim of the drought and Depression of the 1930s and sat vacant for forty years. In 1973, two brothers, Donald and Richard Horst, businessmen originally from Belgrade, purchased the old hotel, began a restoration project and renamed it. When you push open the heavy iron lobby door, you step seventy years into the past. Special attention has been given to the turn-of-the-century decor. Each of the fourteen guest rooms is furnished with antique wooden and brass furniture. The bedspreads are exquisite old-time piecework quilts. Lace curtains adorn the windows, yet each of the rooms has a touch of modern comfort with individual baths, electric wall heaters and air-conditioning.

"In the lobby hang over one hundred pictures of Belgrade residents and scenes, along with many interesting antiques. The dining room has a lush appearance set off by brass chandeliers with flowered glass. A private party room is furnished with antique kitchen and dining items. The cuisine is superb and reasonably priced. Prime ribs, steaks, seafood and home-baked pastries are the specialties of the chef, Warren Johnson, who, along with the co-manager, Grace Jackson, provides warm and exuberant hospitality."   —*Joseph L. Neal*

Open all year.
14 rooms, all with private bath.
Rates $15 double.
Special weekly and off-season rates.
No credit cards.

_____*Crawford*

Fort Robinson
Box 392
Crawford, Nebraska   69339
Telephone: (308) 665-2660

"In the far northwest corner of Nebraska just west of Crawford lies the old Fort Robinson Military Reservation. A very important cavalry post during the Indian wars, it was abandoned by the military in 1948 and reverted to state control. In the 1960s the Nebraska Game and Parks Commission took over the post and has restored a number of the remaining buildings. One of the enlisted men's barracks has been converted to a lodge with a number of very comfortable guest rooms, meeting rooms and an excellent restaurant. The officers' adobe quarters have been restored and made into family units, and the large multiple family residences, built in the early 1900s, are available for large groups. There is a great deal of history and much scenic area around Fort Robinson."   —*Joseph L. Neal*

Open Memorial Day to Labor Day.
24 rooms, all with private bath. Cabins.
Rates $8–$10 double.
Credit cards: Master Charge, Visa.
State park, swimming pool.
Directions: 3 miles west of Crawford on Highway No. 20.

Where are the good little hotels in Boston? Philadelphia? Omaha? Dallas? If you have found one, don't keep it a secret. Write *now*.

Ohio

Granville

Buxton Inn
313 East Broadway
Granville, Ohio   43023
Telephone: (614) 587-0001

"The inn is a charming place to stay in Ohio. It has only three rooms, all different. The dining room serves excellent meals and attracts many from the central Ohio area. The inn was built in 1812 by Orin Granger and was originally called The Tavern. When he died it changed hands several times until Major Buxton bought it in 1865. He ran it for over forty years. Mr. and Mrs. Orville Orr bought the inn in 1972 and have been restoring it with authentic antiques, paintings and furniture."

—*Nancy Michael*

"Small, old, recently refurnished with antiques. It is preferable to its better known and larger neighbor, the Granville Inn. The menu is limited but satisfactory. A nearby restaurant to be tried is in an old country home called Bryn Mawr. Granville is a lovely little town, the home of Denison University."

—*Jean Ogg*

Open all year, except Christmas Day.
3 rooms, all with private bath.
Rates $14 single, $20 double, $22–$50 suite. Special weekly rates.
Credit cards: Master Charge, Visa.
Bar.

_____ *Lebanon*

The Golden Lamb Inn
27 South Broadway
Lebanon, Ohio   45036
Telephone: (513) 932-5065

The westward movement of early America gave the town of
Lebanon a prominent place on the traveler's map, and brought
to its inn a succession of famous visitors. Lebanon was a stagecoach stop and through it passed presidents, eminent writers,
generals, scientists and a host of other memorable guests. It is
not surprising that Lebanon, which retained its sense of history
after the stagecoaches disappeared, has kept alive what is
widely believed to be Ohio's oldest inn, the Golden Lamb. It
was at this inn that a cross and probably weary Charles Dickens
complained in 1842 about the lack of spirits—it was then a temperance hotel. Lebanon, by the way, was the site of Shaker settlements. The inn also played host to Henry Clay, Mark Twain
and no fewer than ten United States' presidents. Today's guests
at the Golden Lamb can sample the area's history not only by
staying in the rooms of the famous, but also by visiting the
Warren County Historical Museum nearby. In spring and
summer the Glendower State Museum, a Greek Revival home,
is open to the public. The Lebanon area is an antique buyer's
haunt.

"The Golden Lamb professes to be the oldest inn in Ohio, dating from 1803, the year that Ohio became a state. This small
inn, the host to many famous writers and historical figures, has
all antique furnishings. (Even restaurant guests are invited to
go upstairs and look around.) The rooms are tastefully and
comfortably appointed. The dining room is popular with locals,
lunching businessmen from Cincinnati and transients. Simple
but good fare."
                    —*Jean Ogg; also recommended by Wanda Dillon*

Open all year, except Christmas Day.
18 rooms, all with private bath.
Rates $22 single to $26 double.
Credit cards: American Express, Master Charge, Visa.

Marietta

Hotel Lafayette
101 Front Street
Marietta, Ohio   45750
Telephone: (614) 373-5522

"Marietta is an old river town and the hotel is close to the river. Be sure to ask for rooms in the old section, which are small but attractive and comfortable. They are reasonably priced. The Gun Room has an extensive menu and excellent food and service."
—*Jean Ogg*

Open all year.
98 rooms, all with private bath.
Rates $17–$21 single, $20–$30 double, $30 suite.
Credit cards: American Express, Diners Club, Master Charge, Visa.
Bar, river festival in September.

Oberlin

Oberlin Inn
North Main and East College Streets
Oberlin, Ohio   44074
Telephone: (216) 775-1111

"Across the street from the Oberlin campus—stately oaks and wide grassy areas make the college grounds look New Englandish—the inn has good food and attractive rooms. There is a 'tearoomy' atmosphere in the dining room."   —*Jean Ogg*

Open all year.
75 rooms, all with private bath.
Rates $19–$24 single, $25–$30 double, $34 suite.
Credit cards: Master Charge, Visa.

Details of special features offered by an inn or hotel vary according to information supplied by the hotels themselves. The absence here of a recreational amenity, a bar or a restaurant doesn't necessarily mean one of these doesn't exist. Ask the innkeeper when booking your room.

Wisconsin

Milwaukee

Pfister Hotel
424 East Wisconsin Avenue
Milwaukee, Wisconsin 53202
Telephone: (414) 273-8222

"In a city not noted for elegance, the Pfister retains a good deal of Old World charm and dignity. Built in 1893, it has always been Milwaukee's most recommended place to stay. That's even more true since a recent refurbishing added more Victorian luster, including an abundance of gilt and marble. The vaulted lobby is especially charming, with its display of Middle European 19th-century paintings. There are 333 rooms in the eight-story original hotel and the twenty-three-story adjoining tower, built in 1966. The original building has more charm, the tower more convenience. European touches continue in the service: Beds are turned down and sweets left each evening, and beds are provided with three sheets. The hotel's Crown Room at the top of the tower is Milwaukee's most popular nightclub, the English Room a favorite restaurant. And the place is convenient—a few blocks from Lake Michigan (for the best view of the lake, ask for rooms 8, 9 or 10, as high as possible in the tower), yet in the downtown shopping district."

—_Paul Salsini_

Open all year.
333 rooms, all with private bath.
Rates $30–$100 single, $40–$100 double, $65–$250 suites.
Credit cards: American Express, Carte Blanche, Diners Club, Master Charge, Visa.
Bars, free parking, game room, nightclub, sauna, swimming pool.
Arabic, French, German, Italian, Japanese, Russian and Spanish spoken.

Part
Five

Plains, Northwest and Alaska

Alaska
Idaho
Montana
North Dakota
Oregon
South Dakota
Washington
Wyoming

Alaska

Skagway

The Skagway Inn
Box 483
Skagway, Alaska   99840
Telephone: (907) 983-2289

"Skagway today boasts a population of 750, reduced somewhat from the 10,000 people who swelled the town during the gold rush of 1898. The main street is almost unchanged, sporting the Pack Train Saloon, the Arctic Brotherhood Hall, the Golden North Hotel and the White Pass and Yukon RR Depot. The National Park Service has taken a low profile in carefully restoring a few buildings, seeking to maintain the frontier spirit of Soapy Smith and his gang.

"The Skagway Inn has the charm of its locale and the warmth of home. Rooms are named for infamous ladies of the good old days, and a player piano in excellent working condition graces the living room. The owners, both natives of the town, love to sit around swapping stories about flying over glaciers, catching seafood in the inlet or cross-country skiing. Coffee and homemade pastries are put out every morning for guests. A highly recommended hotel, and the cheapest place in town to boot."
—*Jean Carlton Parker*

Open all year.
10 rooms, none with private bath.
Rates $25 single, $30 double.
No meals served.
Credit cards: Master Charge, Visa.

Idaho

Boise

Idanha Hotel
Main Street at 10th
Boise, Idaho   83702
Telephone: (208) 342-3611

Idaho became a state in 1890, opening the way to further growth of an area already rich in mining and on the verge of a canal-building age that would turn more and more land into productive acreage. Boise, the state's capital, soon needed a grand hotel.

"The Idanha is the outstanding example of the French chateau style of architecture in the state. This nationally registered landmark opened as a luxury hotel on the first day of the 20th century, and its castlelike towers still grace Main Street. Handsomely restored to its original elegance, the Idanha today features Rolls-Royce limousine service, Victorian accommodation and Peter Schott's continental restaurant."   —*Arthur A. Hart*

Open all year.
100 rooms, all with private bath.
Rates $38–$55.
Credit cards: American Express, Master Charge, Visa.
Two bars, gift shop.

Montana

Essex

Izaak Walton Inn
Box 675
Essex, Montana   59916
Telephone: Ask operator for Toll
            Station Essex 1

"The inn, just off Highway 2 on the southern boundary of Glacier National Park, is surrounded by scenic mountains. It is obvious that the inn was established because of the railroad that passes by the door. A couple of dozen immaculate, but austere, rooms provide visitors with a feeling that they have been transported back to the 1920s. Each room has throw rugs rather than wall-to-wall carpeting, a porcelain sink, more than adequate closet space and central restrooms and showers down the hall a few paces. Part of the charm of staying at the Izaak Walton Inn is bumping into other lodgers, wrapped in towels, heading for their morning or evening baths. Later in the evening, in the elegant basement bar, these same lodgers join in revelry that lasts late into the night under the superb guidance of bartender-owner, Sid Goodrich. Sid's wife, Millie, directs general housekeeping and the restaurant activities. Meals are essentially family style, with orders from an excellent menu. Everyone dines at closely spaced tables in a quaintly furnished dining area immediately adjacent to a large, comfortably appointed fireplace room. This fireplace room is the gathering point for lodgers who may be planning the day's hike into the Glacier Mountain peaks in summer, or deciding which cross-country ski trail to follow during the winters of deep snows.

"One is struck by the simple wooden architecture of the inn. Inside there are varnished floors, beamed ceilings, a rock fireplace and a general alpine look. Throughout the building, there is a touch of the railroad-station theme. This is best exemplified in the bar, which is a museum of railroad memorabilia. Railroad songs are sung around the piano, and some specialty drinks carry various kinds of railroad names. A recent addition to the operation includes a large conference room, beneath which is located a huge sauna, completed in the fall of 1978. The sauna adds an entirely new luster to the end of the hiking, fishing or skiing day. Parking facilities behind the hotel are more than adequate and many 'locals' from the region come to the inn for an evening meal and good fellowship. It is impossible to remain a stranger at the inn for more than twenty-four hours. Breakfasts are traditional affairs designed to satiate the appetites of outdoorsmen: huge pancakes, thick slices of cured bacon, fresh eggs, steaming pots of coffee. Sack lunches for the trail are available. Evening meals concentrate on great quantities of beef, chicken or pork with all the extras.

"The inn is also the local post office for a widely dispersed population of hardy Montanans who have retreated from the more crowded sections of the region. They come to eat, drink, chat, make plans, rent ski equipment, arrange for river float trips down the Middle Fork of the Flathead River, but mostly to stop by the inn as if it were the cracker barrel of western Montana. Informality is the rule. Leave your suits and ties at home but bring jeans, hiking and riding boots and those pieces of gear needed to enjoy the great northern Rocky Mountains."
—*Richard A. Solberg*

Open all year.
24 rooms, 4 with private bath.
Rates $12–$15 single, $15–$20 double.
Credit cards: Master Charge, Visa.
Bar, river rafting, sauna, ski rental shop.
Trains and planes met.

Would you be so kind as to share discoveries you may have made of charming, well-run places to stay in Europe? Please write to *Europe's Wonderful Little Hotels and Inns,* c/o Thomas Congdon Books, E.P. Dutton, 2 Park Avenue, New York, N.Y. 10016. (By the way, a new and greatly expanded edition of this splendid guide is now available at your bookseller's.)

North Dakota

Medora

The Rough Riders
Medora, North Dakota   58645
Telephone: (701) 623-4422

"Around the little town of Medora in the North Dakota Badlands is some of the most spectacular natural beauty in the world. The barren bluffs and buttes, with layers of the earth's history exposed and the deep, shaded ravines carved by the Little Missouri River, are a startling contrast to the prairie. The muted colors, the layers of soil and the textures are beautiful in any light. Medora has been restored to the time when Theodore Roosevelt raised cattle in the area and the Marquis de Mores had a grand plan for a packing plant to process the local beef. The hotel is in the center of town, and is just as it was when Teddy Roosevelt was a guest—complete with wood sidewalk. The hotel is constructed inside and out of rough lumber that has been left unpainted. You feel you are in a true 'cow town' when you climb the center stairway leading to the antique-furnished rooms. The train gently shakes the building as it passes through town. All this is juxtaposed with a fine menu in a dining room that would be expected only in the city. Mornings at the Rough Riders are a delight. The rugged old buttes and incredibly clear sky, and the sounds of breakfast downstairs, make you aware this is a fine way to begin a day."

—Carol Winger

Open from Memorial Day to Labor Day.
9 rooms, all with private bath.
Rates $23 single, $28 double.
Credit cards: American Express, Master Charge, Visa.
Beer and wine license.

Jacksonville Inn,
Jacksonville

Oregon

Government Camp

Timberline Lodge
Government Camp, Oregon   97028
Telephone: (503) 272-3311

"The day that President Franklin Delano Roosevelt drove up the hill from Portland to the slopes of Mt. Hood to dedicate the Timberline Lodge must have been a happy one for him. His 'grand tour' of the West, during the years of World War Two, had been a success. He had been able to take the Union Pacific Railroad to the coast—see a unified nation at work—and enjoy the pleasures he most delighted in. He must have been happy to see the completion of a project close to his heart since the Depression—the Timberline Lodge at Government Camp. In taste it was a bellwether for ski resorts. Masons, craftsmen, carpenters and artisans of many persuasions lived and worked together in an extraordinary freemasonry of art. What they achieved at the lodge was unique for such a highly populistic society as theirs was at that time.

"Despite the changes in taste, the lodge is still respected for its superb design and decor. Its style beggars any facile categorization. The scale of the lodge is monumental: It is nearly 400 feet long, four stories in elevation and dominated by a cupola that is a poetic reflection of the summit of Mt. Hood. Today the lodge is used and enjoyed the year round. Its cathedralesque Grand Hall reflects the Olympian aspect of its surroundings. In a sense, what sculptors had done for the great European cathedrals in carving gargoyles, the craftsmen of Oregon did for the lodge. The newel posts are a singular example of their success in such a specialized area of art. The rooms of the inn are furnished with a special dated feeling. To some they might seem comfortably bland, reflecting the age of their creation. Others may find them campy.

"Food and drink at the lodge are under the close scrutiny of Richard Kohnstamm. It is decidedly hearty, wholesome and good, frequently excellent and occasionally great if not grand. Flamboyance is not the operative word at the lodge—nor is it anywhere in Oregon. On the contrary, understatement is the keystone of life."   —*Dr. Forest M. Hinkhouse*

Open all year.
53 rooms, all with private bath.
Rates $19–$43.50 single, $31–$60 double. Special ski packages.
Credit cards: American Express, Master Charge, Visa.
Bar, pool.
French, German and Italian spoken.

Jacksonville

Jacksonville Inn
175 E. California
Jacksonville, Oregon   97530
Telephone: (503) 899-1900

"I should start with the annual Shakespeare festival held in the nearby town of Ashland. Here they have an outdoor replica of the old Globe Theatre, and they put on three or four Shakespeare plays, many of them obscure enough that we may have read them but will not have seen them. They also produce two or three fascinating contemporary plays each year, such as O'Neill's *Long Day's Journey into Night* and Brecht's *Mother Courage.* All of this takes place in the picturesque town of Ashland. But where to stay for our annual four- or five-day orgy of theater?

"The answer to this question is a resounding vote for the Jacksonville Inn. Jacksonville was a gold rush town in the 1860s, and the main street has been restored—including the inn. Behind its brick facade are eight rooms, all lovingly furnished with Victorian beds, chairs and lamps. Downstairs there is a large and attractive dining room serving first-class meals. The proprietor, Jerry Evans, is a wine buff as well as an expert in Victoriana and has an impressive list of California wines. He also offers one or two Oregon wines, and is waiting for new ones to be developed.

"The atmosphere of the inn, without being arty and crafty, is authentic and done in very good taste. On the outskirts of town is Pioneer Village, a reconstruction of a dozen or so buildings of the gold rush era. George McUne and his son have executed this accurate restoration of buildings, and six covered wagons. Mr. McUne was a wheelwright and wagon master who led a one hundredth anniversary trek with his six wagons along the old southern Oregon Trail. But let us not lose sight of the fact that the hub of these cultural and historical excursions is still the Jacksonville Inn, itself a jewel of Victorian perfection."

—Dr. Joseph B. Wheelwright; also recommended
by Margaret and Don Lee

Open all year, except Christmas Eve and Christmas Day.
8 rooms.
Rates $18 single to $23 double.
Credit cards: Master Charge, Visa.
Bar, restaurant, hunting, fishing.

Portland

Mallory Hotel
729 S.W. 15th Avenue
Portland, Oregon   97205
Telephone: (503) 223-6311

"The Mallory is a bargain city hotel just a couple of blocks from the main shopping mall. It's old, well maintained, exquisitely clean and very inexpensive. (A suite for the four of us, complete with private bath, TV, stereo and all the amenities of a city hotel, cost $22—less than our accommodations in a Motel 6! For that price, we had a living room with queen-size hide-a-bed and a twin-bedded bedroom.) The staff was pleasant and gave a personal touch. The hotel is replete with funky stairways, mail chutes and a pleasant dining room just off the main lobby."

—Margaret Zeigler

Open all year.
144 rooms, 140 with private bath.
Rates $15–$22 single, $17–$26 double, $26 suites.
No credit cards.
Bar.

_____South Dakota

Custer

State Game Lodge
Custer, South Dakota   57730
Telephone: (605) 255-4541

The lodge, near all points of interest in the Black Hills area, is set in the midst of one of the largest state parks in the country—Custer State Park. There are lakes and streams, herds of buffalo as well as deer, elk and mountain goats.

"This is one of my special favorites. The Game Lodge hosted President Coolidge in 1927 and President Eisenhower in 1953."
—_Senator George McGovern_

Open from May 15 to October 1.
67 rooms, in lodge, motel and cottages, all with private bath.
Rates $26 single, $29 double.
Credit cards: Master Charge, Visa.
Pets in motel and cottages only.
Bar, riding, Jeep ride to the buffalo herd, hiking, art exhibit.
German spoken.
Directions: 15 miles east of Custer on Highway 16A. Transportation from depot or airport available for a fee.

Sylvan Lake Lodge
Box 752
Custer, South Dakota   57730
Telephone: (605) 574-2561

"The lodge on top of the hill is built of golden limestone and large logs. Beyond its broad halls are large rooms, providing comfortable quarters for visitors. The dining room, which reflects the culture of the Dakota Indians, provides high-quality food. The chef is justly proud of his variations on the theme of the American steer. Vegetarians would be pleased by the wide range of other dishes offered as entrees or side dishes. The lodge is proud—and with good reason—of its own farm."

—*Dr. Forest M. Hinkhouse*

Open all year.
64 rooms, 60 with private bath.
Rates $22 single, $27–$31 double. Special group rates.
Credit cards: American Express, Master Charge, Visa.
Bar, cross-country skiing, ice skating, hiking, lake swimming and trout fishing.

Washington

Cathlamet

Cathlamet Hotel
Main Street
Cathlamet, Washington   98612
Telephone: (206) 795-8751

"This sleepy little lumbering-fishing town on the banks of the
Columbia River boasts an interesting hotel and restaurant
(Pierre's, next door to the hotel). Both are owned by Pierre
Pype, a former Chicago businessman who fell in love with
Cathlamet and decided to put his expertise and efforts into
making a super eatery and hostelry in this little Washington
town. The hotel is all done in 1920s style (some of the beds
seem to be of the same vintage, alas!) with Art Deco stained
glass in the small upstairs lobby. There is a game room with
pool table for the use of guests. Most of the rooms do not have
private baths, but very clean baths are available down the hall.
The rooms are small, but comfortable, and have sinks in them.
We paid only $22 for two separate rooms without bath and in-
cluding our breakfast of homemade coffeecake and coffee or
hot chocolate. Pierre's is closed Mondays and Tuesdays, so
visits to Cathlamet should be geared to avoid these two days;
the other eating establishments in Cathlamet cannot be recommended."
—*Margaret Zeigler*

Open all year.
13 rooms, 1 with private bath.
Rates $11 single, $15 double, including continental breakfast.
Special two-day rates.
Credit cards: Master Charge, Visa.
Bar.

_____*Coupeville*

The Captain Whidbey Inn
Box 32
Coupeville, Washington   98239
Telephone: (206) 678-4097

"Years ago, when the summer's heat got out of hand in Arizona
(where I was the founding director of the Phoenix Art Museum), I would flee to Seattle and sail on to the magical islands
that are but a ferry's ride away. There, I discovered the Captain
Whidbey Inn on a heavily forested isle that had been discovered by Captain Vancouver. In that sylvan retreat I found
splendid isolation, sunny-crisp weather, a double-storied inn—
nearly a century old, and hewn from Madrona logs—and a
gracious welcome. My hosts, the Stephen Stone family, then, as
now, provide superb hospitality, spacious rooms and strikingly
good food and drink. The inn's library, dominating the second
floor, is made up of first editions and a near-limitless collection
of current international magazines. The inn, with its own dock
on Penn Cove, used to berth ships from Seattle, Tacoma, Vancouver and Victoria. The Captain Whidbey offers guests local
oysters, Dungeness crab, delicate baby lamb or properly aged
beef. The dining room, like the Chart Room, its bar, and the
common room with its field and beachstone fireplace, has
paintings reflecting the beauty of the adjacent land and sea by
Dennis Argent, whom I call the inn's 'artist in residence.' "
                                        —*Dr. Forest M. Hinkhouse*

Open all year.
25 rooms, 14 with private bath.
Rates $15–$25 single, $20–$35 double.
Credit cards: Master Charge, Visa.
Bar, beachcombing, fishing, hiking.
French, German and Spanish spoken.

If you would like to amend, update or disagree with any entry,
write *now*.

Eastsound

Beach Haven Resort
Route 1, Box 12
Eastsound, Washington   98245
Telephone: (206) 376-2288

"This delightful spot on one of the few inhabited islands in the San Juan chain is accessible to the mainland by ferry from Anacortes. We found Beach Haven the most tasteful, rustic, yet well furnished and maintained place on the island. We spent a week here, resting, reading, hiking, boating and canoeing—a perfect relaxation. The accommodations range from one- to three-bedroom rustic cabins to one- to two-bedroom deluxe apartments. All have fully equipped kitchens. Some have fireplaces. They are strung out in a line among the pines that line the western shore—and the sunsets are breathtaking. The small town of Eastsound, the metropolis of the island, has a supermarket, which makes shopping easy. There is a laundromat at the airport. And a number of good restaurants—Bilbo's, the Chambered Nautilus—make dining out a pleasure. Marilyn and Russ Hyslop are the owners-managers of Beach Haven; the tiny store they maintain in their office helps avoid many a last-minute dinner-preparation crisis. Our deluxe two-bedroom apartment cost us $216 for a week."   —_Margaret Zeigler_

Open all year.
20 units, all with private bath.
Rates $25–$60. Special weekly and off-season rates.
No credit cards.

The Outlook Inn
Box 210
Eastsound, Washington   98245
Telephone: (206) 376-2581

"The slowing down begins on the hour-long ferryboat ride from Anacortes. There is the expanse of sky and water, jeweled by wooded islands and the distant snow-capped mountains. Disembarking at the tiny port of Orcas, one drives through several miles of rolling meadow and primitive forest to the quaint village of Eastsound at the end of East Sound Bay. The inn is across the street from the driftwooded beach: The window boxes are full of flowers, and the large windows along the dining room are bordered with the etched designs of another day. Within, the little lobby has soft, red wallpaper, antique wood, copper and houseplants. Louis (just Louis) is our host, and he can be found anywhere from the vegetable garden, the greenhouse or the large modern kitchen to the dining room or the seclusion of his small suite—reading, painting or preparing one of his Sunday 'contemplations' to be given at the wooden chapel for any who wish to attend. Wood for this nondenominational gathering place was gleaned from one of the earliest farmhouses in Washington and rafted to the island.

"The inn's food is famous on the island, always cooked to order. During the growing season salad makings come from the vegetable garden and fresh herbs from the garden or greenhouse. Fish are caught and served the same day. There are herb teas, homemade soups, homemade breads and pies and about twenty wines in stock. The bedrooms are homey and, above all, colorful. Some of the beds and bureaus are antiques. Rooms have adjustable wall heaters and washstands with hot and cold running water, but the bathrooms are those of the old family-style hotel—off the hall, within easy reach of your room. The front bedrooms look out to the Sound with its fade-away borders of steep blue hills. The back bedrooms look out over the pond and gardened hillside.

"There are many activities on the island: tennis, indoor and outdoor swimming, fishing, boating and some horseback riding. The island is an excellent place for bicycling. Hikers (or drivers) can take a trip through Moran State Park with its lakes and waterfall, up Mt. Constitution to the old stone tower for a bird's-eye view of the San Juan islands, the 'floating' snowclad range of the mainland and, right below, the lakes. Orcas is an inspiring place for painters and photographers. Easy trips by ferry or chartered plane or boat can be made to other islands. Jacques Cousteau brings his boat into these waters because the scuba diving is excellent. Others rejoice in the varieties of birds that nest on Orcas or migrate through, in the deer and in the blooming of unusual flowers. Interestingly enough, there are no poisonous plants on the island, no poisonous mushrooms, no harmful animals—nothing that will hurt people."

—*Darthea Stalnaker*

Open all year.
18 rooms, none with private bath.
Rates $16–$21 single, $18–$24 double. Special weekly rates from Labor Day to June.
Credit cards: Master Charge, Visa.

Turn to the back of this book for pages inviting *your* comments.

Port Townsend

James House
1238 Washington Street
Port Townsend, Washington   98368
Telephone: (206) 385-1238

"This charmingly restored Victorian house was built in 1889, at a time when Port Townsend expected to become the New York of the West Coast and to have the terminus of the transcontinental railroad. Neither of these things came to be, and the town withered away, being restored and revamped only in the last quarter century. A breathtaking array of grand Victorian houses stands proudly on a tall bluff above the harbor and the commercial parts of town along the waterfront. James House commands a view out to sea over the sound. Lowell and Barbara Bogart, who own and operate James House with a friendly and personal touch, make any stay memorable. We had the garden suite—two rooms in the brick-walled basement with ground-level windows (we even had a view)—full of antiques, including brass beds, and fresh-scented bowls of rose petals in every room. There was a wood-burning stove, which we used one damp, chilly evening. Outside our suite there was a game room, with bookshelves of reading material, and chess, checkers, backgammon and Monopoly. We ate our breakfast in the kitchen with other guests, enjoying Barbara Bogart's homemade breads (three different ones each morning) and homemade jellies and jams. Port Townsend is at the tip of the Olympic Peninsula and a fine jumping-off point for an exploration of the peninsula itself."   —_Margaret Zeigler_

Open all year.
10 rooms, 4 with private bath.
Rates $24 single, $28 double, suites from $38, including continental breakfast.
No credit cards.
Hiking, library, skiing, water sports.
French spoken.

Would you be so kind as to share discoveries you may have made of charming, well-run places to stay in Europe? Please write to _Europe's Wonderful Little Hotels and Inns,_ c/o Thomas Congdon Books, E.P. Dutton, 2 Park Avenue, New York, N.Y. 10016. (By the way, a new and greatly expanded edition of this splendid guide is now available at your bookseller's.)

Manresa Castle
7th and Sheridan
P.O. Box 564
Port Townsend, Washington   98368
Telephone: (206) 385-3398

"The turreted Manresa Castle, restored to its original Victorian opulence, stands as a hilltop guardian over charming Port Townsend and commands a panoramic view of Puget Sound. The Manresa will definitely not fulfill anyone's idea of a typical ancient, cold and dank castle. It is a warm and inviting hotel. The building was constructed in the late 1800s as a private residence for a wealthy merchant. That was in Port Townsend's heyday, a fascinating story to pursue during a visit. Some years later, with the addition of a large wing, the castle's second calling was to serve as a religious order's retreat until spiraling costs forced its sale and conversion to a hotel. The story of its restoration began seven years ago when the present owners moved in with a dream. The magnitude of the rejuvenation seemed a hopeless and enormous task. When a mere four rooms were completed, I was one of the earliest guests, and could easily be importuned into holding a ladder, shifting a carpet or, at the very least, giving advice. Today the castle enjoys a newfound popularity as a haven of old-fashioned splendor. From its mahogany-paneled bar to its turret suite, it is an excellent example of Victorian architecture. It offers the finest accommodations, one of the best restaurants in the area and, as a bonus, the nicest people you'll find anywhere."

—Kenneth A. Schueman

"This castle atop a hill with walls of solid brick, two feet thick, is an attractive place that the family is continually renovating and upgrading. Recently they did a complete landscaping, planting thousands of tulips and other plants. They added a restaurant with the widest menu—the seafood is extraordinary—and the best quality on the Olympic Peninsula. When I was last there they were working on a two-level dining room with booths decorated with stained glass and a big stained-glass chandelier in the center. Some of the stained glass came from the old chapel—the castle was once a Jesuit retreat. They are doing all the work themselves, this remarkable family. The bar was also designed and built by them, everything from tables to the smallest elements of the decor. I like that old-time concept of knowing how to do things for yourself—and of making use of the resources you have in new ways. The post with gas lamps along the driveway they built from the old bricks of the wall

that ran along the front of the grounds. Inside there are fifty to a hundred oil paintings around the place, and antiques in all the rooms. Port Townsend is a town of about 5,000 people—a sort of arty community with antique stores and art shops. There are people living in retirement and many younger people who have moved up there to escape California and find a more relaxing life."
                                                            —*Jerry Tennant*

Open all year.
39 rooms, 27 with private bath.
Rates $25–$43 single, $28–$46 double. Off-season and commercial rates.
Credit cards: American Express, Master Charge, Visa.
Old English lounge.

_____*Seattle*

The Olympic
Fourth and Seneca
Seattle, Washington   98111
Telephone: (206) 682-7700

"I don't know if this would qualify as a small hotel, but we prefer it when in Seattle on business. The entry hall and reception area are reminiscent of the turn-of-the-century hotels in Europe. Our room—a corner suite—gave us a glimpse of the bay and was pleasantly furnished. It proved to be quite comfortable—we had ample room for spreading papers in the parlor. The delight, though, was the Golden Lion restaurant. The atmosphere was of quiet luxury in good, not-too-ostentatious taste. The sommelier, who has been reigning over the cellar for many years, will offer assistance in selecting wines. When the waiter presents the menu, he also places a snowy napkin near the lady's plate; a rosebud of deepest red rests among the folds. Adjacent to the Golden Lion is the Lion's Den, where you can sip an after-dinner drink while listening to the soothing music of a piano player. Should you desire a modest meal, there is an oyster bar and a coffee shop on the premises: Both serve excellent food."
                                                            —*Louisa L. Becker*

Open all year.
765 rooms, all with private bath.
Rates $37–$49 single, $47–$59 double. Off season rates. Children under 18 free in rooms with parents.
Credit cards: American Express, Carte Blanche, Diners Club, Master Charge, Visa.
Arabic, Chinese, French, German, Greek, Italian, Japanese and Spanish spoken.

Wyoming

Cody

Irma Hotel
1192 Sheridan Avenue
Cody, Wyoming   82414
Telephone: (307) 587-4221

"The Irma Hotel was built by William F. 'Buffalo Bill' Cody and opened on November 1, 1902. It was named for his youngest daughter. During this period he was traveling far afield with his Wild West Show, and he would return to the small town and stay in his suite at the Irma or at his ranch on the South Fork of the Shoshone River.

"Many of the bedrooms have been renovated and named after well-known Cody people, such as Frank Blackburn, the sheriff; Vern Spencer, a guide and trapper, and Caroline Lockhart, novelist and journalist. The dining room has been enlarged recently, a private dining room added and the floors covered in a warm, patterned red carpeting. The cherrywood backbar, presented by Queen Victoria to Buffalo Bill, was made in France, shipped to New York, taken by rail to Montana and then by horse-drawn freight wagon to Cody. The old ceiling was made of metal and showed several bullet holes where some overexuberent cowboy had shot in the air, narrowly missing people in the bedrooms above, when the dining room was a bar. The innkeeper has replaced that old ceiling with new metal, which is almost a replica of the old.

"Many festive occasions have been held in the Irma, such as the annual Trappers Ball and the Stampede Ball—affairs which have unfortunately been discontinued. Wallace Reid, of the old silent-movie days, was once a night clerk here long before his rise to stardom. The hotel, which is on the National Register of Historic Places, is in the heart of the downtown business district on Sheridan Avenue, named after Buffalo Bill's good friend, General Sheridan. Cody is a tourist town only fifty miles from the eastern entrance to Yellowstone Park. Attractions include the Cody Stampede held in July and the Buffalo Bill Historic Center known for its Western art." —*Margaret Martin*

Open all year.
41 rooms, all with private bath.
Rates $21–$23.
Credit cards: American Express, Master Charge, Visa.
Cocktail lounge.

Part
Six

Southwest and South Central

Arkansas
Colorado
Kansas
New Mexico
Oklahoma
Texas

Arkansas

Eureka Springs

Crescent Hotel
Prospect Street
Eureka Springs, Arkansas   72632
Telephone: (501) 253-9766

"The description of Eureka Springs as the 'little Switzerland of America' is a grotesque one. This town is very different, and it can stand comfortably on its own merits. It's a town of steep streets that wind up and down the hillside, of Victorian shops and ornate, fussy houses. It's a town that has become a meeting point for musicians, artists and writers. The two places to stay are the massive Crescent perched high on the hill, or the small New Orleans tucked away on a curve of the main street. Both are exceptional—the choice depends on your mood.

"You sweep up to the front entrance of the Crescent as you would arrive at a Victorian country home, looking over your shoulder for the pomp. The lobby has a stone fireplace and a period reception desk. The Crystal dining room is cavernous, has a handsome wooden floor, a grand piano and, unfortunately, an ugly glass centerpiece that I am always tempted to bump into accidentally. There is a pub on the lower level and from the lounge named Top of the Crescent you can sit in a

wicker chair, grasp your aperitif and look out over the valley.
The rooms have all been restored—lots of footstools, lamps and
marble-topped tables.

"The Hotel had its grand opening in 1886 and was used exclusively by grand people known then as the 'carriage set.' A
period followed when it became a summer resort hotel and a
junior college for women the remainder of the year. Then for
an unhappy three years in the 1930s it was a hospital for the
'curing of cancer'—the operator later being charged with fraud-
ulent practices. Now it is back in business, open all the time,
and owned by a couple of Wichita businessmen.

"The town is full of surprises. For the religious there is the
giant Christ of the Ozarks, a replica of the Holy Land (still in a
very unfinished state) and the great Passion play, performed
from May through October. For the less religious or irreligious,
there is Silver Dollar City, a kind of Disneyland of the Ozarks
(which has a fine national crafts festival in the autumn) and, if
you are lucky, some memorable music. I wandered into a bar
on the main street and listened to a group of musicians who
called themselves (for reasons known only to themselves) something like the Greasy Greens; the three female singers, in
dresses to their ankles, poured out their emotions and their formidable talents to an entranced group of drinkers."

—*David Wigg*

Open all year.
76 rooms, all with private bath.
Rates $26–$32 single, $38–$65 double. Special senior citizens' rate
during September and special group rates.
Credit cards: American Express, Master Charge, Visa.
Bar, gift shop, historical museum, recreation rooms, swimming pool,
tennis court.

New Orleans Hotel
63 Spring Street
Eureka Springs, Arkansas   72632
Telephone: (501) 253-8630

"Eureka Springs must be one of the oddest towns in America
(architectural oddities alone got it at least seven mentions in the
old 'Ripley's Believe It or Not' column). Late in the last century
it blossomed from wilderness to a city of 16,000, when a local
judge experienced a cure from a crippling leg inflammation
after bathing in its spring waters. World War One medical ad-
vances cut the bottom out of the curative-water business, and
Eureka Springs, like many spa towns, shrank to one-tenth its
previous size, but with the architecture of a Victorian hill

town—if you can imagine such a thing—still intact. Tourists returned in the mid-1960s, mostly busloads of fundamentalist Christians come to witness the then-new 'Sacred Projects' established just outside of town by Gerald L.K. Smith (a largely forgotten evangelist now, but one of America's leading preachers of the 1930s). Smith's pilgrims brought others in their wake. In the last decade the old Victorian shops of Spring Street have blossomed into workshops and salesrooms for a more-than-usually-talented cluster of artists and crafts people.

"Eureka Springs is a divided town these days. The Sacred Projects administrators have gathered political muscle, especially among the merchants and innkeepers along the Strip City of nearby Highway 62. Those businesses rely on Smith's buses for their trade. They'd like to see the old town turned into a theme park. But the merchants and residents of the old town prefer it as a living place—one with a past but also a future.

"Phil Schloss is one of the town's interesting newcomers. He recently took over the old New Orleans Hotel—so-called thanks to two rather spartan cast-iron balconies along the facade—and is restoring the place, not to splendor, but to something resembling its original shabby gentility. For example, he found a trove of cheap, old lyre-back washstands in storage. Doubtless early fixtures, they're being stripped, repaired and replaced in the rooms. How nice to see someone restoring a hotel that was never first class and being true to it. Old-fashioned second class (or maybe even third) can be fun to visit, too, it turns out. There are impromptu musical evenings in the high-ceilinged lobby, hearty soups in the ground-floor dining room, sixteen hamburger variations (and two steaks) in a cozy basement pub called The Quarter. A fascinating little hotel in an even more fascinating hidden corner of America. You'll never come to Eureka Springs by chance, but if you're within one hundred miles it's well worth a detour."

—*Mechtild Hoppenrath and Charles Oberdorf*

Open all year.
24 rooms, 18 with private bath.
Rates $20–$24. Lower rates November through April. Special rates available for small groups.
No credit cards.
Cocktail lounge.

Historic Redstone Inn,
Redstone

Colorado

Boulder

Hotel Boulderado
2115 13th Street
P.O. Box 319
Boulder, Colorado   80302
Telephone: (303) 442-4344

"One can only hope that what is happening to the Hotel Boulderado will happen to many, many other fine, older hotels in America. Here was a stately, dignified hotel, built around the turn of the century and owned for forty years by the townspeople of Boulder, that was allowed to become, in the words of the present manager, a 'flophouse.' The same story can be repeated in many other American cities and towns. A hotel that in its day had guests such as Bat Masterson, Helen Keller and Louis Armstrong, deteriorated to a place that 'nice' people ignored. No longer. At last, the mood in America is one of restoration and preservation. A group of local business people have bought the Boulderado and are cleaning it up. They have saved the magnificent lobby with its glass dome and the stairway and banisters made of cherrywood. Now on the Victorian mezzanine lounge overlooking the lobby string quartets and a brass ensemble give concerts. The hotel has attracted no less a guest than Joan Mondale."
—*David Wigg*

Open all year.
53 rooms, 35 with private bath.
Rates $14 single, $25 double. Special weekly rates $85–$160.
Credit cards: Master Charge, Visa.
Bar, entertainment.
French and Spanish spoken.

Denver

The Brown Palace
321 17th Street
Denver, Colorado   80202
Telephone: (303) 825-3111

"This is Denver's answer to the Plaza in New York. Or, more likely, it is what the Plaza would like to be. Anyone who knows the Brown Palace will try to get a room in the old wing. (The new wing, known as the tower, is motelish.) There is an interior court and a stained-glass ceiling in the lobby, which rises nine floors. An American flag hangs from the seventh to the fourth floor. There is a wonderful bar and grill called the Ship's Tavern, with a bartender who really knows how to mix drinks. In the heart of the downtown district, the Brown Palace, which opened in 1892, dates back to the time when visitors arrived by Pullman."   —*Jack Goodman*

Open all year.
476 rooms, all with private bath.
Rates $35–$300.
Credit cards: American Express, Carte Blanche, Diners Club, Master Charge, Visa.
French, German, Greek, Italian and Spanish spoken.

Durango

The General Palmer House
567 Main Avenue
Durango, Colorado   81301
Telephone: (303) 247-4747

"Last summer I took a Continental Trailways' Southwest Tour and the most interesting place I visited was the General Palmer House. It's a modern, charming and moderately-priced hotel in Gay Nineties decor, close to the historic, narrow-gauge railroad depot. The train, a pioneer steam-powered passenger train, makes a run from Durango to Silverton, one of the most rugged, most spectacular stretches of scenery in the whole southwest of Colorado. The General Palmer House has the Grande Palace Restaurant and the Prospector Lounge."

—*Lucille Bates*

"The hotel is centrally located for a visit to the Mesa Verde cliff dwellings, fishing or a visit to the streams and lakes in the nearby San Juan Mountains, and in winter months convenient for skiing and other winter sports at the Purgatory Ski Resort."   —*C. R. Ellsworth*

Open all year.
35 rooms, all with private bath.
Rates $28 single, $34 double.
Credit cards: American Express, Diners Club, Master Charge, Visa.

Strater Hotel
699 Main Avenue
Durango, Colorado   81301
Telephone: (303) 247-4431

"The Strater Hotel is a place that converts overnighters into habitués, and habitués into addicts. Every room pleases: dining rooms, Diamond Belle Saloon, Diamond Circle Theatre, lobbies and shops—but best are the splendid bedrooms. The whole place is furnished in genuine Victorian antiques, no two rooms alike. It's like visiting the mansion of a fabled grandmother who has maintained myriad family treasures in mint condition—plus laid on impeccable plumbing, unobtrusive individual thermostats and three-way light bulbs that work three ways. This is the place to headquarter while you explore the Four Corners marvels which range from San Juan alpine wilderness to Navajo desert. Possibilities unlimited: ski Purgatory, kibitz the local cattle auction, visit Mesa Verde, ride the Silverton train, and much, more more.

"By the time you start to become an habitué, you'll find the staff will give you special coddling, and you'll love wallowing in all that Victorian elegance. In our family there are three generations of addicts; love's labor by the present owners makes it better every year. One caution: Try the Strater at least slightly out of season. They tend to bring in busloads of tour groups. In season, make reservations well in advance."

—*Betty Feazel*

"Durango, an historic little city nestled in the San Juan Mountains, surely must be the most beautiful place in the United States, as well as the friendliest. The Strater is a Durango landmark and has been privately owned since 1882. The present owners, Mr. and Mrs. Earl Barker, and their fine staff, make every effort to make their guests feel welcome. The theater offers family entertainment in the summer: vaudeville acts and plays from the early 1900s. There are two very fine restaurants in the Strater—the Columbian Room and the Opera House Restaurant. Our favorite is the Opera House—we've enjoyed many wonderful meals there, and the decor is lovely. In the summer, the guests are entertained by singers from the theater. After dinner, or the theater performance, you need not leave the hotel for further entertainment. Just step through the lobby and enter the doors of the famous Diamond Belle Saloon. Guests, visitors and local people gather here to enjoy a drink, the honky-tonk piano, singing and visiting, all in a Gay Nineties atmosphere.

"History is not left behind when you step out of the Strater. Two blocks to the east is Rio Grande Land—an area of shops and restaurants restored to reflect the turn of the century. Nearby is the Durango and Rio Grande Depot, home of the famous D&RG Narrow Gauge Railroad. In the summer, this little train chugs its way forty-four miles north to the historic little mining town of Silverton. Just a few miles west is the historic Mesa Verde National Park. It's a fascinating place to take the family to view Indian life of long ago."

—*Linda and Alberta Word*

Open all year.
94 rooms, all with private bath.
Rates $22–$28 single, $22–$32 double, $28–$40 triple or quadruple.
  Ski packages; special rates for government or educational groups.
Credit cards: American Express, Carte Blanche, Diners Club, Master Charge, Visa.
Bar, theater.
Spanish spoken.

_____*Redstone*

Historic Redstone Inn
0082 Redstone Boulevard
Redstone, Colorado 81623
Telephone: (303) 963-2526

John Cleveland Osgood was a financier, coal baron, industrialist and the business partner of such powerful men as J. P. Morgan and John D. Rockefeller. His cousin was Grover Cleveland, the twenty-second president of the United States. In the mining village of Redstone, Osgood built himself a manor house he called Cleveholm, chalets for the married miners and the Redstone Inn for bachelor employees and guests. The inn, built in 1902, was a copy of a Dutch tavern. It had a barber shop, electric lights, a laundry, telephone and steam heat.

"The inn has been kept very much the same as it was in those early days. The rooms are pleasant and comfortable, and the food excellent. The drive from Denver to Redstone is spectacular scenery all the way—through the Eisenhower tunnel to Dillon and Vail, along the Colorado River through Glenwood Canyon, along the Roaring Fork River to Carbondale, then eighteen miles south along the Crystal River to Redstone. Only ten miles to the south of Redstone is Marble, now a ghost town but once the place where high-grade Colorado Yule marble was quarried, from 1907 to 1941. The Redstone Inn is the real Colorado. There are no 'strangers' there, and you have no feeling that you are 'hitting the tourist trail.' "   —*Harriett Morgan*

Open all year.
26 rooms, all with private bath.
Rates $26–$32.
Credit cards: Master Charge, Visa.
Bar, pool, tennis.
Spanish spoken.

Kansas

Harper

Rosalea's Hotel
121 West Main Street
Harper, Kansas   67058
No telephone.

"Rosalea is a frustrated artist. And if artists cannot get recognition or sell their work, then they have to find some other outlet. For Rosalea it is her hotel, in the most unlikely place of Harper—a prosperous, neat community set in the vast wheat-fields of southern Kansas, where the sky comes down to the horizon in all directions.

"This must be America's most eccentric hotel—in the nicest possible sense of the word. In 1968 Rosalea bought the old, decaying hotel in town, a town too small even for the local youths to bother to drag the main street on Saturday nights. She painted the outside of the building red, made part of it an art gallery filled with her own work, called it 'the oasis in the Bible Belt,' gave an understanding ear to the young and the less conventional—and earned the opposition of the intensely conservative townsfolk. They considered her to be a 'hippie' and things far worse.

"She refused to give up through many frugal years and has just completed her tenth year there. A sign in her window, next to two strange, illuminated glass ducks, reads: 'Harper, Kansas, laughed and said it could not be done. Happy tenth Birthday, Rosalea's.'

"Sometimes I almost think that she does not want any guests at all. She has had the telephone removed, so that the only way to get a reservation is to write in advance and include one night's payment. And I heard her murmur recently (I'm not sure whether she was serious) that she was thinking of having a compulsory intelligence test for her potential guests, as she was tired of having unintelligent people stay with her. Groups of six people and more are not encouraged as 'the hotel is not staffed to handle group madness.' She refuses to let you look at any of the rooms in advance before deciding whether to stay—she is tired of having Harper citizens, agog with curiosity, paying nothing and wandering around upstairs, convinced that they are on a grand tour of a brothel.

"She wants interesting people to come and stay, particularly visual artists. She has a special offer whereby an artist (a painter, a photographer, a printmaker) can have a free one- or two-week stay in return for a piece of art. which will be placed on permanent display in the hotel.

"And what are the rooms really like? Is it worth the effort to defeat the obstacles strewn in your path to become an overnight guest? I think so. The rooms have a flavor of the 1960s about them. I have stayed in Room 7, a special honor, as it was the first to be officially decorated. A sign on the wall reads: 'I expect more people have made love in this room since 1968 than in any other room in the hotel.'

"The walls are covered with foil, and on the ceiling is a montage of pictures of famous people such as Nixon, Kennedy and Pope John, and civil rights marchers. A tailor's dummy models a belt and a scarf created by Rosalea, and by the side is a message complaining that no one bought it, so it has been relegated to the Upstairs Permanent Collection. 'How our stupid society,' it concludes, 'loves to see artists struggle and suffer.'

"The room is surprisingly comfortable. The bed is on a raised platform; there is another of those strange ducks in the window; there are two cane chairs originating from the Methodist Church; a fan, and a radio that doesn't turn off unless you unplug it. The bathroom is warm, carpeted, lace-curtained and boasts a handsome tub. There is more sculpture on the walls and a jar of pretty paper flowers sits on the toilet cistern.

"Much of the ground floor is a huge lobby—a fine place with a long, wooden table (ideal to sit around and pound and argue the existence or nonexistence of a deity). The artwork on the walls is made of colored crepe paper, and there are many books, a box filled with 'nice objects to handle' and, in one corner, the office, known as the 'disaster area.'

"And Kansas is not a state that exists just to fly over or to drive through as quickly as possible to get somewhere else. Certainly it still has odd liquor laws (Prohibition lasted until 1948, when it was known as the 'almost dry state'), but it is a state, like many in this part of the country, that grows on you and is hard to forget. It is an awesome experience to drive out into the broad expanses of fields, especially in summer, and see the miles and miles and miles of healthy wheat, or to spot on the horizon a huge cathedral-like grain elevator and watch it grow larger and larger as you approach."   —*David Wigg*

Open May 1 to Labor Day.

12 rooms.

Rates $12.50–$19.50 single, $17.50–$25.50 double. Weekly: 7 nights for the price of 5. Monthly: 4 weeks for the price of 3. Artists: 1- or 2-week stay traded for piece of art.

There is no telephone, so all reservations must be by letter, accompanied by one night's payment in advance. Add 3 percent Kansas state tax.

No credit cards.

*Sagebrush Inn,
Taos*

New Mexico

El Prado

Hacienda de San Roberto
P.O. Box 449
El Prado, New Mexico   87529
Telephone: (505) 776-2630

"Tucked into a New Mexico mountainside, the Hacienda lies roughly midway between Taos and the spectacular Taos ski area. On arrival you are made to feel that each and every member of the Hacienda's management family has been waiting just for you—so warm and personal is the welcome. A complimentary margarita (superb) is brought to your unostentatious but thoroughly comfortable apartment, a crackling piñon wood fire lit in your own adobe fireplace, and you settle in with a purr of complete contentment. So far, our family has enjoyed the pleasures of the Hacienda—the delectable food, warm sun on the terrace with the mountains as a backdrop, the heated swimming pool and adjoining Jacuzzi for overworked muscles and the evenings of Spanish guitar and New Mexico song in the crowded living room—only in late-winter ski season. But we plan to return to the Hacienda in summer and fall—not the least of the reasons being that my nonskiing husband, who normally avoids ski resorts and their denizens like the plague, fell in love with the place (having once been inveigled there) and can't wait to go back to its comforts. As a headquarters from which to explore the Indian pueblos, Spanish villages and the almost endless variety of arts, archeology and scenery of northern New Mexico, the Hacienda is without compare. No request for a particular favorite meal, a ride to the ski area or town, advice on where to find what in Taos, surrounding pueblos or even Santa Fe is too much trouble for the accommodating innkeepers."   —*Mr. and Mrs. R. H. Mix*

Open from Thanksgiving through Easter, and Memorial Day until late October.
5 suites, all with private bath.
Rates $44–$59 in summer. From $40–$50 in winter, including three meals. Special skiers and nonskiers packages.
Credit cards: American Express, Master Charge, Visa.
Bar, heated pool, Jacuzzi, library, sauna.

_____*Pecos*

Tres Lagunas
Route 2, Box 100
Pecos, New Mexico   87552
Telephone: (505) 757-6194

"We have spent about ten days every summer for thirty years here. Tres Lagunas is a beautiful guest ranch of three lakes at an elevation of 7,500 feet in the Sangre de Cristo Mountains, on the Pecos River less than an hour from historic Santa Fe. Modern cabins with fireplaces and maid service, plus excellent meals served in a dining room overlooking a waterfall, allow an entire family time to relax, fish, read, hike, horseback ride, shop in Santa Fe or see the mountains and the scenic area around, which is steeped in Indian, Spanish, Mexican, New Mexican and Anglo history."   —*Fred Zimmerman, Jr.*

Open Memorial Day to Labor Day.
5 rooms in lodge, 6 cabins sleeping 4 to 8.
Rates $47 single in lodge, 6-person cabin $225, 4-person cabin $150, deluxe cabin $63 single, $50 double per person. Children free to age 5; $27.50 each, ages 6 through 11. All rates include three meals.
Credit cards: Master Charge, Visa.
Bar, pool, horseback riding.
Spanish spoken.
Guests met at Lamy railroad station or at Santa Fe municipal airport.

Santa Fe

The Inn at Loretto
211 Old Santa Fe Trail
Santa Fe, New Mexico   87501
Telephone: (505) 988-5531

"This is a charming Old World inn of quiet elegance. The classic adobe style of the building is consistent inside and out. The plaza, heart of Santa Fe, is only a block away, as are many of the best shops and museums. The rooms are appointed simply yet most comfortably. There is adequate parking, but you walk most places in Santa Fe."   —*Harry Kennedy, Jr.*

Open all year.
141 rooms, all with private bath.
Rates $36–$44 single, $44–$60 double, $85–$125 suites.
Special monthly rates.
Credit cards: American Express, Carte Blanche, Diners Club, Master Charge, Visa.
Bar, sauna, shops, swimming pool.
Spanish spoken.

La Fonda
100 East San Francisco Street
Santa Fe, New Mexico   87501
Telephone: (505) 982-5511

"La Fonda—the inn at the end of the Santa Fe trail—makes much of its past. In the hotel that stood on that site in the 19th century, Captain Stephen Watts Kearney celebrated his conquest of New Mexico for the United States, General H. H. Sibley was quartered when the Confederates took the city in 1862, General and Mrs. Ulysses S. Grant danced at a grand ball in 1880, and no less a person than Billy the Kid washed dishes in the kitchen. However, that building was demolished in 1919 and the present soft-cornered pueblo-style hotel took its place. It dominates the surprisingly small, modest plaza (nothing grandiose here, nothing to compare with many of those dramatic plazas in Mexican cities), reflecting the fact that Santa Fe was a minor, northern outpost of the Mexican empire.

"Lobbies of large hotels in the middle of towns should be lively, bristling with gossip: a place for meeting people by arrangement or unexpectedly. Too few still have that function now. La Fonda has been and still is the city's meeting place. Its tiled lobby is large, ideal for sitting and watching, while just to one side is the Plazuela, an enclosed patio, where food is served from early in the morning until late at night. It's often crowded and consequently the service is sometimes slow, but that may be because diners, understandably, tend to linger over their food (the sunlight streaming through the glass roof) and they are rarely in a great rush to let someone else have their tables. The bedrooms are traditional New Mexican, which means fine wooden furniture. The atmosphere, described by the owners as 'the rustic elegance of Spanish hospitality' (well, yes, we know what they mean) is relaxing.

"Outside on the plaza, walk slowly in the clean thin air. The height is 6,999 feet above sea level, so it is cool in the shade and in the evenings. In front of you is a slice of New Mexican history—the Palace of the Governors built in 1610 and the open-air market where the Indians continue the tradition of selling jewelry and leather goods. There are many restaurants within walking distance—gentle places with good jazz and soft-spoken waitresses and satisfying, if not too adventurous, food. But the whole atmosphere of Santa Fe is like that—tranquil and accepting.

"There is no problem about getting transportation to the airport, but be warned that if you arrive, as I did, on one of the not-too-frequent Amtrak trains, do not expect a busy station, a line of cabs and noisy hustling taxi drivers. The station is miles from the city, and when the train pulls out, you can be left standing alone and seemingly abandoned in glorious countryside, like a Hitchcock hero waiting for something threatening to happen. I could not persuade a taxi to come out from the city, nor could the only railroad official offer any suggestion. Luckily, I hitched a ride with a young couple—studious and calm (even though the back seat was aswarm with progeny). You can probably persuade the taxi to make the journey out from the city but reserve one well in advance—the porter in the lobby will probably help."   —*David Wigg*

"The food is not wonderful, but La Fonda itself is absolutely charming."   —*Wendy Werris*

Open all year.
170 rooms, all with private bath.
Rates $35–$45 single, $41–$51 double. 10 percent discount for senior citizens. Special ski packages.
Credit cards: American Express, Carte Blanche, Diners Club, Master Charge, Visa.
Bar, pool. 16 miles from Santa Fe Ski Basin.
Spanish spoken.
Shuttlejack limousine service provides transportation from Albuquerque airport to the hotel.

Taos

La Fonda
Box 1447
Taos, New Mexico   87571
Telephone: (505) 758-2211

"The literary industry that surrounds the work of D. H. Lawrence is getting a little out of hand, and literary pilgrimages can be a bit phony. But during his gypsy life Lawrence did spend some time in spectacular places, and this was one of them. Here in the mountains of northern New Mexico he lived for a while with his wife, Frieda, and after he died in Europe in 1930 she had his ashes brought here from France to be placed in a tiny building a few yards from their ranch house. Frieda is buried beneath a massive stone slab a few paces to one side. The ranch house is now owned by the University of New Mexico. The place was deserted when I arrived there early one morning in March—just a few friendly donkeys ambling about. The view is worth the short climb: An avenue of pine trees slopes down the hill to the long, long stretch across the valley floor leading to the distant, snow-capped mountains. The visitors' book at Lawrence's grave is interesting to glance through. The pilgrims, inspired perhaps by the clear air, quote his poems or lapse into their own versions of Lawrentian free verse.

"The ranch is a few miles north of the tiny town of Taos, with its buildings of adobe. On one side of the minute plaza is the La Fonda hotel, with its fine, high-ceilinged lobby, fireplace and walls covered with art, weaving and photographs. On his office walls, the manager has a few of Lawrence's erotic paintings that, unbelievably, caused so much official outrage when they were exhibited in London in the 1920s. Guests of the hotel may look at the paintings, but frankly, they are not very good and certainly not very erotic. There are also photographs in the office of some of the literary personalities who at one time or another made their way through this part of New Mexico.

"La Fonda's bedrooms are smallish, neat and agreeably simple. You can eat at one of the restaurants nearby—one has a veranda overlooking the Taos plaza, where local artists and drop-outs, as well as more conservative types, lounge during happy hour. There is an Indian pueblo on the outskirts of town and a Kit Carson museum full of bric-a-brac."   —*David Wigg*

Open all year.
22 rooms, 19 with private bath.
Rates $21.40 single, $32.10 double.
No credit cards.
Restaurant and bar.
Spanish spoken.

Sagebrush Inn
P.O. Box 1566
South Santa Fe Road
Taos, New Mexico   87571
Telephone: (505) 758-2254

"The town of Taos is not a melting pot, but rather a potpourri of Taos Indians (the original inhabitants), Hispanics descended from the conquistadores and what are loosely referred to as Anglos. For years it has been a haven for artists, lovers of nature and beauty and seekers of an independent and unhurried life-style. The Sagebrush Inn also has these characteristics. The decor of the lodge and the guest rooms includes some fine paintings. The lovely view from the north window of the Sangre de Cristo range and mystical Taos Mountain, the sight through the 'geranium window' of the Talpa Mountains, the enclosed open-roof intimate patio dining area and the garden patio for noon luncheons all give meals something special to look forward to.

"The inn is a social mecca for the townspeople and has more native flavor of Taos than any other hotel in town. The large lobby, bar and entertainment area complete with piñon wood in the fireplace, southwestern artifacts and giant tumbleweeds on the rafters, lends itself to comfortable socializing. Just to take a seat there is to be involved within minutes in conversation with someone, perhaps a resident artist (R. C. Gorman is a Sagebrush regular), classical singers, guitarists, actors, silversmiths, miners, ballerinas, gallery owners or animal trappers. Several nights a week there is musical entertainment. If one prefers more privacy, there are waiters who will gladly and promptly bring dinner or drinks to the rooms. There is horseback riding from the inn's stable, tennis, swimming, hiking in the nearby pastures or sunning in the courtyard. The town of Taos offers some eighty art galleries, many unusual shops, jewelry stores, shopping malls, madrigal singers, live theater, movies, challenging ski slopes and breathtaking views in every direction."   —*Marilyn Foust*

Open all year.
32 rooms, all with private bath.
Rates $20 single, $30 double.
Credit cards: American Express, Carte Blanche, Diners Club, Master Charge, Visa.
Bar, pool, riding, skiing, tennis.
French, German and Spanish spoken.

Oklahoma

Tulsa

The Hotel Mayo
Box 2101
Fifth and Cheyenne
Tulsa, Oklahoma   74101
Telephone: (918) 583-2141

"Should you be going to Tulsa soon, insist on staying at the Mayo hotel downtown near Fifth and Cheyenne. This marvelous old hotel, built in 1925, is being lovingly restored and all that is good is being carefully retained—the crystal chandeliers, the honest-to-goodness heavy ceramic tiles, the carved moldings, the intricate wood paneling, the polished brass handrails, the marble stairs leading upward and onward to even more fascinating nooks and crannies tucked away on the mezzanine, the marble baseboards and wainscoting in public rooms, the tables with legs thick as tree trunks and, on top of all this, the friendliest soul sister this side of the Mississippi hovering about in the coffee shop.

"It may take an extra minute or so to figure out how to operate all the dials and faucets that control the old-time showers in the suites, but the rewarding geysers of steaming water make the challenge worth the effort. Nary a speck of masquerading plastic did I spy anywhere on the premises. Right now I'm looking for some kind of excuse (any old kind will do, thank you) to get me back down that highway to Tulsa. After a night of fun and frolic, it's fun strolling down those marble steps for hot coffee and boiled grits. Take me back to Tulsa. Who needs Paris in the spring?"
—*Jo Gardenhire*

Open all year.
450 rooms, all with private bath.

Rates $35 single, $41 double, suites $45–$250. Special weekly and
monthly rates.

Two restaurants, coffee shop, private club.

Credit cards: American Express, Carte Blanche, Diners Club, Master Charge, Visa.

French and German spoken.

Texas

El Paso

Hotel Paso del Norte
115 South El Paso Street
El Paso, Texas   79901
Telephone: (915) 533-2421

"They say more cattle have been traded in the lobby of the Hotel Paso del Norte than any other place in the world. This legend just might be true—the hotel has been home away from home to cattlemen of the American Southwest since it opened on Thanksgiving Day in 1912. The dream hotel of Zach T. White, pioneer El Paso businessman and developer, has been the showplace of the community ever since. A favorite headquarters for conventions of all sizes, the hotel is located just a block from the Convention Center and from two bus terminals, near the train terminal and convenient to transportation to Ciudad Juarez, fifth largest city in Mexico, which lies just across the bridge at the far end of El Paso Street.

"The Ben Dowell Saloon, which opened in 1978, has waitresses in can-can outfits and antique furnishings as a reminder that the hotel stands on the site of El Paso's most famous early saloon, operated by Dowell, a veteran of the Mexican War and the town's first mayor in 1873. On the opposite side of the spacious lobby is the Union Depot restaurant and bar, also in period decor reflecting the town's heritage as a cross-country and international rail center. The hotel's east entrance opens on the Camino Real, the trade route between Santa Fe and Mexico City when the area was part of New Spain. The lobby itself—where cattle trading takes place in hushed voices—is notable for walls faced with cherrystone, golden scagliola and black serpentine marble, and is dominated by an awesome Tiffany stained-glass dome. The hotel remained in the family of Zach White until 1971 when his daughters sold it to the TGK Investment Company."   —*Nancy Hamilton*

Open all year.
130 rooms, all with private bath.
Rates $22 single, $25–$29 double, $21–$85 suites. Special weekly and monthly rates.
Credit cards: American Express, Carte Blanche, Diners Club, Master Charge, Visa.
Bar, walking distance from Mexico.
French and Spanish spoken.

_____*Jefferson*

Excelsior House
211 West Austin Street
Jefferson, Texas   75657
Telephone: (214) 665-2513

"The Excelsior House is—in my experience—one of America's unique and charming hotels. To me the fascinating thing about it is the picture it presents of a bygone way of life. To spend the night there is to take a step back in time. An ambiance of history fills every room. The Excelsior was built in the 1850s with a wing added about twenty years later. In the old, open hotel register you can see the names of several Presidents—Ulysses S. Grant, Rutherford B. Hayes and my husband, Lyndon. It is said that Robert E. Lee was also a guest. The pages are filled with the signatures of most of the famous players, minstrels, actors and drama groups that toured in the early days. What exciting visions they conjure up! The furnishings speak of that period of American history. The old player piano came from Europe to New Orleans and was shipped up the Mississippi to the Red River and then the Bayou. In the 1870s paddle steamers carrying both freight and passengers landed at Jefferson.

"A group of volunteers—the Jesse Allen Wise Garden Club—owns and operates the Excelsior. This remarkable group of women restored the old hotel to new life and usefulness—and the product they have created is marvelously inviting. They laughingly say that with all of them jointly deciding on wallpapers and resolving the problems of paying for the restoration, it was enough to give you hope that the United Nations itself might succeed." —*Mrs. Lyndon B. Johnson*

"A visit to the Excelsior House is a return to the late 19th century when Jefferson was a thriving center of commerce and shipping, with a population of over 35,000. In those days this was one of the great hotels of Texas. Among the visitors it attracted from all over the world were the Whitneys, Vanderbilts and Jay Gould, the great railroad tycoon whose private railroad car is still parked across the street from the hotel. Today the Excelsior stands in a Jefferson of under 3,000 people.

"The highlight of a stay at the Excelsior is breakfast in the garden, where Cissie McCampbell, the manager, serves her famous orange muffins, accompanied by perfectly prepared ham, eggs, grits and fresh orange juice." —*George Underwood III*

"Our favorite guest room is the Diamond Bessie Room, a room filled with early Texas furniture highlighted by a canopy bed and a solarium facing the courtyard. Our favorite pastime in the solarium is watching hundreds of hummingbirds feed on the flowers of the trumpet vines on an old brick wall."
—*Walter T. Osborn*

Open all year, except the first weekend in May.
14 rooms, all with private bath.
Rates $12–$14 single, $16–$18 double. Presidential suite $30. Children free.
No credit cards.
Only breakfast served.

New Jefferson Inn
124 Austin Street
Jefferson, Texas   75657
Telephone: (214) 665-2631

"Jefferson is a lovely place in the spring and fall, situated in the beautiful pine forests of northeast Texas. Once a booming town, it is now quiet and peaceful. The citizens, who care about their heritage, restored many of the lovely homes and the downtown historic area. One thing that cannot be restored is the river channel where palatial steamboats carried freight and passengers to New Orleans. Many a bride and groom spent their honeymoons, as did my parents, aboard the old paddlewheel boats on their way to Southern plantations on the Mississippi River in Louisiana. After some restoration, the New Jefferson Inn reopened recently to the delight of my husband

and myself. The inn has the air of the late 1800s in east Texas, with rooms furnished in the Victorian manner. The proprietor, 'Red,' makes everyone feel at home, serving delicious breakfasts of biscuits, ham, grits and eggs, as well as lunch. Dinner is served on weekends." —*Mr. and Mrs. Kenneth Wickett*

Open all year.
22 rooms, all with private bath.
Rates $20–$22.50. $30 suite.
No credit cards.

San Antonio

St. Anthony Hotel
300 East Travis
San Antonio, Texas   78205
Telephone: (512) 227-4392

"Overlooking a particularly hideous public square in downtown San Antonio, the St. Anthony is one of the last of the great old hotels of the American Southwest. Recently refurbished, the narrow but ornate marble lobby is a good place for an afternoon cocktail, the bar is small but superb and the two restaurants better than average. The larger restaurant serves Mexican specialties the day round and thus provides an interesting, if fiery, way to wake up at breakfast. Accommodations are large and comfortable, although leaning toward the striped-wallpaper school of decor, and there are the usual phones, color television and air-conditioning. The bathrooms are huge and equipped with all the usual conveniences, including a shower stall as large as an elevator. The staff is mostly young and very competent, with a sprinkling of old Mexican retainers whom nothing, absolutely nothing, surprises. Room service is a fair cut above the usual horror and there is parking on the premises." —*L. J. Davis*

Open all year.
400 rooms, all with private bath.
Rates $36–$40 single, $46–$50 double.
Credit cards: American Express, Carte Blanche, Diners Club, Master Charge, Visa.
Three bars, restaurants, nightly entertainment in the lobby bar.
French, German, Japanese and Spanish spoken.

Where are the good little hotels in Boston? Philadelphia? Omaha? Dallas? If you have found one, don't keep it a secret. Write *now*.

Part
Seven

Far West
and Hawaii

Arizona
California
Hawaii
Nevada
Utah

Arizona

Grand Canyon

El Tovar Hotel
Grand Canyon, Arizona   86023
Telephone: (602) 638-2631

"At the decidedly abrupt edge of the southern rim of the Grand
Canyon, at Bright Angel's Point, is this small hotel, which is
something of a lodge. Despite that identification, it is a very
grand place in the manner that a Teddy Roosevelt would appreciate. Canyon limestone and ponderosa pine logs make up
its structure. Its facade is abutted by a vast front porch with a
seemingly endless line of comfortable chairs arranged for maximum viewing of the canyon. Inside, its great hall is dominated
by one of the most vast chimney pieces ever conceived. The
rooms are ample, if somewhat rustic, and strenuously punctuated by the rhythmic insistency of the steam heat in the early
morning hours. El Tovar's food and drink—done in the tradition of the Santa Fe Railroad's Harvey Girls—is of high quality. The wine list, too, is probably one of the better ones in the
Southwest.

"El Tovar has always attracted a worldly society. Victoria
('Vita') Sackville-West spent a fair time in residence at the
lodge during World War II and celebrated it in a moving if epi-

sodic book recalling her life 'hibernating by the rim.' Scores of her countrymen have followed, undoubtedly attracted by the drama of her tome. The rooms, with their ample mullioned windows and their view, have inspired some of the great artists and photographers. One European diplomat said that El Tovar was one of America's great landmarks. I think him right. In a sense it serves as a chronicle of the Southwest from the days of the 'noble savage' to those of the Anglo rancher. El Tovar is used by all—artist, traveler, rancher and local."

—*Dr. Forest M. Hinkhouse*

Open all year.
123 rooms, all with private bath.
Rates $38–$42, $70–$85 suites.
Credit cards: American Express, Carte Blanche, Diners Club, Master Charge, Visa.
Bar, hiking, mule rides.

Paradise Valley

Hermosa Inn
5532 North Palo Cristi Road
Paradise Valley, Arizona   85253
Telephone: (602) 955-8660

Lon Megargee, a cowboy artist, built this rambling hacienda in 1930, guided by inspiration and without, the story goes, formal blueprints. He had completed some paintings for the Arizona State Capitol. He later became better known for his paintings called *Black Bart* and *Cowboy's Dream.* When Megargee decided to move on, he left behind a building that became a guest ranch. Much of the original structure is still there: the beehive fireplaces, the secret passages and huge doors.

"The inn has a resort feeling within what could be considered metropolitan Phoenix. The fun and pleasures of the city's restaurants, museums and shopping areas are only minutes away by car. Yet the inn is in a residential area, which creates a noncommercial atmosphere. Although rooms have been added, the old charm of the old home remains. There is a delightful dining room where good food and a fireplace (burning in season) add to the ambiance. The grounds are magnificently landscaped in the cacti and rock motif typical of the area. There are tennis courts for those who insist on activity, and a pool that is part of the lovely setting. One of the loveliest experiences is staying in a *casita,* a small apartment where one can enjoy a quiet breakfast overlooking the desert garden. From the inn, Camelback Mountain is clearly and magnificently present."

—*Muriel Burnstein*

Closed from June 15 to August 31.
20 rooms, 4 villas, all with private bath.
Rates $36–$45 single, $36–$90 double, $80–$150 villas (2 bedrooms).
Credit cards: American Express, Master Charge, Visa.
Bar, pool, tennis, shuffleboard, bicycles to rent.
French, German, Italian and Spanish spoken.

_____*Scottsdale*

The Inn at McCormick Ranch
7401 North Scottsdale Road
Scottsdale, Arizona   85253
Telephone: (602) 948-5050

"The Inn at McCormick Ranch is not typically Arizonan. It is a green oasis in the desert. While many other resorts emphasize the Western atmosphere, McCormick features rolling lawns shaded with numerous trees and a lake. It is almost like a transplanted Eastern inn, although the architecture of the buildings is Mexican-Western. We had a very spacious corner suite overlooking the lake and enjoyed the privacy of a small balcony—privacy, that is, if you don't count the ducks, geese and a lone pelican who adopted us after we shared our breakfast with them. There are sailboats and pedal-boats on the lake and fishing equipment can be rented if you wish to try your luck. There is a swimming pool near the bar and restaurant. The only complaint I would have is that there were not enough umbrellas near the pool for redheads like me, who burn to a crisp without beneficial shade.

"There is only one restaurant on the premises and, if you wish to enjoy a window table overlooking the lawns and the lake, it is a good idea to make an early reservation. The food is not of gourmet standards but good, and the service, by a very young staff, is smiling, courteous and efficient. Try the bison steak—a different and quite palatable experience. Each afternoon in the bar, you can also order a shrimp basket for the modest sum of 50 cents. The inn has a small boutique where you will find all that you have forgotten at home. And, a nice touch, the lady who runs the place will ask you if you wish to reserve a newspaper since they sell out very quickly. She will save it for you and it will be brought up to your room with your breakfast tray."
—*Louisa L. Becker*

Open all year.
126 rooms, all with private bath.
Rates $20–$76 single, $25–$82 double, depending on the season.
Credit cards: American Express, Carte Blanche, Master Charge, Visa.

Golf, tennis, pool, Jacuzzi, sauna, sailing, boating, putting green, shuffleboard, bar.
German and Spanish spoken.

Tucson

Arizona Inn
2200 East Elm Street
Tucson, Arizona   85719
Telephone: (602) 325-1541

"Every desert city, be it Marrakech or Tucson, has its oasis, its caravansary. Not too far from the heart of Tucson—and hard by the University of Arizona—is the Arizona Inn. There, within a dozen acres, are immaculate gardens. The inn's dusty pink walls, decidedly Andalusian in feeling, are elaborated with wood and iron grilles and endless cascades of flowers. Within the rooms are creature comforts that echo a taste of a more leisurely age. Lunch is served beside a cobalt-blue pool. The food is imaginative. An endless mosaic of salads tempts all but a diet-stricken Hollywood starlet. Dinner in the cathedral-ceilinged great hall is likely to be preceded by drinks in the adjacent cantina. The university provides a rich offering of concerts, exhibitions and even planetary viewing in the recently completed observatory. Those doggedly searching for the exotic can take a run down to the nearby border town of Nogales, where fun and games are available for all tastes."
—*Dr. Forest M. Hinkhouse*

Open all year.
85 rooms, all with private bath.
Rates $29–$43 single, $37–$48 double, from May 1 to December 31.
   $56–$82 single, $62–$88 double, from January 1 to April 30.
   American plan and MAP available.
Credit cards: American Express, Carte Blanche, Master Charge, Visa.
Bar, heated pool, English croquet, putting green, tennis.
French, German and Spanish spoken.

Hacienda del Sol
Hacienda del Sol Road
Tucson, Arizona   85718
Telephone: (602) 299-1501

"The hacienda is in the foothills of the Santa Catalina Mountains, two miles outside the city of Tucson. In 1930 it was developed as a private school for asthmatic girls, mostly from the

East: New York, Boston and Philadelphia. The original building was designed along Spanish lines of adobe materials, thus maintaining the Spanish and Western character. In 1941 the school failed and the property was sold and developed as a resort. The building required considerable alteration, such as converting single rooms to double and constructing a new dining room and kitchen. Since then there have been some four or five owners, each one making improvements and building cottages, owners' apartments, a swimming pool, recreation buildings, exercise rooms, tennis courts and a corral. The food is excellent; the chef is from Norway and serves on the King of Norway's yacht in the summer months when the hacienda is closed."

—*R. T. Johnstone; also recommended by Robert Acomb*

Open November 1 to May 1.
36 rooms, 7 suites, all with private bath.
Rates $45–$65 single, $85–$100 double, $125 suites, including meals. Special family rates.
No credit cards.
Bar, heated pool, riding, shuffleboard, tennis, therapy pool.
German, Norwegian and Swedish spoken.

The Lodge on the Desert
306 North Alvernon Way
Tucson, Arizona   85733
Telephone: (602) 325-3366

"This is a sprawling combination of large, Spanish-style rooms, many with beehive fireplaces. The center of the grounds is the pool area, which is beautifully landscaped and has a tranquil view of the mountains in the distance. Here is an oasis of peace and quiet right in the heart of the city—although sometimes you can hear traffic noise. The restaurant is very good. There are many pleasant diversions in the area, best of which is the natural beauty of the desert."   —*Muriel Burnstein*

Open all year.
35 rooms, all with private bath.
Rates $52–$84 single, $68–$100 double, including three meals, from December 15 to May 1. Lower rates other times. European plan also available.
Credit cards: Master Charge, Visa.
Bar, swimming pool.
Spanish spoken.

La Valencia Hotel,
La Jolla

California

Beverly Hills

L'Ermitage
9291 Burton Way
Beverly Hills, California   90210
Telephone: (213) 278-3344

"It is beautiful, it is quiet, old-fashioned, gracious and elegant, with touches that almost all over the world disappeared with World War Two—and you can really call it a hotel. It has no rooms, only suites, all beautifully appointed. There are no convention crowds, no noisy groups, no boisterous guests. The street is almost like a street in Paris with its trees, boutiques and sidewalks wide enough and safe enough to take a stroll. The restaurant serves excellent food and is for the exclusive use of hotel guests. If you prefer room service, you will receive hot food, beautifully presented and graciously served. There is a fireplace in your suite, you receive a daily newspaper and, if you leave your shoes at your door (oh, French hotels of my youth revisited), they will be polished before you wake. That 'ne plus ultra' is L'Ermitage." —*Louisa L. Becker*

Open all year.
120 suites, all with private bath.

Rates $95–$350, including continental breakfast.
Credit cards: American Express, Diners Club, Master Charge, Visa.
Bar, rooftop pool, Jacuzzi, 24-hour room service.
French, German, Italian, Russian and Spanish spoken.

Big Sur

The Ventana Inn
Big Sur, California   93920
Telephone: (408) 667-2331

"Some of its early guests—scarcely two years ago—saw the
Ventana as a sort of California equivalent to an excellent country inn somewhere along a French coastline. To me, that pa-
tently slick simplification is only a partial description. Furthermore, it is somewhat demeaning.

"Ventana, perched on a ridge of the coastal mountains bearing the same name, is decidedly much more. It is an environment that celebrates its magnificent situation. The wise man
behind the idea had the singularly good taste to select Kipp
Stewart—an internationally known designer who happened to
live nearby on an adjacent escarpment—to be his 'taste-maker.'
Stewart saw the situation there on the precipitous cliffs of the
country called Big Sur—with its endlessly ramified forests on
one side and the limitless Pacific on the other—as an opportunity to design a very special establishment. Moreover, he saw
that the situation allowed for two areas of physical concentration. The living accommodations, with its pool and saunas and
morning room, were situated away from the relative hurly-
burly of the restaurant and bar and its continguous general
store. The latter sells nearly everything within the human
ken—as well as the handsome canvases of Stewart himself.

"The bar and restaurant are capacious, done in low-keyed—
yet psychologically warm—tones which force the guest's eye
beyond to the sea and to the mountains. From them, presum-
ably, he receives his strength. Banquettes are upholstered in
handsome Oriental rugs and heavily textured stuff.

"All, however, had been set as a stage for the superb cuisine
of Jeremiah Tower. He, like Ventana's 'patron,' was determined to bring a grand cuisine to an inn removed from the
nearest centers of population—Carmel and Monterey—by
nearly an hour. Tower's paternal grandfather had lived in the
former when it was thought to be an artists' colony and was
known in most circles as Carmel-by-the-Sea. The grandson, the
chef, had a great deal of the poet in him when he first came to
the inn. He had also the determination, buttressed with knowl-

edge and credentials, to create a temple of food rather than just another very, very beautiful roadhouse there on Highway One—the Great Pacific Route. He introduced the finest of regional food, using the best of local raw materials of the area. Fortunately, the fish and the shrimp and the beef and the wild boar—all on the very ample yet disciplined menu—were all available locally. Specialty items, all very important in the final analysis, had to be shipped from San Francisco, nearly 150 miles away. The operative word was logistics.

"After the Lucullan repast, the guest is delighted to stroll through the copse to his quarters. There, all is wonderfully quiet except for the tranquilizing murmur of the wind in the pines. The rooms, extraordinarily commodious, lend themselves to quiet comfort and reflection. The cares of the city seem light years away and sleep comes easily. In the morning a breakfast tray can be brought to your room where you may elect to enjoy it on your balcony overlooking the land Robinson Jeffers so loved and heralded in his verse.

"If you prefer, you can go to the morning room and enjoy your juice, brioche and coffee with other guests. Chances are, however, that they may be over a book while they sip their coffee. Ventana, in the final analysis, is a very private place."

—*Dr. Foust M. Hinkhouse*

"The Ventana Inn, set on the side of a hill in the sheltering woods across the road from the drama of the Big Sur coast, is in complete harmony with the surrounding wilderness. The separate structures have the clean, natural lines and casual community that we Easterners associate with the California spirit. Each suite has blond wood walls, a private porch and brightly colored quilts that match their crafted headboards. Even the soap is true to the naturalness of the whole. Breakfast is shared by all the guests around the fire in the main house. A neighboring general store offers local wine (not especially recommended) and Monterey Jack cheese for picnics on the beach."

—*Laura Rose Handman*

Open all year.

24 rooms, all with private bath.

Rates $67–$87 double, $150 suite, including breakfast. Two-night minimum on weekends.

Credit cards: American Express, Carte Blanche, Diners Club, Master Charge, Visa.

Hiking, saunas.

French and Spanish spoken.

Rates quoted were the latest available. But they may not reflect unexpected increases or local and state taxes. Be sure to verify when you book.

Carmel

Normandy Inn
P.O. Box 1706
Carmel, California   93921
Telephone: (408) 624-3825

"Carmel is an enchanting area divided by Ocean Avenue with its wide spreading palms, groups of rhododendrons and other colorful flowers in season. On either side of the avenue are small shops, packed closely together. There is a clean, sandy beach where children and dogs run freely, joggers take their daily exercise, families picnic, enthusiastic surfers enjoy their sport and sandcastles are built in competition. Only a few blocks east of the ocean—beyond which and within easy walking distance are a concert hall, a theater, a movie house, innumerable art galleries and restaurants—stands the Normandy Inn. The front steps are decorated with blooming flowers. The walk leading to the newer rooms is lined with potted geraniums, and beyond that is a garden patio with easy chairs and a heated swimming pool. Just across the side street are two cottages with enclosed patios. The main office is small, neat, unpretentious. Adjoining it is the breakfast room where a fine continental breakfast is served. In the Normandy-style section of the inn, around a courtyard, are double rooms with bathrooms, well-furnished tiny kitchens and a space with mirrors and drawers. Some of the double rooms have fireplaces in addition to steam heat, where hearth fires, if needed, are laid daily with wood provided by the management. Having traveled abroad and in this country I have chosen to return to the Normandy for twelve successive years because I consider it a most unusual place to stay for a few weeks."

—*Frederica Mitchell; also recommended by*
Robert Hochhauser

Open all year.
45 rooms plus three houses, all with private bath.
Rates $20–$39 single, $36–$41 double, $57–$61 suites, $67–$85 homes, including continental breakfast.
No meals except breakfast.
No credit cards.

Pine Inn
Ocean Avenue
Carmel, California   93921
Telephone: (408) 624-3851

"This turn-of-the-century inn, which still maintains its Victorian flavor, is on busy Ocean Avenue. Always good, with a charming atmosphere, and right in the heart of Carmel for those who like to wander through the shops and the art galleries." —*Mrs. Bartley M. Harloe*

Open all year.
49 rooms, all with private bath.
Rates $27–$70.
Credit cards: American Express, Master Charge, Visa.
Bar, beach swimming.

The Sandpiper Inn
2408 Bayview Avenue
Carmel, California   93923
Telephone: (408) 624-6433

"When I have stayed at the Sandpiper Inn, with its practically unobstructed view of the ocean about a block away, I have enjoyed very much the morning coffee hour. The host or hostess greets the guests over a cup of coffee before a roaring fire, breakfast having been served in one's own room. The conversation drifts from what they know about Scottish legends or the stock market, to the fabulous inns where they have stayed. I loved going back to my spacious bedroom with the antique furniture and comfortable bed, and the feeling that I was far away from the rush of the big cities, and even from little Carmel, which could be reached within five minutes, yet seemed remote because of the quiet that had been created at the tree-surrounded Sandpiper Inn." —*Mrs. Russell J. Matthias*

Open all year.
15 rooms, all with private bath.
Rates $30–$42, including continental breakfast. Special off-season rates.
No meals except breakfast.
Credit cards: Master Charge, Visa.
French, German and Italian spoken.

Sea View Inn
Box 4138
Carmel, California   93921
Telephone: (408) 624-8778

"The small town of Carmel is really an enchanted village full of craft shops, European-style eateries and homes whose owners very cleverly translate even the smallest yard into an elegant and private garden. The inn, a restored Victorian house, offers the traveler a special experience in lodging and is definitely not

for those who prefer large color television sets over the quiet sounds of the village and nearby Pacific Ocean. The inn is owned and managed by the Hydorn family, all natives of California, who go out of their way to make each guest's stay pleasant and comfortable. Each of the eight guest rooms has its own enchanting decor, and a sprinkling of antiques adds a feeling of quaint security and stability to the establishment. Continental breakfasts, accompanied by fresh California fruits and juices, are served at the fireside in the front parlor every morning. And, in the evenings, sherry and port."   —*Susan M. Lee Bales;*
also recommended by Rita F. Murphy

Open all year.
8 rooms, 4 with private bath.
Rates $20–$28, including continental breakfast.
Breakfast only served.
Credit cards: Master Charge, Visa.
Arabic and French spoken.

Vagabond House
Fourth and Dolores Streets
P.O. Box 2747
Carmel, California   93921
Telephone: (408) 624-9988

"Carmel-by-the-Sea began at the turn of the century as a colony for artists and a summer home for the affluent of San Francisco. Over the years, the area has been home to Robinson Jeffers, John Steinbeck, Fernand Léger, Alexander Archipenko and Ansel Adams. Just south of Carmel are the highlands and Big Sur, where the mountains, land, sky and sea merge into one of the world's most splendid natural sights. In addition to its windswept cypress trees and dazzling beach, Carmel is known for its fine restaurants, unique inns, artists' studios and unusual shops. Nestled in this gorgeous piece of real estate is Vagabond House. Service at the Vagabond is as extraordinary as its scenery. Errands are run for you, free transportation to and from Monterey airport arranged, dinner reservations obtained, unlimited logs and free coffee supplied—just some of the ways the Vagabond spoils its guests. Fresh flowers and fruit welcome a guest, and the rooms are filled with original art works and antiques from all over the United States."
—Truman and Ver Jean Chaffin

"No description would be complete without a mention of the flagstone courtyard that all the rooms face. Old and very large live oak trees occupy the center, and these are adorned with hanging baskets of fuchsias, tuberous begonias, ferns and many other plants. Camellias, rhododendrons and azaleas circle the trees, and each room and balcony has its plantings of flowers and greenery. Squirrels that chatter through the branches of the oaks are fed each morning from the office."   —*Grace A. Bixby*

Open all year.
12 rooms, all with private bath.
Rates $32–$50, including continental breakfast.
Only breakfast served.
Credit cards: Master Charge, Visa.
Decanter of wine in each room.

_____*Columbia*

City Hotel
P.O. Box 1870
Columbia, California   95310
Telephone: (209) 532-1479

"Columbia as a town is a fascinating daguerreotype of the past: quaint, isolated and frozen into the late gold rush era of the Sierra foothills. The City Hotel is a wooden-verandaed, brick-fronted building stretching back into the 1850s. It has been completely restored with a crystal-lighted dining room, frontier saloon and upstairs bedrooms furnished in old Victorian style with polished brass bedsteads, cuspidors, pitcher-basin wash-stands, beveled lead-glass mirrors and all the trimmings, including customary modern plumbing and lighting conveniences as well.

"But charming though it is as a wayside inn, it is the dining room that will, in my mind, earn the City Hotel its greatest claim to fame. The chef, for many years at one of San Francisco's most renowned restaurants, is a master at his trade. I have never tasted more delectable vegetables *en croute,* more delicate soufflés or excellently prepared wilted spinach salad. I am something of an amateur cook myself and can usually at least match the quality of the restaurants in which I eat, but I have yet to come near the cuisine of this room. The wine list, too, is unique in that it is exclusively California's best, and chosen only from small, family-owned wineries. I know of no better selection anywhere. The service is impeccable, the decor demure and the food exquisite. While I am loath to give away one of my few remaining secret hideaways in California, I also feel talent and hard work deserve recognition and applause. I tip my glass to the City Hotel!"   —*Harold J. Seger*

Closed December 24 and 25.
9 rooms, all with half-bath.

Rates $33.50–$42.50, including continental breakfast.
Credit cards: Master Charge, Visa.
Bar. Hotel is in Columbia State Park, near open gold mines and the summer theater of the University of the Pacific.
French spoken.

Coronado

Hotel del Coronado
1500 Orange Avenue
Coronado, California   92118
Telephone: (714) 435-6611

"This hotel, though now much enlarged, has atmosphere and old-fashioned charm. It also has historical interest: The Prince of Wales, later Edward VIII, stayed here and the dinner service for the prince is on display in one of the vitrines. Wallis Simpson also was a frequent visitor at the time her husband was an officer at the naval base on Coronado—no, their paths did not cross then! Other illustrious guests have spent time at the hotel. Some old rooms have very dated plumbing, which even leaks, but all in all it is a gracious old lady worthy of mentioning."
—*Louisa L. Becker*

Open all year.
575 rooms scattered among several buildings, all rooms with private baths.
Rates $45–$105, suites $85–$195, penthouse apartments $175–$275.
Credit cards: American Express, Master Charge, Visa.
2 bars, pool, tennis, beach, spa.
French and Spanish spoken.

Garberville

Benbow Inn
2675 Benbow Drive
Garberville, California   95440
Telephone: (707) 923-2124

"This is an old English, Tudor-style inn near the Redwood country, 200 miles north of San Francisco. The rooms are comfortable, but not fancy. There are no TVs or phones—something we find to be a very pleasant change. The dinner menu is large, ranging from lamb, pork and beef dishes to seafood, including fresh broiled fillet of salmon when in season. A buffet lunch is offered opposite the cocktail lounge. During the summer you can swim in the Eel River, which runs by one side of the inn, or in Benbow Lake, on the other side, where there is a small but nice state park. A golf course is within walking distance."   —*David and Donna Mullin*

Closed from December 1 to March 30.
70 rooms, 68 with private bath.
Rates $20–$36 single, $22–$42 double.
Credit cards: Master Charge, Visa.
German spoken.

_____*Gualala*

St. Orres
P.O. Box 523
Gualala, California   95445
Telephone: (707) 884-3303

"St. Orres is an experience you relive each time you visit this hideaway on the rugged Mendocino coast. You are in another world the moment you motor up the curved drive, park and glance around for a friendly puppy who runs to greet visitors. Once again you comment on the stained-glass and oak front doors as Eric, Ted or Rosemary greet you as long, long friends. You go up a spiral staircase to your second-floor room—each room is different, finished in warm woods. There is a view of the Pacific and a surrounding forest, no TV or radio and a queen-size quilt-covered bed just like when you were a kid growing up on the farm. The sunken dining room, with its rustic timbers, is a showplace, with more stained glass and overhead planters along the walls. When we dine, our minds are already made up: rack of lamb, even more tender than filet mignon. The soup and salads are light, leaving room for a neat surprise called lemon mousse. At continental breakfast you meet the other guests and hear their first impressions—about the super 'his and hers,' perhaps, with its combination minipool and oversize shower."   —*Violet and Pete Peterson*

Open all year, except for two or three weeks in March.
8 rooms, no private baths.
Rates $35–$45, including continental breakfast.
Credit cards: Master Charge, Visa.

Turn to the back of this book for pages inviting *your* comments.

La Jolla

La Valencia Hotel
1132 Prospect
La Jolla, California   92038
Telephone: (714) 454-0771

Fourteen miles north of San Diego the seaside resort town of La Jolla has been attracting the rich and the famous since it became a boom area in the post-World War I years. In 1926 a hotel was built, in careful replication of the Spanish style, that would become synonymous with La Jolla's sparkling beachfront in the minds of writers and the new crop of screen celebrities growing up in Hollywood. The hotel, first called Los Apartamentos de Sevilla—it was designed as an apartment-hotel—was soon renamed La Valencia.

"La Valencia is the kind of hotel that becomes part of its visitors' autobiographies. Something memorable—the hotel itself and its ambient charm—always happens when one stays there. To find an excuse for getting back to it is my idea of how to combine pleasure with business.

"To register in La Valencia is to enter a world of solid comfort and graceful pleasure. The staff combines cheerfully unobtrusive efficiency with old-fashioned courtesy. The place is beautiful in the Spanish style and immaculately maintained. My favorite place for lunch or dinner is the Whaling Bar and Grill. And the view of the Pacific Ocean from the other main dining room, the Sky Room, is a feast for the eye that quite matches the culinary feast. That is another thing about La Valencia: the food is never less than very good and more often it is superb. The kitchen and service always remember precisely what one has ordered, and the service maintains its dignity. The wine list is excellent and the prices sane. La Valencia is not staffed by robots with their palms out for tips, but by wonderfully helpful professionals who know their jobs perfectly and appear to enjoy doing them.

"The swimming pool, with its Jacuzzi hot spring bath, is a splendid place to relax. One of the most refreshing things in the world is a swim in this pool before one of La Valencia's excellent breakfasts. But the point of being at La Valencia is that it is the best hotel of any I know in which to have a relaxing and civilized time. It is a haven of the good life. If Henry James were alive today, I think he would include it as one of the enduring places of beauty on the American scene. I say *American* because La Valencia is not imitation English, or French, or anything but the generous American manner. At La Valencia that manner is a rare blend of dignity and authentic hospitality, without a trace of folksy back-slapping or phony friendliness. Rather, La Valencia deserves a national award as one of the most civilized places in the United States. Yet there is not the slightest stuffiness about it. It is on no nostalgia trip. La Valencia is the real thing in the real world, which only proves that the good and graceful things of life are still amply available somewhere—if you know where to go." —*Professor Philip Rieff; also recommended by Louisa L. Becker*

Open all year.
100 rooms, all with private bath.
Rates $45–$65 single, $50–$65 double. Oceanfront suites $75–$140, according to season.
Credit cards: American Express, Master Charge, Visa.
Bar, heated pool, exercise room, putting green.
French, German and Spanish spoken.

Little River

Heritage House
5200 Highway 1
Little River, California   95456
Telephone: (707) 937-5885

"The Heritage House nestles in a cliff a hundred feet above, and smack in the midst of, the most majestic coastline in the world. Getting to and exploring beyond this inn carries you past towering forests, soaring cliffs and unique hamlets. Mendocino, the quintessential 'New England' village, is but six miles to the north and the architecture of the inn reflects that East Coast time and place, but the climate here is more temperate, the ocean, while thunderous, is more pacific and redwoods tower all around. This could only be northern California. The main house of the inn, initially an 1877 residence, is now divided into well-proportioned dining, reception and sitting rooms. Guest cottages have been added, reflecting the more merciful architectural development of subsequent eras. Each bears an appropriate name, not a number (the Schoolhouse, Stable, Ivy and Country Store). Almost all accommodations offer an ocean view (ranging from nice to thrilling) and some fireplaces and stoves. There is a slight and pleasant atmosphere of 'old money' throughout. Guests are in for many delicious surprises. The meals are both sumptuous and elegant, prepared and served with a degree of care and feeling suitable for old friends. (As we sunned on our veranda we saw the young man who had served us our luncheon now tending the flowers. Both pursuits were conducted with such an air of dedication and repose we were put in mind of a country physician.) Here 'repeat business' takes on a new meaning. Couples book years in advance for anniversaries—beginning, as we did, with our wedding night. Their children follow suit. It is, indeed, a heritage house. Newcomers are welcome but advised to book well in advance, especially for the summer season. With no TV or phones, just strolling, lolling, dining, conversation, motoring to nearby vistas and picturesque hamlets, this is a setting for an elegant country weekend, unique to California and unique in California."   —*Richard and Wendy Kahlenberg*

Open from February to the Sunday after Thanksgiving.
52 rooms, all with private bath.
Rates $49–$77 single, $64–$92 double, $105 suites, including two
    meals.
No credit cards.
Bar.

Little River Inn
Little River, California   95456
Telephone: (707) 937-5942

"Despite the neighborhood attractions, the Little River Inn invites indolence. We never rode the Skunk (a steam line for railroad buffs), or rented a canoe or paddleboat to explore the Big River, or sought activity at the Mendocino Tennis Club. The greatest exertion that gave pleasure was picking up shells and rocks on the beach. The highlight always came before a commendable seafood dinner in the lodge, when we enjoyed the slothful luxury of opening a California vintage as an aperitif at sunset while we studied the awesome changes in the thundering, sparkling, rolling or savage sea.

"On our second visit we were accompanied by another couple and were given the honor of staying in a ranch house on its own private headland. It was once the inn owner's family home. We enjoyed blissful privacy and the lullaby of the buoy's bell. We'd contrive odd, short excursions so we could return at noon with picnic lunches to savor while sitting on the glassed porch or flowered terrace facing the ocean. After dinner we'd make a fire and sip port in our own living room. A smaller party could request one of the four units in the modern motel-style annex that have fireplaces and face a rugged headland with waves crashing around its base. Families might want one of the older cottages that look comfortable and large. Singles may be happiest in one of the few rooms in the main house, a New England-type mansion built in 1853 and converted to an inn in 1939. It also houses the restaurant, bar and offices. A nine-hole golf course, a forested and canyoned state park and a Pacific beach are steps from the inn. Two miles away the restored Victorian village of Mendocino has boutiques and craft shops to lure the tourist dollar and a cheese-and-wine merchant with a selection unmatched in many sophisticated urban areas. The tallest redwoods are a half-day auto excursion north. These are the heaven-caressing giant sequoias, not the drive-through hulks of southern California. After an hour your sense of scale becomes warped and you can't appreciate the grandeur. Your sense of appreciation is even more taxed if you visit the Pygmy Forest where a freakish set of circumstances dwarfed trees up to fifty years old to make them look like twisted three-year-old saplings. You can take a pass on this."   —Camille J. Cook

Open all year.
50 rooms, all with private bath.
Rates $28–$44 single, $30–$46 double, $36–$80 suites and cottages.
No credit cards.
Bar, golf course.

_____*Los Alamos*

The Union Hotel
362 Bell Street
Los Alamos, California   93440
Telephone: Ask operator for area code 805: Los Alamos 2744

"Nowadays there is something other than the Santa Barbara Biltmore or the Madonna Inn to comfort travelers who weary en route between Los Angeles and San Francisco. The Union Hotel awaits in Los Alamos (California, not New Mexico) on U.S. 101, a town not a bit larger now than in the 1880s when its hotel opened. Owner Dick Langdon, an enterprising Los Angeles emigré, and Jim Radhe, his baumeister in residence, have recreated another era: Victorian, Western, perfect. There is a salon, a dining hall and, beyond the swinging doors, the bar where Langdon sometimes plays the upright piano. The furnishings are right for the period—being suitably 'crowded.' Dinner and drinks are sturdy and oddly wholesome, perhaps because their recipe books date from the 1800s. After dinner there's no TV, no phones. Instead, there is brandy, sinfully fresh fruit popovers and shooting pool in the upstairs salon. There is even a well-stocked library. A great part of the charm of the place is chatting with other guests. In the bedrooms you find a carafe of wine and two glasses waiting. Some of the rooms share a bath. And, are you ready for this? The bathtub is sheet copper, authentically postbellum.

"Langdon, consistent in his quest for a total period experience, plans someday to provide his guests with period costumes and turn-of-the-century autos for motoring in the beautiful surrounding countryside. Breakfast is served punctually and family style. Check the time and don't be late. On each table a bottle of brandy sits next to the coffeepot. Like everything else, just the way it was in the old West."

—*Richard and Wendy Kahlenberg*

Open only Fridays, Saturdays and Sundays.
14 rooms, 7 with private bath.
Rates $40–$50, including breakfast.
No credit cards.
Badminton, croquet, Jacuzzi, pool, touring car.

Los Angeles

The Biltmore Hotel
515 South Olive Street
Los Angeles, California   90013
Telephone: (213) 624-1011

"When the Biltmore opened on October 1, 1923, it was the largest hotel west of Chicago. Indeed, more than half a century later its 1,072 rooms hardly qualify it as a 'little' place. But we feel some attention is due it. Like the Clift in San Francisco, the Biltmore *feels* much smaller than it is. Messages come to the room by courier, not blinking light. The plants in the rooms are real and growing. The desk clerk remembers your name. On the weekends tea is served in the lobby—in Los Angeles! And it is important to note that the hotel is in Los Angeles. Not Burbank or Marina del Rey or Beverly Hills or Anaheim, but good old downtown L.A. The area is reviving. The brassy new Bonaventure (now there's a *big* hotel) has given it clout, but the Biltmore gives it class.

"The hotel was taken over in early 1976 by two architects, Gene Summers and Phyllis Lambert (the latter one of the heirs to the Seagram fortune). They've spent about $22 million on renovations. Both were longtime associates of the minimalist master Mies van der Rohe. Mies would probably be appalled at the high Italian-Spanish Renaissance glitter of the Biltmore lobby, but he was the one who said, 'God is in the details,' and what details these are! Plaster medallions, hand-painted tiles, gilded beams and gesso work, murals by an Italian, Giovanni Smeraldi, who trained at the Vatican. All have been lovingly renewed to the point where you expect Douglas Fairbanks to dash in any minute in wing collar and tails, tossing his camel-hair overcoat to a bellman in a pillbox hat.

"Original details in the bedrooms had been largely lost by 1976, so Summers and Lambert thoroughly remodeled those, with a little help from the Pop master Jim Dine, who designed rugs, lamp bases, wall friezes and prints. Many rooms even have their own Dine sculptures. His work blends very nicely, thank you, into Smeraldi's downstairs. No, the Biltmore is by no means a little hotel, but it has been given that kind of attention. It's a big hotel for people who hate big hotels."

—Mechtild Hoppenrath and Charles Oberdorf

Open all year.
1,072 rooms, all with private bath.
Rates $49–$66 single, $59–$76 double, $100–$1,000 suites.
Credit cards: American Express, Carte Blanche, Diners Club, Master Charge, Visa.
Bar, convention rooms, entertainment, lobby lounge, restaurants.
French, Japanese and Spanish spoken.

MacCallum House,
Mendocino

Mendocino

MacCallum House
P.O. Box 206
Mendocino, California   95460
Telephone: (707) 937-0289

"MacCallum House was a wedding gift to Daisy Kelley from her father in 1882. Today, it is indeed a delightful gift to the traveler. This historic Victorian inn, situated near the rugged coast of northern California, has an enviable view of the Pacific Ocean. Enter the white picket gate and ascend the stairs to a welcoming entrance. In the foyer one is introduced to the Kelley-MacCallum family: mounted on the side wall is a glass case of photographs and a resume of the heritage of the house. Choosing a room, whether in the main house or separate cottages, is not easy, unless one is set on an ocean view. Each room has its unique charm and warmth and all are impeccably clean. Armoires, bedsteads, Tiffany lamps and tables are enhanced by well-chosen wallpaper, homespun bedspreads and batiste curtains. The upstairs sitting room affords relaxed reading. Here for your choice is interesting literature, historical papers and the pièce de résistance: several volumes of Daisy Kelley Mac-Callum's fascinating and informative scrapbook. The day is complete with dinner in the residence dining room (a favorite, freshly caught salmon), followed by a visit to the Gray Whale Bar in the glassed-in porch overlooking the ocean."

—_Helen M. Menken_

Open all year.
20 rooms, 1 with private bath.
Rates $41.50–$78.00, including continental breakfast. 10 percent discount on stays of 5 or more nights.
Credit cards: Master Charge, Visa.
French spoken.

Mendocino Hotel
45080 Main Street
P.O. Box 587
Mendocino, California   95460
Telephone: (707) 937-0511

"Mendocino, situated on bluffs high above the Pacific, north of San Francisco, is a village founded about the time of the California gold rush. It has been declared an historic monument. The architecture is Victorian and American Gothic, with many patterns of shingle, weathered or in crisp white, blue and yellow. Many of the houses or cottages are shops or galleries of fine quality. The atmosphere of creativity is an inspiration to artists, writers and those of us who enjoy their works. Then there is the magnificent sea, smashing waves and huge rock formations, wonderful for fishermen, naturalists and photographers. Nearby are the awesome redwood forests and the famous 'skunk' trains that take one on the old logging route over trestles, through tunnels, by steam engine.

"Coming home to the hotel is another joy. It faces the bay and is comfortably 'done' in the best Victorian tradition. The parlor or lounge will have a fine fire to gather around, and perhaps a chess game going on in a corner. The bar is attractive—in the Art Nouveau motif of the late 19th century. The bedrooms have canopied brass beds, with wallpaper and drapes in softly patterned colors to match. If the nights are cool, Oscar the pigeon might come in through the window to roost on top of the wardrobe until morning. He is friendly, elusive and determined. The restaurant has delicious meals served by gracious young ladies dressed in gowns of the period."

—*Dorothy Burgert*

Open all year.
26 rooms, 12 with private bath.
Rates $21.50 single, $26.50–$65 double, including breakfast.
Credit cards: Master Charge, Visa.
Bar.

Mokelumne Hill

Hotel Leger
Main Street
Mokelumne Hill, California   95245
Telephone: (209) 286-1401

"The Mother Lode Country, as the vicinity of Highway 49 is called, is one of the few areas of California where asparagus ferns do not sprout in the windows of trendy cafes and where historical artifacts have been allowed to molder gracefully. One can drive for days checking up on towns with names like Angel's Camp and Volcano, where things have never been the same since the gold rush days of the mid-19th century. Each town bears its version of the International Order of Odd Fellows hall, a post office/general store and hotel.

"The Hotel Leger offers a pleasing combination of historic authenticity with modern convenience. The hotel bar features Victorian decor and rowdy humor, while the restaurant serves up unusually delicious prime rib. Guests can linger after dinner on the long porch of the building fronting the main street or take a refreshing dip in the pool concealed in the leafy back yard. The owners are proud to show off the old wine cellar, the vaudeville theater next door and the historic objects found around the property. All in all, a delightful stopover for the wistful prospector." —*Jean Carlton Parker*

Open all year, except for two weeks in January.
13 rooms, 7 with private bath.
Rates $19.50 double.
Credit cards: Master Charge, Visa.
Bar.

Nevada City

National Hotel
211 Broad Street
Nevada City, California   95959
Telephone: (916) 265-4551

"Reputed to be the oldest hostelry in continuous operation in California, the venerable and historic National Hotel of picturesque Nevada City first opened its doors to the public in 1854. Today, it combines authentic Victorian gold rush atmosphere with modern comforts, pool and a popular cuisine. The bar is the social hub of town. The National is surrounded by numerous shops and fine restaurants, catering to local as well as tourist trade. Gas streetlights, stately homes and ornate sidewalk porticoes add their embellishments to a once-fabled mining town anchored peacefully amid the tall pines along the banks of Deer Creek. The hotel, museums and shops operate year round, with visitors returning often to enjoy the distinct seasons and holiday decor of this important heritage center, located on a scenic highway between Sacramento and Lake Tahoe. Because of the many cultural events held at the historic Nevada Theatre—Mark Twain once lectured there—it is well to make reservations at the National, particularly on weekends." —*James W. Lenhoff*

Open all year.
28 rooms, 23 with private bath.
Rates $16 single, $35 double.
Credit cards: Master Charge, Visa.
Bar, swimming pool.

All innkeepers appreciate reservations in advance; some require them.

Pacific Grove

The Gosby House Inn
643 Lighthouse Avenue
Pacific Grove, California   93950
Telephone: (408) 375-1287

"A restored Victorian mansion, full of leaded glass, brass and wood. There is an antique doll collection displayed in the entry parlor. Nearby is Cannery Row, made famous by John Steinbeck; Carmel-by-the-Sea, and the coastline of Big Sur. A breakfast, which comes with the room charge, is served in the common room. The inn is right on Lighthouse Avenue, about two blocks from the bay front. The rooms were attractive and clean."   —*Mrs. Bartley M. Harloe*

Open all year.
15 rooms, 5 with private bath.
Rates $22–$30 single, $28–$32 double, including continental breakfast.
No credit cards.

Piercy

Hartsook Inn
Piercy, California   95467
Telephone: (707) 247-3305

"The inn is actually a collection of rustic cottages hidden away in a thirty-acre grove of redwoods on both sides of U.S. Highway 101. One lodge contains a gift shop, lobby and dining room, serving simple but excellent fresh fare. The location on the banks of the Eel River affords bathing and fishing; the river's gentle current will carry you slowly downstream, and you can hike back up for another ride. Trails from the inn lead hikers off into the redwoods—to Richardson Grove, to the Hartsook Giant (fifty-nine feet in circumference), to a lookout point above the Eel River. Some cabins have kitchens in them; others are only bedrooms and baths. The total tariff for our two-bedroom cabin (with dressing room and bath), four dinners in the inn dining room and four breakfasts came to under $70."   —*Margaret Zeigler*

Open April 15 to November 1.
62 rooms, all with private bath.
Rates $22–$32, housekeeping units from $40.
Credit cards: Master Charge, Visa.
Hiking trails, river swimming.

Rancho Santa Fe

The Inn at Rancho Santa Fe
Box 869
Rancho Santa Fe, California   92067
Telephone: (714) 756-1131

The Rancho Santa Fe area was little more than a barren waste when, in 1845, the last Mexican governor of California granted almost 9,000 acres of it to Juan Osuna, a Spanish soldier of fortune who had become alcalde of the Pueblo of San Diego. In 1906 the Santa Fe Railroad bought the grant from Osuna's heirs and named it Rancho Santa Fe. The railroad had an ambitious plan: The area would be planted with eucalyptus trees that in time would grow into an endless supply of railway ties. Unfortunately, the wood turned out to be unsuitable for the purpose, and the railroad was left with lush scenery but still useless land. By 1923 the railroad company had decided to turn part of the area over to citrus crops and develop the rest as a residential community. A guesthouse was built to accommodate prospective buyers: It became the centerpiece of an inn that in turn has become the focal point of a community.

"The inn is located in the center of an old-fashioned village mostly inhabited by the very rich of good breeding (not the nouveaux riches—although some have infiltrated, but few to date). It resembles some of the old-fashioned inns I have visited in New England and the setting is beautiful. The cottages are well appointed and comfortable and meticulously clean.

"The 'buts.' Rancho Santa Fe is a residential village and has one street and one restaurant besides those at the inn—though at this writing I understand that a little restaurant in the Patio arcade has been bought by a restaurateur from Amsterdam who has managed one of the finest establishments in that city. You need a car. There is no bus service or other public transportation. If you do have a car then Del Mar or La Jolla and San Diego are easily accessible for choice restaurants and entertainment.

"Most of the guests at the inn seem to be in the senior citizens' class of higher means—many are Easterners in search of clement skies or aficionados of horse racing during the Del Mar season (July to mid-September)."   —*Louisa L. Becker*

Open all year.
75 rooms, all with private bath.
Rates $26–$60. Special rates for cottages and suites.
Credit cards: American Express, Master Charge, Visa.
Dogs allowed in cottage rooms for a $6-a-day charge.
Swimming pool, golf, tennis.

Guests can be met at Del Mar or Lindbergh field for a modest charge.
French, German and Spanish spoken.

_____*Reedley*

Hotel Burgess
1726 11th Street
Reedley, California   93654
Telephone: (209) 638-6315

"I was in Reedley on business, the hotel's sign outside of town caught my eye and I found the Burgess a delightful place. It has been completely restored and the rooms are done with a variety of international themes such as the San Francisco room, the Polynesian room, the Indian room, the Brazilian room, the Austrian room, the French room, the Moroccan room, the Oriental room and the U.S. Today room."   —*Joseph L. Neal*

Open all year.
17 rooms, all with private bath.
Rates $16–$30 double, $30 suite.
No meals served.
Credit cards: Master Charge, Visa.

_____*St. Helena*

The Wine Country Inn
1152 Lodi Lane
St. Helena, California   94574
Telephone: (707) 963-7077

"The towels are so deliciously thick at the Smith family's Wine Country Inn that you can't stick them in your ear. Each room is artfully and individually decorated in country style. Some are accented with framed examples of Grandma Smith's stitchery, and others have weathered barn siding as paneling. Some of the rooms have fireplaces with kindling properly laid on the days it is cool enough for a fire. Other rooms have the comfort of private terraces or balconies. Only breakfast is offered here—warm baked goods and California juice and fruit in season. It is served in the entry-level common room, and it gives the opportunity for meeting fellow guests to compare notes on the sights, restaurants, winery tours and tasting rooms of the Napa Valley. One of the family (most often son Jim) will be on hand to offer tourist advice while he refills your coffee cup.

"The building (new in 1976, with an addition started in 1978) sits tall on a treeless plot in the center of the Napa Valley, one of the foremost wine-producing regions of the United States. We might be able to claim 'of the world,' because a product of this valley recently won a blind tasting event in Paris. The event made headlines in wine journals. The inn is off Route 12/29, which is studded with tasting rooms that give away glasses of vin ordinaire and sell finer bottlings. There is a minimal tourist interest outside the wineries. The town of Sonoma restored some buildings pertaining to early California history that may be visited en route from San Francisco. In Calistoga, a few miles north of the inn, a not-too-elegant hot spring spa may be enjoyed. A missable sight in the area is the local geyser, an authentic geothermal phenomenon—but if you've seen the original, this 'Old Faithful' will look as though the keeper had opened the valve of a garden hose as soon as the required number had paid their admission fees. Various shopping malls sell antiques, imports, fashion and craft items, foodstuffs for picnics and, of course, wine. An old mill in a state park on Route 12/29 offers a good picnic site. Be warned that most of the fine restaurants in the area are closed Mondays." —*Camille J. Cook*

Open all year, except for December 18–23.
25 rooms, all with private bath.
Rates $43–$46 single, $45–$48 double, including breakfast. Special weekly rates.
Only breakfast served.
Credit cards: Master Charge, Visa.

San Diego

Half Moon Inn
2303 Shelter Island Drive
San Diego, California 92106
Telephone: (714) 224-3411

"Polynesian architecture—relaxed, but has class. Breathtaking view of basin with sailing ships and all pleasure craft. Beautiful surroundings and easily accessible, although it is better if you have your own transportation. A favorite of movie and television artists. By comparison all others on Shelter Island are definitely run-of-the-mill." —*Louisa L. Becker*

Open all year.
142 rooms, all with private bath.
Rates $34–$40 single, $40–$50 double. Some larger suites $88–$135.
Credit cards: American Express, Carte Blanche, Diners Club, Master Charge, Visa.
Marina, pool, putting green.

Little America Westgate Hotel
1055 Second Avenue
San Diego, California　92101
Telephone: (714) 238-1818

Those who see hope that the day is not far off when small and elegant hotels—not necessarily old or restored ones—can again thrive in American cities, point to the Westgate. Built in an urban-renewal area, the hotel was dedicated from the start to a kind of luxuriousness commercial hotels (as this one is) had long since forsworn. The interior is deliberately Grand European (while fitting a California life-style, they say; and for some that will be a hard concept to accept). Many of the antiques and paintings are real treasures—among them an 18th-century marble fireplace worth a reported $150,000. An incongruous imitation or a contemporary version of past glories? Let the guest decide.

"It is truly a great hotel with period furniture and decor in exquisite taste. The service is excellent and the Fontainebleau restaurant does serve superbly prepared food. The personnel is courteous and attentive. In fact, it is rather incongruous to see a guest in sports clothes or resort attire. One almost expects to see a courtier or a lady in velvet and lace descending the grand staircase. It is all that the brochure claims it is.

"But, have you ever thought of mounting a diamond of the purest limpidity and best cut in common metal? The brochure mentions that the hotel is ten minutes from the airport and near the Community Concourse, but it doesn't say that the neighborhood is the eyesore of San Diego as well. But if you can overlook the slums around it, I would classify the Little America as one of the most beautiful and gracious hotels in the United States."　　　　　　　　　　　　　　　—*Louisa L. Becker*

Open all year.
223 rooms, all with private bath.
Rates $52–$67 single, $58–$73 double, suites up to $395.
Children under 12 free.
Credit cards: all major ones.
French, Italian, Spanish and Swahili spoken.

American hotels and inns generally list rates by the room, assuming one person in a single, two in a double. Extra people in rooms normally incur extra charges. Where rates are quoted per person per day, at least one meal is probably included under a modified American plan (MAP). A full American plan would mean three meals are included.

San Francisco

The Cartwright
524 Sutter Street
San Francisco, California   94102
Telephone: (415) 421-2865

"The Cartwright is removed but one block from Union Square and just steps away from cable cars that take you with ease to Nob, Russian or Telegraph Hill, or to Ghiardelli Square and Fisherman's Wharf, the financial district or Grace Cathedral. The Adams family have long owned a hotel that reflects the prewar period, which was, perhaps, the greatest epoch in comfort and elegance in this city. While the hotel has preserved that look, it has been comfortably modernized as a family-type hotel in the best sense. Continuity is manifest in the 'guest histories' so sedulously maintained by the staff and the bell captain who has been with the Cartwright for a quarter of a century. His log is truly an international one. Somehow the staff knows that, on special occasions, the English and Continental visitors would enjoy a basket of fruit and a bottle of a choice vintage from the Napa Valley, and that certain Australian and New Zealand guests, if they could have their druthers, would prefer a bottle of cold beer from their own domains.

"From here it is easy for the first-time visitor to America or to San Francisco to stroll up Sutter Street, on to Union Square and Post Street and window shop in the art galleries and specialty shops that are just a step or two from the handsome if unpretentious marquee of the hotel. The regular visitor is fully aware that some of the greatest of San Francisco's nearly limitless cuisines are but a short stroll away, as are the great clubs."
　　　　　　　　　　　　　　　—_Dr. Forest M. Hinkhouse_

Open all year.
119 rooms, all with private bath.
Rates $24–$30 single, $28–$38 double, $32–$42 twin, $55–$65 suite.
Breakfast only served.
Credit cards: American Express, Master Charge, Visa.
Arabic, Dutch, French, German, Japanese and Spanish spoken.

El Cortez Hotel
550 Geary Street
San Francisco, California   94102
Telephone: (415) 775-5000

"If you are looking for a reasonably priced, pleasant hotel within easy reach of Union Square, you couldn't do better than the El Cortez. Architecturally, it is an amazing mixture of Mexican and twenties American. Once in our room, we discovered comfortable beds, a clean bright bathroom, a dressing room and a small but well-equipped kitchen. The latter is a boon, saving the money one usually spends in hotels on room service. The hotel has a restaurant, which looked promising. But when we weren't cooking for ourselves, we explored the vast range of ethnic restaurants around the town. We certainly prefer to stay at the El Cortez than at any of the ritzier but more expensive hotels in the center of San Francisco."

—Maggie and Andrew de Lory

Open all year.
170 rooms, all with private bath.
Rates $22–$24 single, $28–$30 double. Suites $56–$62.
Special rates for groups of 15 and over.
All credit cards.
French, German and Spanish spoken.

El Drisco Hotel
2901 Pacific Avenue
San Francisco, California   94115
Telephone: (415) 346-2880

"This is seldom found in conventional travel books—it is supposedly one of the few hotels that existed before the big earthquake. It is small, quaint, located in Pacific Heights, high on a hill, an area of old mansions, many of which are still private homes. Don't eat in the hotel; the dining room is out of an Agatha Christie novel. Be sure and request an outside room or a suite with a view." *—Jean Ogg*

Open all year.
42 rooms, all with private bath.
Rates $28–$31 double, $35–$42 suites.
Monthly rates.
Credit cards: Master Charge, Visa.
Spanish spoken.

Four Seasons–Clift Hotel
Geary and Taylor Streets
San Francisco, California   94102
Telephone: (415) 775-4700

"With 402 rooms and suites, this hotel can hardly call itself 'little.' But this is San Francisco, after all, city of the Mark Hopkins, the St. Francis, the Fairmont and what must surely be the most soaring Hyatt of them all. Next to them, the Clift is a country inn. And little is as little does. The Clift feels small enough that *Fortune* magazine, in October 1974, called it one of the world's eight great little-known hotels; that must be some measure of size. The Clift does things in a small way. There's a proper concierge, a morning paper with the room service breakfast (alongside weightless croissants and tiny pots of Scottish marmalade and jam), free shoeshines and a small brochure in each room outlining a walking tour of the neighborhood. The hotel was purchased a couple of years back by the Canadian Four Seasons chain, which could have spelled trouble. But Four Seasons' president, Isadore Sharp, has a commitment to excellence (we've experienced it in his Montreal, Toronto and Vancouver hotels), and he's promised to keep the Clift the intimate, secret place it's always felt like. So far, he seems to have succeeded. As for the surrounding city, it's always felt a bit self-satisfied to us. But any place that's been called the most beautiful in America by Alistair Cooke, Georges Pompidou and Nikita Khrushchev can be forgiven that."

—*Mechtild Hoppenrath and Charles Oberdorf*

"The Clift—as it is known to cognoscenti—is immediately contiguous to San Francisco's major legitimate theaters, department stores, specialty shops, ladies' and gentlemen's clubs and some of the city's most distinguished restaurants. One of the last of such is the Redwood and another the French Rooms within the Clift; the first celebrating its glory in Art Deco designs in laminated wood, heightened by four major paintings by Gustav Klimt, and the second the bon ton one associates with the very best of France's five-star hotels. The latter is undoubtedly the West's most beautifully proportioned and decorated dining room in the grand manner. The Clift is small enough for singularly good service, yet large enough for the attention its clientele would expect of a human-scaled grand hotel. Mr. Allport, its stellar concierge of thirty-two years, is exceptional. Likewise, Greta, the housekeeper—also a San Francisco institution—will execute nearly any of the guests' wishes. The Clift has its own French laundry which is amazingly fast and good."   —*Dr. Forest M. Hinkhouse*

Open all year.
402 rooms, all with private bath.
Rates $51–$80 single, $66–$96 double, $120–$250 suites.
Credit cards: American Express, Carte Blanche, Diners Club, Master Charge, Visa.
Bar.
Dutch, French, German, Japanese and Spanish spoken.

The Raphael
386 Geary Street
San Francisco, California   94102
Telephone: (415) 986-2000

"A marvelous, centrally located hotel with European overtones, it is a short distance from the shops, theaters and restaurants. The rooms are very well furnished and have two telephones each. If the Raphael is full, which it often is, the staff will help you to find another hotel."   —*Harry Kennedy, Jr.*

Open all year.
150 rooms, all with private bath.
Rates $33–$49 single, $47–$61 double, $80 suites.
Credit cards: American Express, Diners Club, Master Charge, Visa.
Bar, restaurant open 24 hours.
Chinese, French, German, Hungarian, Italian, Korean and Spanish
  spoken.

The Washington Square Inn
1660 Stockton Street
San Francisco, California   94133
Telephone: (415) 981-4220

"Washington Square Inn is situated at the foot of Telegraph Hill—the very heart of San Francisco. Despite its proximity to the financial center of the West, the best of the city's restaurants, its stores, shops and theaters—and a blessedly short ride to the opera, the symphony orchestra and the museums—it is graced with a quiet, low-keyed elegance. That charm is reflected in its superbly appointed rooms, which feature, alternately, English and French antiques and the handsome paintings and watercolors of such contrasting talents as Noal Betts and Dennis Argent. The merger of such antiques and art creates an extraordinarily comfortable milieu for the weary traveler from anywhere or an overnight visitor who came to 'the city' just for a change of scene. The inn is kitty-corner from the Venetian Gothic Revival Church of Saints Peter and Paul and from Mama's Restaurant. Thus soul and body, body and soul are well served. For the delectation of its guests, breakfast is served in the rooms on Staffordshire, or at an aging oak table situated directly in front of a roaring fire. At teatime, the thin, crisp cucumber sandwiches hark back to those served in an oaken parlor at Brown's Hotel in London.

"The inn reflects its situation in the heart of San Francisco's

Italian neighborhood by providing for the needs and pleasures of its guests. Its concierge can arrange theater, opera or concert tickets, a private secretary, a special tour—perhaps to Muir Woods or to Pebble Beach—or nearly anything else one might need. In these times, the inn seems to be exactly what is needed by the visitor to San Francisco who would like to avoid yet another typically internationalized hotel or a plasticized motel."

—Dr. Forest M. Hinkhouse

Open all year.
15 rooms, 11 with private bath.
Rates $38–$85 single, $43–$90 double, including continental breakfast.
Only breakfast served.
Credit cards: American Express, Master Charge, Visa.

San Luis Obispo

The Madonna Inn
100 Madonna Road
San Luis Obispo, California   93401
Telephone: (805) 543-3000

"San Simeon, William Randolph Hearst's castle, is just a few miles north, but we prefer Alex Madonna's monument to himself. Hearst had pretensions to taste; Madonna had no pretensions at all. Where to begin to describe this outrageous hotel? How about in the men's washroom of the coffee shop? The sinks are copper, set into a copper counter. The mirrors are copper paella pans with mirrored bottoms. The urinal, a solid copper trough flushed by an overhead waterwheel. Beginning to get it? How about the room where we stayed, the Daisy Mae. The walls are rough-hewn boulders. So are the floors and ceilings, the shower and the washbasin. In fact, anything that can be a boulder is one. The only exceptions are the bed, the toilet, two night tables, the TV and two strands of daisylike light fixtures. The boulder sink has no waterspouts. You turn the tap and hear a gurgling overhead to one side. Then down over the rocks and out from two little waterfalls come the hot and cold torrents. The shower works the same way. The inn's dining room is all pink—but that means *all* pink, right down to the cash register tapes. No pane of glass in the place that isn't stained or etched. No length of wood uncarved or unturned. No public wall that isn't a mural. Each of the hundred or so rooms is a different fantasy. Alex Madonna's castle is like a man so ugly he's handsome. Unlike Hearst's place, it should not be missed."   *—Mechtild Hoppenrath and Charles Oberdorf*

Open all year.
109 rooms, all with private bath.
Rates $33–$42 single, $40–$70 double, $55–$80 suites.
No credit cards.
Bar.
Spanish spoken.

Sutter Creek

Nine Eureka Street
P.O. Box 386
Sutter Creek, California   95685
Telephone: (209) 267-0342

"There are several good reasons for visiting northern California's gold country: its beautiful rolling highlands, the nostalgic aura of the gold rush days that pervades the small Western towns of the Mother Lode, and the unique experience of unwinding at Nine Eureka Street in Sutter Creek. The spacious sitting room, with its interesting memorabilia and wonderful collection of books, is meant for lingering. The guest rooms are a delight to the connoisseur of the past—each as individual in feeling and decor as only the inn's proprietress (no novice in the art of innkeeping) could have fashioned. For those who read in bed, she has provided excellent lighting, as well as a galaxy of reading material. At breakfast time, guests gather in the sunlit dining room to find a table refreshingly laid with elegant silver and china. Fresh orange juice in a tall crystal pitcher, slices of melon or other fruit, homemade bread and pastry, with steaming coffee, are complimentary—and a happy start to a day of browsing in the numerous antique shops of Sutter Creek, or exploring nearby Jackson, Mokelumne Hill, Ione, Volcano, Amador City, Fiddletown and other historic attractions of the gold country."   —*Rita F. Murphy*

Open all year.
5 rooms, all with private bath.
Rates $22 double, including light breakfast.
Breakfast only served.
No credit cards.

Sutter Creek Inn
75 Main Street
Sutter Creek, California   95685
Telephone: (209) 267-5606

"In a warren of buildings behind the 1859 Keyes-Voorhies home, Jane Way installed a series of hideaway accommodations. Each is individually decorated with old pieces of comfortable contemporary furniture. Some units have beds suspended on chains: Sleeping on a swinging bed gives much of the pleasure of a hammock with none of the spine-bending discomfort. It is also more predictable and less active than a water bed. The nonadventurous may use blocks provided to stabilize the furniture.

"Established in 1966, the inn was one of the first modern country inns to open in California. Each room is furnished with a carafe of California sherry, and those who get to the dining room before the breakfast bell may pour brandy into their morning coffee. A hearty hot breakfast is served at long tables in the main house, and the assembled guests become an instant extended family, united in their pursuit of sight-seeing the Mother Lode country. Abandoned gold mines, toppled tailing wheels and ancient Indian village sites are to be explored. In Amador City a museum (erratic hours, check ahead) houses working-scale models of mine structures. If you travel between March 24 and April 21, a drive past Daffodil Hill near Volcano should be enjoyable. In winter there is snowmobiling and skiing."   —*Camille J. Cook; also recommended by Sue Swezey*

Open all year, except January 1–15.
17 rooms, 15 with private bath.
Rates $25–$65, including breakfast. Special weekly rates.
Only breakfast served.
No credit cards.

_____*Volcano*

St. George Hotel
2 Main Street
P.O. Box 275
Volcano, California   95689
Telephone: (209) 296-4458

"Volcano, California: a 90-degree turn to the left, two blocks, a 90-degree turn to the right. And that, lined with a few stone buildings, is all that remains of this once-booming Mother Lode town. But its charm is in its quiet: a charm which is shared by the St. George Hotel. This three-story masonry block wrapped in white-columned verandas cannot have changed much since it was built in 1862 nor has its comfortable interior, except for the addition of amenities considered essential today. Sarah's home-cooked meals are something not to be forgotten. Pasta, pies, rolls, everything is prepared from scratch in more than ample quantities. Chuck Inman, the proprietor, is usually

found behind the bar amid dusty bric-a-brac accumulated over countless years. There, Chuck, or his wife, Marlene, holds forth out of a seemingly bottomless supply of tales and anecdotes. Though modern motel accommodations are available in a separate annex, the quality of the St. George experience is to be found in the old hotel. Autumn colors and spring daffodils are two of Volcano's delights."
                —Harvey Black; also recommended by David H. Melnick

Closed from January 1 to about February 17, and on Mondays and Tuesdays.
19 rooms, 6 with private bath.
Rates $12.50 single, $18.50 double. Special Saturday rate of $50 double, including breakfast and dinner.
No credit cards.
Bar, swimming hole.

_Yosemite

Ahwahnee Hotel
Yosemite National Park
California   95389
Telephone: (209) 372-4611

"At the bottom of the valley's verdant floor, hard by the Merced River, which is fed by Yosemite Falls—and previously, a series of ramified glaciers—is the Ahwahnee Hotel. Made of fieldstone and redwood by conscientious and dedicated architects and draftsmen in 1927, it has just the right number of rooms for a mutuality of convenience and privacy. Despite its location near the heart of one of America's most visited national parks, the guest feels a sense of tranquility and elegance when he enters the stone gates abutting the hotel's own private park. There the weary traveler can find perhaps not exactly nirvana, but at least a surcease from crowds, noise and confusion. The Ahwahnee's food is grandly served in a handsome, cathedral-ceilinged dining room with a prospect of El Capitan—the mighty monolith dominating Yosemite Valley. Fastidious care has been taken in the preparation of the food enjoyed by its guests, be they overnighters or in residence for such an occasion as the legendary days of Christmas. The able administration has done a signal job in the selection of its staff, be it in the kitchen, dining room and bar, or elsewhere. The guest is left in a state of delight with the efficiency, warmth and good looks of those who always seem eager to please, to assist in making the visit more pleasant. How very unlike the usual, highly vacuous 'Have a good day' greeting and farewell one has in all too many of the American hotels—be they franchised or not.

"The six-story structure—which seems ever so squat and homey in contrast to the perpendicular walls nearby—has received and housed a near-legendary number of presidents, let alone emperors and kings. It has been said that such a critic as Frank Lloyd Wright found it to be grand yet not imperious. The Ahwahnee is comfortable for the weekender who wants to get away from urban tensions. The naturalist, in search of the Sierra Nevada's unique flora and fauna, or the unabashed romantic is likely to be thrilled to the bottom of his socks by the four (or are they really five?) waterfalls nearby: Yosemite (which is made up of two falls), Bridalveil, Vernal and Ribbon. It is all very, very awesome. Truly there, within the Ahwahnee's great halls, its library, its card room or along one of its great loggias, one finds a special respect for space and proportion. At the Ahwahnee, man seems to be decidedly at peace with his environment." —*Dr. Forest M. Hinkhouse*

Open all year, except for three weeks immediately after Thanksgiving.
121 rooms, all with private bath.
Rates $42 single, $50 double.
Credit cards: American Express, Master Charge, Visa.
Bars, game room, putting golf, swimming pool, tennis.
French, German, Japanese and Spanish spoken.

Yountville

Burgundy House Inn
6711 Washington Street
Yountville, California   94599
Telephone: (707) 944-2711

Set in the heart of the Napa Valley wine country, this inn with its thick stone walls was built in the 1870s, and was originally a brandy works.

"There are some fine country French antiques in this inn. We had a large bedroom with French doors and a bath—a deluxe suite. Although they serve only breakfast, there is a good Italian restaurant next door that served good homemade pastas and sauces." —*Nell Thomas*

Open all year.
18 rooms, 13 with private bath.
Rates $35 single, $45 double, including breakfast.
No credit cards.
Free wine.
German and Spanish spoken.

Magnolia Hotel
6529 Yount Street
Yountville, California   94599
Telephone: (707) 944-2056

This handsome stone building, built in 1873 as a hotel, was used at one stage (according to the present owner, Bruce Locken) as a bordello. The hotel has a swimming pool, a sauna and a restaurant (open from Thursday to Sunday) that boasts a wine cellar with a selection of over 200 wines. The inn, in fact, overlooks vineyards.

"Each room is different and is filled with French antiques. The dining room is small, beautifully intimate and very French in feel, with crystal and lace tablecloths."   *—Nell Thomas*

Open all year.
9 rooms, all with private bath.
Rates $48–$65, including breakfast.
No credit cards.
Japanese and Spanish spoken.

Hawaii

Honolulu

Colony Surf
2895 Kalakaua Avenue
Honolulu, Hawaii   96815
Telephone: (808) 923-5751

"For those who have never visited Oahu and dream of swaying palms, balmy breezes and romantic moonlit nights on sandy beaches, the awakening to the reality of today's Waikiki is rude.

In my case it was disappointing. It had been ten years since we visited Honolulu and those years have left an indelible mark on the town. Waikiki has become a concrete jungle of hotels and condominiums reaching to the sky. The sidewalks are crowded. Hotels fill every available inch of land and construction is still going on. Judging from the volume of visitors, I would recommend early booking: Our hotel, for instance, had no further vacancies for three months. We chose to stay in the Colony Surf on the beach at the foot of Diamond Head. No large overcrowded lobby here, but rather a quiet, small reception area with courteous and smiling people ready to welcome guests and answer questions. The crisp white of the woodwork and the spring green of the carpeting and wallpaper create a refreshing and serene atmosphere. With very little time lost in formalities, we were escorted to our 11th floor suite, an airy and sunny place with an immense window running along the whole width on the ocean side. A floral arrangement in a silver bowl added an uncommercial touch that we found to be true throughout our stay.

"The hotel is not inexpensive, but it offers many advantages that make it far superior to a room on the beach at Waikiki. Besides, all suites are equipped with kitchenettes fully stocked with dishes, flatware, cooking utensils, refrigerator, gas stove and dishwasher. There is a little grocery store around the corner. Should you wish to go to the market, bus fare anywhere in town is only 25 cents. A few steps away from the Colony Surf is the Colony East, where you will find smaller accommodations, though still suitable for families. That building is not on the beach, but overlooks a park and Diamond Head. The Colony East has a disco for the young, a beauty salon and a travel bureau.

"Dining at the Colony Surf is an adventure in fine cuisine. Michel's is an award-winning restaurant and richly deserves its reputation. The atmosphere is that of an elegant French dining room with crystal chandeliers, period furniture and formally attired waiters. The view of the beach and the ocean is unrestricted. During our stay at the hotel we chose to breakfast in our room, and used Michel's room service. The food reaches you promptly and warm, with juices properly chilled and the Kona coffee deliciously fragrant. The *Honolulu Advertiser* will be delivered to your door each morning. At night, a few orchid blossoms will be placed on your pillow by the maid who turns down your bed."
—*Louisa L. Becker*

Open all year.
100 rooms, all with private bath.
Rates $65–$115 single or double in Colony Surf, $55–$65 in Colony East. Suites $200–$350. $10 extra for third person in any room.

Credit cards: American Express, Carte Blanche, Diners Club, Master Charge, Visa.

Bars.

French, German, Japanese, Korean, Laotian, Spanish and Taiwanese spoken.

Nevada

Gold Hill

The Gold Hill Hotel
P.O. Box 304
Virginia City, Nevada   89440
Telephone: (702) 847-0111

"On entering Gold Canyon, flamboyant with color in the fall, the little town of Gold Hill whisks you back to the era of the gold and silver kings of the 1870s and 1880s. Many of the buildings are gone, of course, the victims of strong winds, heavy snows and desert sun—not to mention souvenir hunters. Prospectors began rushing the area in 1859, with the discovery of the great Comstock Lode, and it was well on its way to fame and fortune. On May 1 of that year, Vesey's Boarding House sprang up on the main street. The two-story building of mellowed brick and wood and white-painted railings still lends a charm of the pioneer West. Only its name and owners have changed over the years. The Gold Hill Hotel is now owned by Fred and Dorothy Immoor, who celebrated their twentieth anniversary at the hotel in 1978. The hotel snuggles against the sagebrush-covered hills within the shadows of the Crown Point Trestle, where millions in gold and silver ore were shipped to the mills on the Carson River by the Virginia and Truckee Railroad."   —*Dorothy Paulsen*

"The small hotel has five rooms, a banquet room for weddings and the old original bar where the overnight guests gather to talk or cook their own steaks. Up the rock-walled stairway there's a community bathroom with a chilly stone floor and an old-fashioned bathtub. The bridal suite at the end of the hall has a four-poster bed and a turn-of-the-century picture of Cupid on the pink walls. The other rooms are furnished with period pieces from Virginia City and the Gold Hill area. Morning brings the sun and the smell of coffee into your room. Guests are greeted downstairs by Dorothy's delicious brew and Fred's good-natured banter. They tell you how they've raised four children while acknowledging their years of labor. You realize the significance of the sign outside: 'This is the first edifice known to Nevada to be worthy of the name hotel.' "

—*Jim Beazley; also recommended by Wilbur E. Wieprecht*

Open all year.
5 rooms, no private baths.
Rates $18.50. No breakfast. Dinner by arrangement.
No credit cards.
Cross-country skiing, tavern, water sports.
Spanish spoken.

Utah

Midway

The Homestead
700 North Homestead Drive
Midway, Utah   84049
Telephone: (801) 654-1102

"A number of buildings make up the Homestead—the Virginian House, the Farmhouse, the Ranch House, the Barn, the Mill House, Valley View and the Guest House. It is like an old farmyard with cottages. The Homestead, at an altitude of 6,000 feet, is east of Salt Lake City, near the Park City recreation area. There is an indoor thermal pool—known as a 'hot pot,' which has temperatures between 85 and 92 degrees."

—Jack Goodman

Open all year, except Christmas Day.
43 rooms, all with private bath.
Rates $24–$37, $40 suite. Children under 17 free.
Credit cards: Master Charge, Visa.
Cross-country skiing, riding, sauna, snowmobiling, tennis.

Salt Lake City

Carlton Hotel
140 East South Temple Street
Salt Lake City, Utah   84111
Telephone: (801) 355-3418

"A clean, inexpensive hotel, well located in the historic downtown area of the city. A favorite with European visitors, it is rather an ordinary-looking building of red brick and white-painted pillars. Neat but not gaudy. There's no bar but there is a coffee shop." *—Jack Goodman*

Open all year.
125 rooms, 65 with private bath.
Rates $9–$14 single, $12–$17 double. Special weekly rates.
Credit cards: Master Charge, Visa.
Coffee shop.

Part Eight

Canada

Alberta
British Columbia
New Brunswick
Nova Scotia
Ontario
Quebec

Alberta

Waterton

The Prince of Wales
Waterton, Alberta   TK0 2M0
Telephone: (402) 226-4841

"The Prince of Wales is another of those Canadian resort hotels built in the 1920s by a railroad—in this case, the Great Northern—in a style known hereabouts as 'chateau.' The Prince departs from the style in having far fewer rooms than most (eighty-two) and in its wood, not stone, construction. The site is spectacular: a promontory looking due south along Waterton Lake, which reaches through two ridges of the Rockies into Montana. Ten minutes' walk away is the town of Waterton, much cozier than Banff and more relaxed. On most afternoons, beautiful mule deer stroll along the main drag, begging food from strangers. All around the town and the lake is Waterton National Park—again, smaller than Banff, but as beautiful, more accessible and much less crowded. On the Montana side of the border is the much larger Glacier National Park, where the owners of the Prince of Wales operate four more lodges. The Prince is the jewel in the collection, though. All rooms open onto balconies that surround its seven-story-high lobby. All are wood paneled, with private baths and telephones, but no radios or televisions—'deficiencies,' says the owner, Don Hummel, 'that are going to continue.'

"Another tradition he plans to carry on is chamber music with dinner, played by two or three undergraduate musicians hired each summer. One can lament the overcivilizing of parks these days, but there's civilization and civilization. We see nothing untoward about watching a sunset over the Rockies while sipping dry sherry and listening to *Air on a G String*. The musicians are the most aptly selected of the hotel's employees. As in most other Canadian park lodges, the rest of the staff— waiters, chambermaids, desk clerks—are drawn from universities for the short season. Their cooking seldom rises above the ordinary (though soups have been reliably wholesome) and the service, especially early in the season, can stumble. Still, in our experience, there's been an unprofessionally cheerful enthusiasm about these young staffers that has more than compensated."   —*Mechtild Hoppenrath and Charles Oberdorf*

Open from June 10 to September 18.
82 rooms, all with private bath.
Rates $32–$36.
No credit cards.
Boating, cocktail lounge, riding.
German spoken.

Qualicum College Inn,
Qualicum Beach

British Columbia

Qualicum Beach

Qualicum College Inn
P.O. Box 99
Qualicum Beach
British Columbia   V0R 2T0
Telephone: (604) 752-9262

"Qualicum College Inn—once a private boys' school—is on the east coast of Vancouver Island, nestled among countryside thickets just beyond a rolling green golf course overlooking the strait. You enter the inn through castle doors. The reception area has hand-crafted medieval-style decor. Each of the bedrooms is identified by the name of a British royal-family member. Just off the lobby is a library-sitting room. Pictures of classroom activities, of tournaments played and trophies won are arranged on the walls, along with other mementos of the good old days when Qualicum was an exclusive boarding school. You frequently come across entrances marked Headmaster, Gymnasium or Laboratory. Down a winding, red-carpeted stairway is a candlelit dining room, where an internationally accredited chef, the pride of the inn, treats his guests to his favorite selection of dishes—among them a seven-course medieval meal. What a treat it is to spend a long summer evening dining on the seaside patio. A leisurely whirlpool or sauna, a refreshing dip in the heated pool, a bit of classy disco music on weekends and a nice tall nightcap in the lounge give a perfect end to any day."   —*Mary-Anne Tinney*

Open all year.
50 rooms, all with private bath.
Rates $20 single, $24 double, from June 23 to September 11. Lower rates at other times. Special packages.
Credit cards: American Express, Master Charge, Visa.
Bar, jazz weekends, private beach, sauna, pool.

New Brunswick

Grand Manan

The Marathon Inn
North Head at Grand Manan
New Brunswick   E0G 2M0
Telephone: (506) 662-8144

"The inn stands on a hill overlooking the fishing village of North Head on Grand Manan Island, about twenty miles off the coast of New Brunswick in the Bay of Fundy. The bright, spacious front parlor with a Franklin stove and bay windows, the antique furnishings and decorations in every room and the cheerful ambiance of the service all help to recall the Victorian origins of this hotel. The Marathon was built in 1871 by a retired sea captain, and it served for many years as a small resort for wealthy Americans from Boston, New York and cities farther south. The bedrooms are unaffectedly quaint and the bill of fare—especially the seafood—is authentic and tasty. The new proprietors, Fern Leslie, her son Jim and his wife, Judy, will welcome you and assist you in any way they can, from filling you in on local customs and geography to helping you plan a day trip to Machias Seal Island to view the puffins and other seabirds that nest there. The Leslies have already introduced a new attraction to the Marathon: the summer Dulse Festival, a folksy-artsy musical show and all-around good time. Dulse, by the way, is an edible—in fact, delicious—seaweed indigenous to Grand Manan and good for what ails you.

"Grand Manan is a special place, not simply because it is an island: It is special even as islands go. Naturally its separation from the mainland tends to preserve and animate a clearly defined territorial culture, and to pass on this way of life from one generation to the next. But native Grand Mananers fairly shine with pride of place, with a very unfashionable, premodern, almost inscrutable sense of belonging—to the island and to each other. Even visitors find themselves yearning to return without really understanding why. Willa Cather, for example, came year after year to her cottage overlooking Whale Cove, and flourished there in creative privacy. Ever since the island was first settled nearly two hundred years ago, writers and painters have found Grand Manan to be strangely inspirational, as have countless bird watchers from Audubon himself to the annual flock of purest amateurs. Helen Charters, an artist and friend of mine who lives on the island, says that Grand Manan is a 'primal point.' Extremes are possible here. Powerful rhythms are present. This explains why there are so many churches on the island: Fundamentalism is a response to fundamentals. Though they are conscious of their history, Grand Mananers live by legends, both lovely and grim; and though the island is prosperous, even affluent, true Grand Mananers are more liable to suffer from grand passions than from existential angst, and are more likely to be found on the wharves and beaches and cliffs watching storms and sunsets than in their living rooms watching television. The beauty—and the danger—of Grand Manan is indestructible. The people, and whatever it is that shapes them and compels them, will not be undone by visitors."

—*Michael Brian Oliver*

"Whether balsam-scented from the highland woods to the west or from the east with a damp chill of fog and the smell of herring smokehouses, the breeze is always there to remind you of the sea and its dominance over all island activities. The relationship between the fishing industry and tourism can best be described as coexistence, but you are never in doubt that the latter was, is and will always be, secondary to the former. If you search the island hard enough, there are a few random tennis courts, and we passed on our bicycles a stretch of landscape that looked much like a golf course. But we would recommend leaving these sports—and your car—behind on the mainland. Everywhere there are birds in great variety and staggering quantity. Proprietors of several herring smokehouses welcome visitors, and you will have a chance to sample this distinctive product. One should keep in mind the formidable logistics of food shopping for the inn, most of which must be done on the mainland. The menu will occasionally be limited and may feature some improvisations or 'standbys,' but these are always well prepared and tasty. If the beds leave something to be desired from the standpoint of comfort, your vigorous day and the sea air will ensure you a sound night's sleep."

—Mr. and Mrs. William G. Sayres

Open all year.
36 rooms, 5 with private bath.
Rates $32 single, $30 double per person, including breakfast and dinner. Lunch on request.
Credit cards: Master Charge, Visa.
Heated pool, mopeds and bikes to rent, tennis.

_____*Sackville*

Marshlands Inn
73 Bridge Street
P.O. Box 1440
Sackville, New Brunswick   E0A 3C0
Telephone: (506) 536-0170

Since Sackville is about midway between the Bay of Fundy and Northumberland Strait, it usually has a warmer temperature in winter and a cooler temperature in summer than the rest of New Brunswick. It is on the edge of the Tantramar Marshes and about an hour's drive from beaches and a few miles from Fort Beausejour and its museum.

"We visited the inn in the first week of October because we wanted to look at the changing leaves. The inn is an old white house surrounded by trees—our room was large and quaint, with soft beds, embroidered hand towels and a footed bathtub. The meals were excellent—we met for drinks in the parlor before dinner (I had lamb curry) and then moved back into the parlor for coffee. Before bedtime, we were offered hot chocolate. There is a wildlife preserve nearby and we watched the 'tidal bore'—the tide rises quickly in a narrow river, about forty feet in one hour."

—Mrs. Yetta G. Samford, Jr.

Closed from early November to February.
16 rooms, 8 with private bath.
Rates $20–$24 single, $24–$35 double.
Credit cards: Master Charge, Visa.

Rates for Canadian entries are quoted in Canadian dollars.

_____*St. Stephen*

The Elm Lodge Inn
477 Milltown Boulevard
St. Stephen, New Brunswick   E3L 1K2
Telephone: (506) 466-3771

"While most of the tourist traffic to the Maritime Provinces enters Canada via Calais and St. Stephen, those who are in search of a quiet country inn will choose a better way. About two miles before Calais on the Bangor road is a sign on the left indicating the Milltown Border Bridge, which leads the traveler from Milltown, Maine, to Milltown, New Brunswick. On either side, the St. Croix River provides beautiful scenery. Clearing the small customs office, the tourist drives past the little Memorial Park and soon sees on his left the sign: Auberge Elm Lodge Inn—*auberge* being French for inn. The tourist *from* the Maritimes coming into St. Stephen will ignore the usual border point and drive on up through lovely riverside country through Milltown, finding Elm Lodge on his *right* at the other end of the village.

"The gracious old house stands proudly in lovely grounds. It is said to be 120 years old and was once the home of a doctor and later a nursing home for old ladies. In 1974 Pat and Zena Garbutt bought the old house and restored it with loving care. The elegant entrance hall with its white paint and red velvet flocked walls and crimson carpet warmly welcome the visitor and, through open doorways, you glimpse a bar and antique-furnished dining rooms. In winter, lamps are lit and great log fires blaze. Upstairs, beautiful and well-equipped bedrooms can house twenty guests. The honeymoon room contains an old restored four-poster; there are family suites and a suite with bedroom and sitting room suitable for a salesman who wishes to entertain business friends. Dinner at the Elm is an occasion—not just a meal. You are served with salad and delicious home-baked breads and the aperitif of your choice while your steak or fish is cooked to your requirements." —*Evelyn Ward*

Open all year except December 24–27.
9 rooms, 4 with private bath.
Rates $18.50–$29 single, $25–$42 double. American plan also available.
Credit cards: American Express, Master Charge, Visa.
Bar, entertainment.

Rates for Canadian entries are quoted in Canadian dollars.

Nova Scotia

Baddeck, Cape Breton

Inverary Inn
Box 190
Baddeck, Cape Breton
Nova Scotia   B0E 1B0
Telephone: (902) 295-2674

"Being Europeans originally I suppose we subconsciously were always looking for one of those family-run smaller hotels or inns we were used to. Well, we found one right here in our own beautiful province of Nova Scotia. A perfect retreat even for a weekend or for longer if you want to leave daily pressures behind or work and sketch quietly without a deadline. The inn was originally an old farmhouse. The barn is made over so that upstairs there are comfortable bedrooms and downstairs a very cozy lounge with a fireplace. The carriage house is a craft shop with first-class local crafts such as hooked rugs and quilts. The MacAulays who own the place are outgoing and friendly and make you feel welcome and at ease. The beautiful antiques and old fireplace give the place an atmosphere hard to equal anywhere else. The food is excellent and it is served in the attractive dining room overlooking the Bras d'Or Lakes.

"One weekend recently the weather changed suddenly. It turned cold and rainy. Disappointed tourists entered the lounge from outside and complained about the unfortunate turn of events. They had planned to visit such places as the old French fort, Louisbourg, or drive along the beautiful 200-mile Cabot Trail. But the weather was trying to spoil their day. Then Dan MacAulay came in and lit the fire in the large fireplace. People started to gather around. I sat somewhere in the back in one of those comfortable antique easy chairs and watched. It did not take long before people were all swapping tales and having a wonderful time. It was not a lost day after all. The next day was warm and sunny. One of those Cape Breton surprises."

—Anneke Betlem; also recommended by
Peggy and Gordon Thompson

Open from May 1 to November 1.
70 rooms, 60 with private bath.
Rates $15–$30 single, $18–$35 double, $35–$50 cottages.
Credit card: Visa.
Lake swimming, licensed dining room, sailing, swimming pool.

Ontario

Algonquin Park

Arowhon Pines
Huntsville P.O.
Ontario   P0A 1K0
Telephone: (705) 633-5661

"In addition to the usual assortment of North Americans, guests at Arowhon Pines one recent weekday included a technical writer and a medical student from West Germany, a distinguished Dutch surgeon taking a break from a lecture tour, three independently holidaying British couples and two Swissair pilots and their wives. The Pines, as friends call it, rarely advertises in any medium more international than the _Toronto Globe and Mail;_ the Europeans had all learned about it through word of mouth. Eugene and Helen Kates took over the lodge from Eugene's elderly mother in 1970. Since then they've adhered to one of Eugene's gruff-voiced tenets. 'Look,' he rumbles, 'we're in the business of selling three things: a bedroom, a dining room and a setting. The setting is superb . . .' (he's right: The Pines adjoins a lake near the southern corner of a 3,000-square-mile provincial park that is a favorite of Canadian naturalists, canoe-trippers and landscape painters) '. . . but that's beyond our control, so we have to do our best with the other two.'

"Architecturally, the dining room is no problem. Broad, hexagonal, jutting over the lake, it was built in the late 1930s by two brothers, Paul and Jack Lucasavitch. Of necessity they used only hand tools, plus a team of horses to winch into place the enormous central cast-iron chimney. Still solid as Canadian Shield granite, their construction has been applauded in several books on fine log buildings. As for its wares, the Pines's baker produces fresh breads and cakes daily, and each summer the Kateses have managed to steal yet another bright young chef from some major Toronto restaurant; their reputation for food has gone consistently up. It had better: Eugene's daughter Joanne writes prickly restaurant reviews for the *Globe and Mail.* Toronto guests know that, and expect the Pines to meet her exacting, and very public, standards. (N.B. The sale of alcohol is forbidden in Ontario's parks. If you want wine with your meals—and they deserve it—you must bring your own. The hotel provides stemware, mixes and corkscrews.) Fifty bedrooms are clustered in small buildings scattered through the densely wooded grounds. Each cabin has a common lounge area with a fireplace, comfortable chairs and sofas, a small refrigerator and an eclectic collection of books. Helen Kates is a compulsive antiques hunter, so many of those stripped-pine pieces are authentic 'old Canada.'

"Canoeing is our recreation of choice. There's an easy but fun whitewater creek leading to the Pines's lake from one to the north. There are wolf howls at night, loon calls at dawn. We've seen dozens of bird species, bear on almost every trip and twice a moose. The canoes are free. So are the tennis and shuffleboard courts, rowboats, small sailboats, swim docks, picnic lunches and well-marked trails through the bush. There are small charges for outboard-motor-equipped fishing boats and for baby-sitting. No tipping: *servis compris.*"
—*Mechtild Hoppenrath and Charles Oberdorf*

Open May 19 to October 9.

50 rooms, all with private bath.

Rates $47.50–$62 single, $38–$47.50 double per person, including three meals. Special weekly rates. Discount of 20 percent from May 19 to June 30.

No credit cards.

Badminton, canoeing, lake swimming, sailing, shuffleboard, tennis, wind surfing.

Winter address for correspondence: 147 Davenport Road, Toronto M5R 1J1. Winter telephone: (416) 923-7176.

Rates for Canadian entries are quoted in Canadian dollars.

Alton

The Millcroft Inn
Box 89
Alton, Ontario   L0N 1A0
Telephone: (416) 791-4422

"Toronto's most elegant country retreat was created three years ago out of an old knitting mill, $3 million and a lot of imagination. To ensure quality, the hotel is managed—though not owned—by the people from the Windsor Arms Hotel (in Toronto). Rooms in 'the Mill,' all twenty-two of them, are furnished with Canadian antiques. The twenty crofts on the hill are a longer walk from the heart of things—from the tennis courts, the outdoor pool, the bar and the dining areas. Management by the Windsor Arms Hotel guarantees above all fine food imaginatively prepared: homemade sherbets and ices, salads of such uncommon ingredients as celery root, perfect drinks, vegetables grown in the inn's own garden and often picked moments before serving. Meals are not cheap. Prices can easily pass $50 for two with wine. But many Toronto food fanatics drive two hours for the pleasure of paying that, without even spending the night."
—*Mechtild Hoppenrath and Charles Oberdorf*

Open all year.
42 rooms, all with private bath.
Rates 50–$69.
Credit cards: American Express, Diners Club, Master Charge, Visa.
Bar, exercise room, outdoor pool, sauna, whirlpool.

Elora

The Elora Mill
77 Mill Street West
Elora, Ontario   N0B 1S0
Telephone: (519) 846-5356

"Until 1973 this hotel was known as Drimmies Mill, a gristmill powered by the thundering waterfall that now crashes past the best tables in the cocktail lounge. Two families bought and refitted the old mill, transforming it into the crown jewel of this town of 2,500, which had already attracted a fair number of Sunday drivers with its artists' and craftsmen's workshops, its natural setting (hard by a deep limestone gorge full of caves, waterfalls and rapids) and the beautiful surrounding countryside, largely farmed by buggy-driving Mennonites. We prefer the food at the less expensive, Basque-style Café Flore, just down the street, to dinners at the Mill. Or we go on a Saturday and assemble lunch from the Mennonite farmers' markets in nearby Kitchener and Elmira. In August the town of Fergus, just down the road, stages one of Canada's more important festivals of 'highland games,' complete with bagpipes and flying cabers. In winter the Elora Gorge Conservation Area becomes one of the province's best cross-country skiing areas, the better for knowing that the Mill will have a nice hot buttered rum on hand at the end of the run. The area is unusually pretty and cozy, with the Mennonites giving it special interest, but it is not well known, even in nearby Toronto. Alas, it soon will be."

—Mechtild Hoppenrath and Charles Oberdorf

Open all year.
16 rooms, all with private bath.
Rates $32–$49 single, $36–$54 double.
Credit cards: American Express, Master Charge, Visa.
Cocktail lounge.
German spoken.

Niagara-on-the-Lake

The Angel Inn
224 Regent Street
Box 268
Niagara-on-the-Lake, Ontario   L0S 1J0
Telephone: (416) 468-3411

"Oscar Wilde once suggested that 'Niagara Falls must be the second major disappointment of American married life.' He was speaking of the 'natural wonder,' but the sentiment applies equally to the two towns of that name—in New York and Ontario—and to their accommodations. On the Canadian side, though, just about twenty minutes' drive downstream from the cataract of kitsch, stands a charming little town of 12,000 with not one, but four recommendable inns. Niagara-on-the-Lake, where the river flows into Lake Ontario, was the first capital of Upper Canada (now Ontario) from 1792 to 1796, after which it reverted to a sleepy rural existence for some 150 years. Its cache of colonial and early-19th-century buildings, however, always set it a little apart from neighboring towns in eastern Canada's fruit belt, and over the years many were bought and restored by wealthy families from Toronto and Buffalo. By the 1950s a few Queen Street shops were catering to this carriage trade. Then, in 1962, the Shaw Festival opened in the old (1848) Court House, and summers have never been the same since. The

Shaw company, now housed in a stunning 800-seat theater, rivals the Stratford (Ontario) Shakespeare Festival as a draw for local audiences and performers. Between the towns there's no contest; Niagara is a far nicer place. We like it in midwinter, when the tourists are gone and the snow creaks underfoot in the big parks and on the restored ramparts of Fort George. Even in July, though, one need only walk about twenty paces off Queen Street, the main drag, to be alone in one of the prettiest 19th-century towns on the continent. Of all the inns, the eleven bedrooms at the Angel are certainly the most charming: four-poster beds, lots of antiques."

—Mechtild Hoppenrath and Charles Oberdorf

Open all year.

11 rooms, all with private bath.

Rates $20 single, $25 double in winter; $27.50 single, $30 double in summer (April 30 to September 30). Special two-day weekend packages in winter.

Credit cards: American Express, Diners Club, Master Charge, Visa.

Bar, patio.

German spoken.

The Oban Inn
160 Front Street
Box 94
Niagara-on-the-Lake, Ontario L0S 1J0
Telephone: (416) 468-2165

"The Oban has one of the finest bars anywhere in Canada—spiked cider made with a fireplace 'spike' in January, a Pimm's No. 1 Cup in summer that is perfection, and a piano that's an after-curtain-calls hangout for Shaw Festival actors."

—Mechtild Hoppenrath and Charles Oberdorf

Open all year.

23 rooms, all with private bath.

Rates $22 single, $30–$39 double. Special midweek and weekend packages from November 1 to April 1.

Credit cards: American Express, Master Charge, Visa.

Bar, gardens, lake sailing, terrace.

German and Portuguese spoken.

Rates for Canadian entries are quoted in Canadian dollars.

The Pillar and Post Inn
48 John Street
Box 1011
Niagara-on-the-Lake, Ontario L0S 1J0
Telephone: (416) 468-2123

"This inn is less historically authentic than others in the town. It's a fairly recent recycling of an old industrial building with all the modern conveniences like sauna and outdoor pool and mostly 'reproduction antiques' in the rooms. But it does have pretty quilts and fireplaces in some bedrooms."
—Mechtild Hoppenrath and Charles Oberdorf

Open all year.
60 rooms, all with private bath.
Rates $38 single, $43 double from May 1 to September 30. Lower rates at other times. Special two-day packages.
Credit cards: American Express, Diners Club, Master Charge, Visa.
Bar, craftshop, fitness club, gallery, sauna, swimming pool.

Prince of Wales Hotel
6 Picton Street
Box 46
Niagara-on-the-Lake, Ontario   L0S 1J0
Telephone: (416) 468-3246

"Dining adequately is no problem anywhere in Niagara-on-the-Lake, but dining splendidly is impossible. To the extent that it still reflects some excellent past management—by Toronto consultants Nicholas Pearce and David Barrette—the Prince of Wales remains the best place to eat. A restored and enlarged hotel of Victorian vintage, the closest one to the Shaw theater, it is also a reasonable place to sleep. In any other town this size it would be a treasure."
—Mechtild Hoppenrath and Charles Oberdorf

58 rooms, all with private bath.
Rates $30–$39 single, $39–$45 double, $55–$95 suites. Special weekend rates.
Credit cards: American Express, Master Charge, Visa.
Bar, exercise room, platform tennis, saunas, swimming pool, whirlpool.
German spoken.

If you would like to amend, update or disagree with any entry, write *now*.

Toronto

The Windsor Arms Hotel
22 St. Thomas Street
Toronto, Ontario   M5S 2B9
Telephone: (416) 979-2341

"The Windsor Arms' owner, George Minden, delights in excellence. He has, for instance, a passion for cars. A few years ago he noticed that the city had no one properly selling or servicing the *great* machines—by Rolls-Royce, Ferrari, Aston-Martin. So he opened Grand Touring Automobiles to do that. Then, when he heard that Aston-Martin, maker of his favorite machines, was on the brink of closing, he assembled some investors who rescued the company and produced the daring Lagonda. Minden loves Italian food, too. Feeling that Torontonians were getting nothing like the full spectrum of that country's cooking, he opened 'Noodles,' still a dazzling flash of Milan-style chic, one of the few places in town to serve *polenta* and the only one with truly superb Italian wines. But the Windsor Arms is Minden's flagship. A fading residential hotel when he acquired it in the late 1950s, he's transformed it into Toronto's finest. His first move was to rebuild the basement into three dining rooms—the Restaurant, the Grill and the Wine Cellar, known collectively as Three Small Rooms. They remain the standard against which the city's many excellent eating places are measured. Then he refitted the bedrooms, individually, often with valuable antique pieces. Carefully attended, they have nonetheless remained more reasonably priced than rooms in the city's larger chain-linked hotels. A new, informal dining room, the Courtyard Café, serves spectacular cakes and ice creams to live chamber music; it's become a cliché of Canadian journalism to note that the nationally published interview began over *kir* and artichokes vinaigrette in the Courtyard. The hotel is on a quiet side street, but only half a block from fashionable Bloor Street, a two-minute walk from the even more elegant Yorkville district, and a five-minute ride on Toronto's antiseptic subway from Canada's centers of commerce and finance. An announced addition will doubtless dilute guests' feelings that after twenty-four hours everyone on the staff knows their names. But George Minden has expanded his domain of excellence with great care in the past, and we're sure the Windsor Arms will grow gracefully."
—*Mechtild Hoppenrath and Charles Oberdorf*

Open all year.
81 rooms, all with private bath.
Rates $32–$51 single, $40–$60 double.
Credit cards: American Express, Diners Club, Master Charge, Visa.

Quebec

Hudson

Auberge Willow Inn
208 Main Street
Hudson, Quebec   J0P 1A0
Telephone: (514) 458-4656 or 5021

"This inn has a perfect name, as there are many willow trees in the area. It is about thirty-five miles west of Montreal. The grounds behind the inn go down to the Lake of Two Mountains, and from your table you can see sailboats passing by in the summer. In winter you can watch cross-country skiers. The inn has quite a few antiques and is decorated with good taste. The food is plentiful and is pleasantly served by either the innkeeper or his efficient helpers. Some of the bedrooms have four-poster beds, and everything is spotless." —_Britt Rottbollp_

Open all year, except Christmas Day.
13 rooms, 8 with private bath.
Rates $15–$20 single, $20–$35 double. MAP available. Special weekly rates.
Credit cards: American Express, Master Charge, Visa.
Bar, swimming pool.
German and Spanish spoken.

North Hatley

Hovey Manor
Box 60, North Hatley
Quebec   J0B 2C0
Telephone: (819) 842-2421

"I have been at Hovey Manor both in winter and in summer and it is hard to say which season is more beautiful. In the winter it has billows of glorious snow and all the winter sports, and in summer it has lovely lawns sloping to the lake and all the summer sports. The exterior of the manor is a replica of Mount Vernon; the interior has the warmth and coziness of a coach house and tavern. But the nicest thing about the place is the hospitality of Robert Brown and his wife, Betty."
—Jeannette Virgin

"The rooms in the main building are furnished in simple early North American style and are very comfortable, if not soundproof. The lovely sitting room–library with its fine fireplace is a charming room in which to relax, read, chat with old and new acquaintances and friends or share a drink before dinner. Nearby, the Carriage House, with its enormous fireplace, is full of antiques. Here (and in the beautiful old gardens as well) are served drinks throughout the week and marvelous steak dinners on Saturday nights. The Carriage House also has some very small guest rooms that are less expensive than those in the main house. Cottages are also provided for families. At Hovey Manor one can be active or inactive, according to one's own inclination. Some come to rest, some to write and some for the variety of activities on and off the premises. Summer stock may be enjoyed at the nearby Piggery and at Bishop University. The works of artists and artisans may be seen in town."
—Clara Loomanitz

Open all year.
34 rooms, 32 with private bath.
Rates $16–$25 single, $32–$50 double. Special 6-day minimum, MAP rates.
No credit cards.
Beach, tennis.

Details of special features offered by an inn or hotel vary according to information supplied by the hotels themselves. The absence here of a recreational amenity, a bar or a restaurant doesn't necessarily mean one of these doesn't exist. Ask the innkeeper when booking your room.

_____*St. Jovite*

Grey Rocks Inn
Mt. Tremblant
Box 1000
St. Jovite, Quebec   J0T 2H0
Telephone: (819) 425-2771

"We wanted a place to take a ski vacation in the Northeast and chose Grey Rocks on the advice of friends, some of whom had visited there two or three times. The inn is in the Laurentian Mountains and both skiing and skiing instruction are offered throughout the winter. We wanted a room in the inn itself (one could also stay in separate chalets) and were pleased to find large, comfortable accommodations. The food was served family style and was delicious and plentiful. The owners even joined us for dinner one evening and, as a friendly gesture, provided our table with our choice of wines from their well-stocked cellars. The inn, which has several bars, offers game rooms at night for cards and chess. There are some organized activities for those interested."   —*Philip and Debbie Fretz*

Open all year.
225 rooms, 180 with private bath.
Rates $35–$52 single, $31–$41 double per person, including all meals.
Credit cards: American Express, Carte Blanche, Diners Club, Master Charge, Visa.
Bar, pool, golf course, tennis, marina, stables.

Maps

Drawn by Donald Pitcher

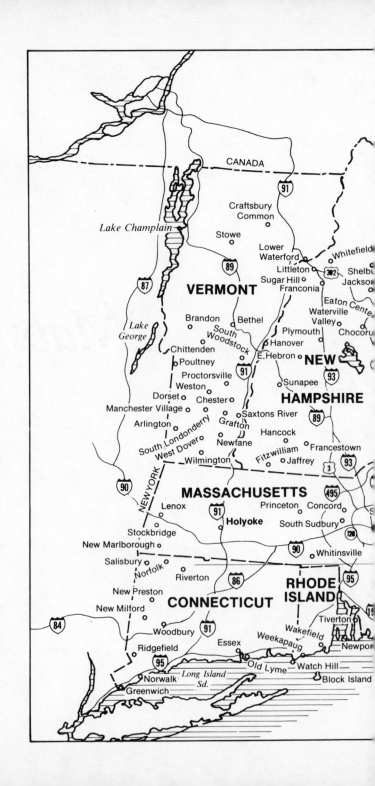

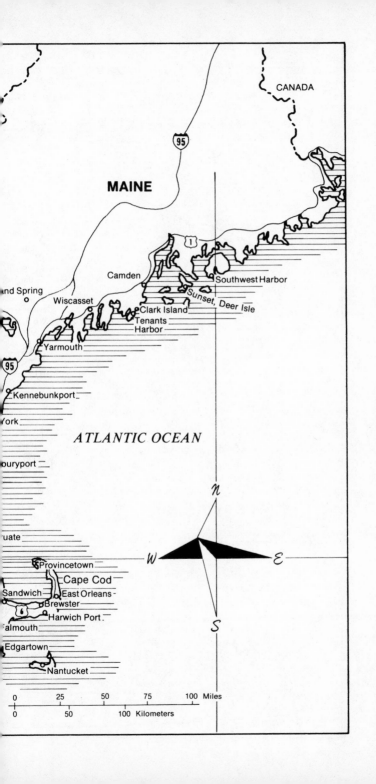

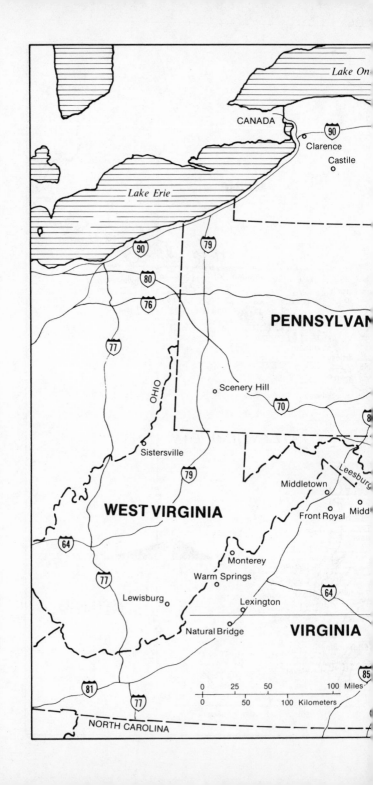

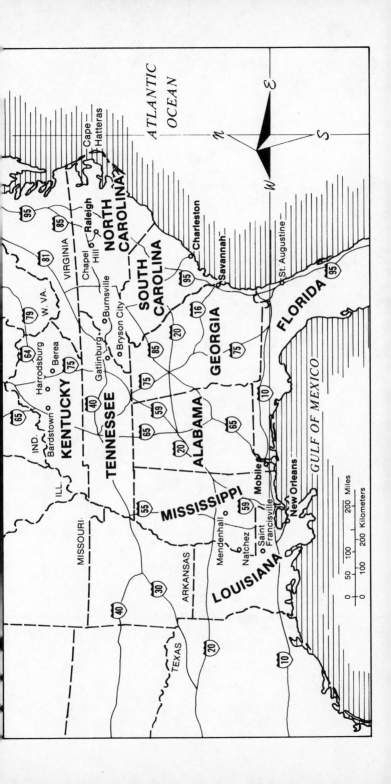

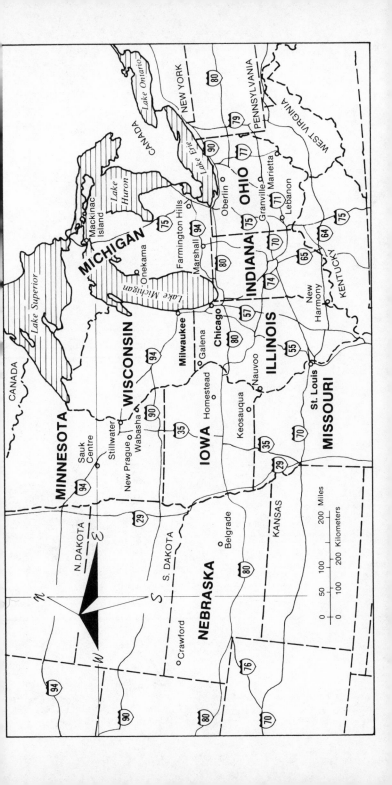

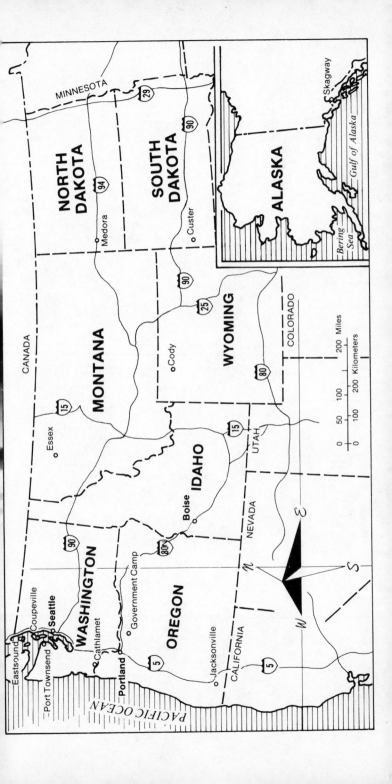

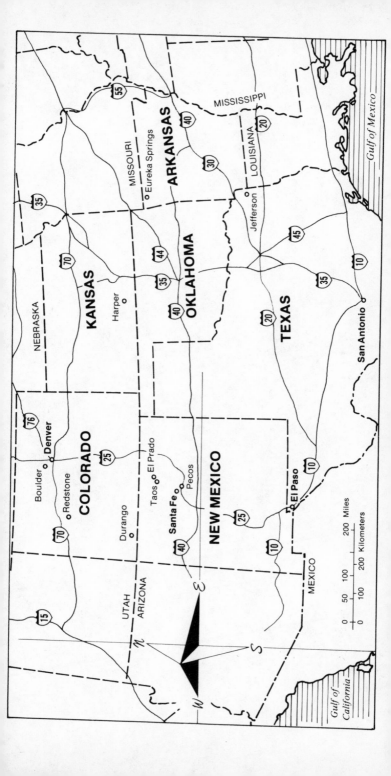

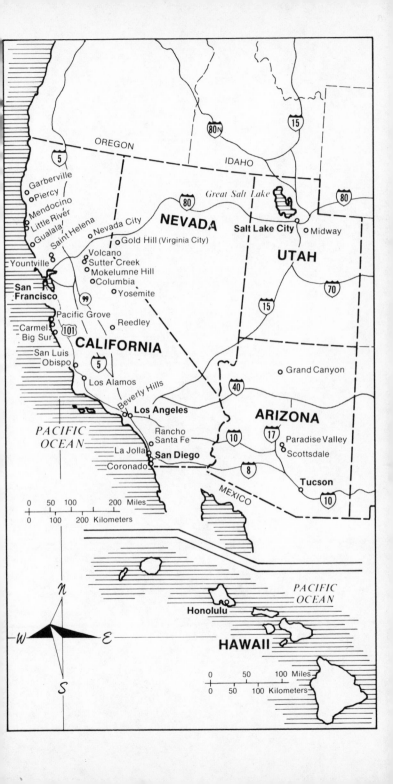

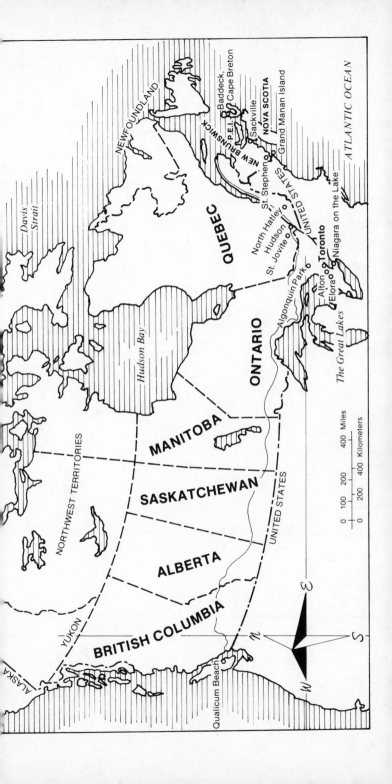

If you have found this book useful, you may want to obtain these three new Dutton titles:

Europe's Wonderful Little Hotels and Inns
edited by Hilary Rubinstein

500 places with special charm. 200 of them new to this freshly revised edition.

Visiting the Gardens of Europe
by Harriet Bridgeman and Elizabeth Drury

A fact-filled handbook of European gardens open to the public—1,200 gardens in twenty-two countries. It contains all the essential information on each—where to find them, what plants they feature, their histories, hours, layouts and tours—as well as descriptions which in themselves are a pleasure to read.

The Wine Taster's Guide to Europe
by Anthony Hogg

A country-by-country, region-by-region guide to on-the-spot visits, tours and winetastings at vineyards, cellars and distilleries throughout Europe. Over 300 establishments, with addresses, phone numbers and names of contacts.

Hotel
Reports

The pages that follow are for you to use to amend, criticize or update entries in this book, or to suggest new entries for our next edition. When you nominate a hotel or inn, please tell other travelers about the region or neighborhood as well as the hotel itself; this is particularly helpful when you write about areas of the country not familiar to many people. There is no need to include a lot of factual information (prices, number of rooms, etc.) with your entry: This is supplied by the hotels and inns. What you will give us is the spirit and character of the places you find. There is no need to confine your comments to a single page. It is important that you send your comments soon, so that this guide can be kept as up-to-date as possible. And thank you for sharing your finds with other people like yourself.

To:
The Editor
America's Wonderful Little Hotels and Inns
345 East 93rd Street
New York, N.Y. 10028

Name of Hotel _____

Address _____

_____

Date of most recent visit _____ Duration of visit _____

☐ New recommendation   ☐ Comment on existing entry

Report:

Signed _____

Name and address (printed, please) _____

_____

Note: Unless we are asked not to, we shall assume that we may publish your name if you are recommending a new hotel or supporting an existing entry.

To:
The Editor
America's Wonderful Little Hotels and Inns
345 East 93rd Street
New York, N.Y.   10028

Name of Hotel _____

Address _____

Date of most recent visit _____ Duration of visit _____

☐ New recommendation   ☐ Comment on existing entry

Report:

Signed _____

Name and address (printed, please) _____

Note: Unless we are asked not to, we shall assume that we may publish your name if you are recommending a new hotel or supporting an existing entry.

To:
The Editor
America's Wonderful Little Hotels and Inns
345 East 93rd Street
New York, N.Y.   10028

Name of Hotel _____

Address _____

_____

Date of most recent visit _____ Duration of visit _____

☐ New recommendation   ☐ Comment on existing entry

Report:

Signed _____

Name and address (printed, please) _____

_____

Note: Unless we are asked not to, we shall assume that we may publish your name if you are recommending a new hotel or supporting an existing entry.

To:
 The Editor
 America's Wonderful Little Hotels and Inns
 345 East 93rd Street
 New York, N.Y.   10028

Name of Hotel _____

Address _____

_____

Date of most recent visit _____ Duration of visit _____

☐ New recommendation   ☐ Comment on existing entry

Report:

Signed _____

Name and address (printed, please) _____

_____

Note: Unless we are asked not to, we shall assume that we may publish your name if you are recommending a new hotel or supporting an existing entry.

To:
The Editor
America's Wonderful Little Hotels and Inns
345 East 93rd Street
New York, N.Y.   10028

Name of Hotel _____

Address _____

_____

Date of most recent visit _____ Duration of visit _____

☐ New recommendation   ☐ Comment on existing entry

Report:

Signed _____

Name and address (printed, please) _____

_____

Note: Unless we are asked not to, we shall assume that we may publish your name if you are recommending a new hotel or supporting an existing entry.

To:
The Editor
America's Wonderful Little Hotels and Inns
345 East 93rd Street
New York, N.Y.   10028

Name of Hotel _____

Address _____

_____

Date of most recent visit _____ Duration of visit _____

☐ New recommendation   ☐ Comment on existing entry

Report:

Signed _____

Name and address (printed, please) _____

_____

Note: Unless we are asked not to, we shall assume that we may publish your name if you are recommending a new hotel or supporting an existing entry.

To:
The Editor
America's Wonderful Little Hotels and Inns
345 East 93rd Street
New York, N.Y.   10028

Name of Hotel _____

Address _____

_____

Date of most recent visit _____ Duration of visit _____

☐ New recommendation   ☐ Comment on existing entry

Report:

Signed _____

Name and address (printed, please) _____

_____

Note: Unless we are asked not to, we shall assume that we may publish your name if you are recommending a new hotel or supporting an existing entry.

To:
  The Editor
  America's Wonderful Little Hotels and Inns
  345 East 93rd Street
  New York, N.Y.   10028

Name of Hotel _____

Address _____

_____

Date of most recent visit _____ Duration of visit _____
☐ New recommendation   ☐ Comment on existing entry
Report:

Signed _____

Name and address (printed, please) _____

_____

Note: Unless we are asked not to, we shall assume that we may publish your name if you are recommending a new hotel or supporting an existing entry.

To:
The Editor
America's Wonderful Little Hotels and Inns
345 East 93rd Street
New York, N.Y. 10028

Name of Hotel _____

Address _____

_____

Date of most recent visit _____ Duration of visit _____
☐ New recommendation   ☐ Comment on existing entry
Report:

Signed _____
Name and address (printed, please) _____

_____

Note: Unless we are asked not to, we shall assume that we may publish your name if you are recommending a new hotel or supporting an existing entry.

To:
The Editor
America's Wonderful Little Hotels and Inns
345 East 93rd Street
New York, N.Y.   10028

Name of Hotel _____

Address _____

Date of most recent visit _____ Duration of visit _____

☐ New recommendation   ☐ Comment on existing entry

Report:

Signed _____

Name and address (printed, please) _____

_____

Note: Unless we are asked not to, we shall assume that we may publish your name if you are recommending a new hotel or supporting an existing entry.

To:
The Editor
America's Wonderful Little Hotels and Inns
345 East 93rd Street
New York, N.Y. 10028

Name of Hotel _____

Address _____

_____

Date of most recent visit _____ Duration of visit _____

☐ New recommendation ☐ Comment on existing entry

Report:

Signed _____

Name and address (printed, please) _____

_____

Note: Unless we are asked not to, we shall assume that we may publish your name if you are recommending a new hotel or supporting an existing entry.

To:
   The Editor
   America's Wonderful Little Hotels and Inns
   345 East 93rd Street
   New York, N.Y.   10028

Name of Hotel _____

Address _____

_____

Date of most recent visit _____ Duration of visit _____
☐ New recommendation   ☐ Comment on existing entry
Report:

Signed _____

Name and address (printed, please) _____

_____

Note: Unless we are asked not to, we shall assume that we may publish your name if you are recommending a new hotel or supporting an existing entry.